Screams & Nightmares

The Films of
WES CRAVEN

Screams & Nightmares

The Films of
WES CRAVEN

Brian J. Robb

OVERLOOK PRESS
WOODSTOCK • NEW YORK

Moline Public Library
MOLINE, ILLINOIS

SCREAMS & NIGHTMARES
THE FILMS OF WES CRAVEN
ISBN 0-87951-918-5

First Published in the United States by
The Overlook Press, Peter Mayer Publishers, Inc.
Lewis Hollow Road
Woodstock, New York 12498

First edition
10 9 8 7 6 5 4 3 2 1

Screams & Nightmares: The Films of Wes Craven copyright © 1998 Brian J. Robb. All rights reserved.
Cataloguing-in-Publication Data is available from the
Library of Congress
Design by Chris Teather
Production by Bob Kelly

Photo credits: p146 (top) © Jeffrey Fenner
Every effort has been made to contact the relevant copyright holders. Any omissions will be corrected in future editions.

Acknowledgements:

Primary thanks are due to Wes Craven for taking the time at various points over the past ten years to talk with me in depth about his films, his career and his life. The majority of the material in this book comes from these interview sessions. The first two were carried out between Brian J. Robb, Brigid Cherry and Wes Craven at the Savoy Hotel in London (28 June 1988) and on the Paramount lot in Los Angeles (12 September 1994). Other material came from letters and telephone conversations between Wes Craven and the author, with a major telephone interview on 22 January 1998.

Thanks are also due to my wife Brigid Cherry, without whom our interviews with Wes Craven would not have been as productive, I'm sure — and for sticking with the book (and me) for the past decade.

Despite Wes Craven's unstinting help, it would not have been possible to put together a comprehensive examination of his career without acknowledging the debt I owe to everyone who has interviewed Craven through the years, and to the magazines which have published those interviews. It's impossible to name them all individually, but magazines which have covered Craven's work have included *Starlog*, *Fangoria*, *Cinefantastique*, *Starburst*, *Fear*, *Empire* and *Premiere*. Material in this book was also drawn from production notes issued by various distributors for each of Craven's films and from various newspaper accounts of Craven at work.

I'm also indebted to my colleagues at the British Film Institute where I worked when Craven visited in 1988 for a retrospective of his films. More recent — and invaluable — assistance came from John Riley at BFI Information Services.

I must thank everyone at the offices of Wes Craven Films for their attention during the speedy production and post-production of *Scream 2*. Thanks are also due to everyone at the various film distribution and publicity offices who has helped. I also owe a debt to Mike Wingate at C&A Video in Edinburgh for tracking down Craven's more difficult-to-obtain work on video. Finally, thanks also to David Barraclough and Gillian Christie at Titan for their support and help through the writing of the manuscript.

Manufactured in the United States

For Brigid, who always asks the right questions.

Contents

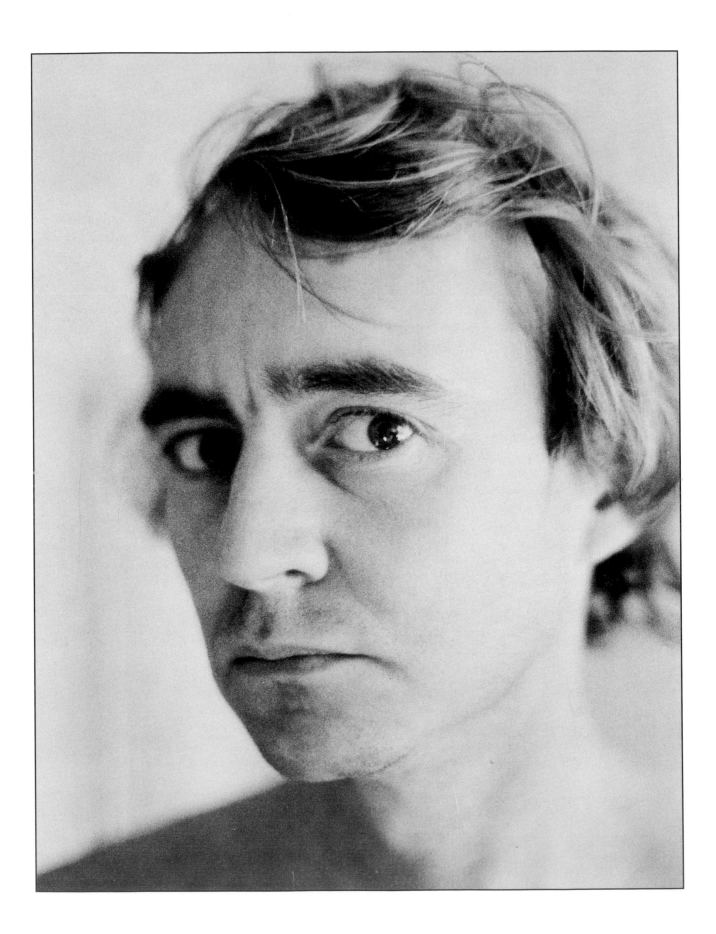

Nightmare Man

Wes Craven began his directing career in 1972 with *The Last House on the Left*, still seen as a shocking and controversial film a quarter of a century later. Banned in Britain, it was one of the notorious 'video nasties' caught up in the tabloid fever which led to the 1984 Video Recordings Act. It wasn't until 1977 that Craven released another completed film, *The Hills Have Eyes*, about a family of ferocious mountain mutants. These two movies alone quickly gained the reluctant horror director a cult following.

Much more was to come over the following twenty-five years, from the unleashing of bogey man Freddy Krueger, who dominated commercial horror cinema for most of the eighties, to the more rewarding and mature *The Serpent and the Rainbow* and *The People Under the Stairs*. It was his triumphant post-modern return to the earlier haunt of Elm Street in *Wes Craven's New Nightmare* that relaunched Craven as a horror brand name and prepared the way for the phenomenal response to *Scream* and its shockingly successful sequel.

It's still a tremendous surprise today to people when they encounter Craven and find that the man who has committed these often disturbing images to the cinema screen is softly spoken, sharply intelligent and always prepared to justify his activities. 'There's basically two ways of looking at this,' says Craven of public perception of his horror persona. 'One is that I'm a frightening person making films; another is that I'm a person who understands how people are afraid, and who's making films about that fear and how to overcome it. I think I fall into the latter category. But people tend to project things: that's

frightening, that's from outside, that must be resident in the person who's presenting it. But I think all of these fears and all of these personae are within all people. It's just that I seem to be skilled in identifying them and bringing them out through characters.'

It's a skill that Craven discovered relatively late in life, only taking up film-making after his thirtieth birthday, following a successful academic career, including a spell as a teacher. Dubbed by the press as 'the Don among the dead men', the 'Sultan of Slash', a 'gentleman terrorist' or even the 'Doctor of Fear', Craven laughs at people's reactions to him. The two careers he's enjoyed seem as incompatible as his personality and the films he makes: 'I'm sort of amused by that seeming dichotomy. I think that if you're a quiet, genteel person, there's probably a lot of rage in you that doesn't get expressed. You need an outlet for that. I deal with my dark side the way kids do at Halloween — I play with it. I'm terrified by the general tone of this world — it feels to me as if life is a series of life-or-death struggles of the species. This entire world is steeped in blood; it's part of the game. So, unless you wrap yourself in a coma, you recognise that you're part of it. One of the ways that I can get rid of a little of that tension is to make crazy, violent films where I have a measure of control over that level of madness.'

Now enjoying unparalleled critical and commercial success, Craven has reached the pinnacle of his career after twenty-five years of struggling to make films. His uphill battle has been against the conditions under which he has had to work; against inadequate budgets and production

Opposite:

Doctor of Fear — Wes Craven at the beginning of his film-making career.

schedules; against the censors who have tried (and in some cases succeeded) to control what he can show to audiences; and against the studios and producers who have given Craven the chance to realise his cinematic visions, only to insist on their own commercially driven 'shock' endings.

With hindsight, it has all been worthwhile, even if much of his career development has been haphazard: 'When I'm interviewed, I'm always aware that people are under the impression that I'm following a much more controlled path than I really am. It's much more of a random thing.'

Craven's body of work has coherently and

Below: A boy and his dog — Wesley Earl Craven aged eleven.

consistently explored a series of themes. The concerns which would dominate his movies, including one generation's betrayal of the next and the breakdown of the family, developed out of his own formative years: 'There are many reasons I return to this theme, including the fact that I come from a broken family myself. Mostly though, it's to do with my feeling that the next generation is getting short shrift. The break-up of the nuclear family and the breakdown of the environment all point to the next generation somehow being discounted.'

Following the success of *Scream* and *Scream 2*, no one in Hollywood or the wider film world can now discount Wes Craven. He has repeatedly shocked and entertained audiences with his often nightmare-inspired visions. Now, with a self-penned novel, a new television franchise at Fox and his sponsorship of up-and-coming filmmakers, Wes Craven is using the power of his horror brand name to escape the genre which he felt stereotyped him as a 'guru of gore'.

'Even at their most ferocious, like my earlier films, I think my work has always had an openness about it, especially in my treatment of characters,' says Craven, always keen to have his genre films regarded as more than just gruesome entertainment. 'Even the worst and most heinous person in my films had a side that is human and is vulnerable. I think even the people who have been depicted as the best can have a side that is evil. I have really very few apologies for my films, except I wish they could be better in some ways.'

As he enters what must be the final phase of his film-making career, Craven feels that perhaps he's been too laid back for his own good about his work: 'I could have done better if I'd been stronger as a person and screamed at people more. If I want anything as a director it's to be more ferocious with people who are trying to fuck with me. That's not a big part of my nature, but directors need that. It's necessary in some ways, in the trench warfare of making a film. There are legions of people who want to diminish the film in one way or another — make it safer, make it easier, make it cheaper — and you find yourself constantly fighting to keep other people's hands off your films.'

Battles with producers, studios and film censors have dominated Craven's career, affecting the outcome of many of his films and causing him to attempt to give up making horror films altogether on more than one occasion. His fans have to be thankful that Craven did persevere during the difficult years, as his work has become more and more satisfying for audiences as it has matured.

The story of Wesley Earl Craven begins on 2 August 1939. He was born into a strict, deeply religious, working class Baptist family who lived in Cleveland, Ohio. Craven's childhood years, spanning World War Two and the great consumer boom of the fifties, he recalls as being mainly happy times, but, as he discovered later, he didn't know any better and had no other models with which to compare his own experiences. The biggest events of Craven's life during these years were the divorce of his parents and the subsequent death of his father when he was aged only five. The emotional impact of these crises has shown up repeatedly in his films.

Craven prefers to talk about his work rather than about his private life, whether it's his childhood, his parents or his own family of two children and two ex-wives. He does, however, recognise that his background has had a profound and direct effect on his creative and imaginative life: 'I don't feel very comfortable with [my family history]. I was raised under a very spiritual environment. A great amount of time, energy and study was spent on things other than the physical or material reality of this world. That sort of stuck with me. Much of that fundamentalist world is concerned with good and evil. As I worked my way out of that, spiritually and intellectually, into whatever world I'm in now, I nonetheless was set on that path of examining things in the largest scenario possible quite early.

I think that was good.'

Often the most effective sequences in Wes Craven's films are drawn from his remembrances of childhood fears. It's a well of inspiration he returns to again and again, to spine-tingling effect: 'I think what's really frightening are fears that were realised in the first five years of life. Like fear of darkness, of abandonment, the school bully or fear of your own body. And so I try to base my films on those early, early fears.'

As a child, Craven was afraid of bullies at school, and one in particular was to unwittingly inspire a horror movie icon. 'Freddy Krueger was named after a boy that got his newspapers on the same corner I did, and he used to try to beat me up,' he admits.

One of Craven's strongest childhood memories is of the nightmares he suffered from. Later in life he was to take great pleasure in using his dreams constructively in his film-making, and he has now left the nightmares behind: 'I don't get nightmares. I used to when I was a kid, and I think part of making the movies that I make is to process those nightmares into films and thereby get control of them. It's like putting the genie

Left: A scholar and a gentleman — Craven's high school yearbook picture.

back in the bottle.' The Bible teachings Craven was subjected to on the role of sin stayed with him right through childhood, and there's nothing like the fear of God or the Devil to spark off nightmares in an imaginative child.

While Craven was later grateful for the outlook on the world his upbringing gave him, after he left home he was painfully aware that there was also a huge downside. '[One] of the bad things that came out of that, obviously, was the fact that it forbade a lot of things, things that everybody is deserving of, from movies to sex,' he notes. 'It tended to be a very secretive world. They did not discuss a lot of things. That really influenced me and now I have this overwhelming urge to know the truth about everything. I

subscribe to far more magazines and newspapers than I can ever read and I have books coming out of every orifice in my house.'

This determination to find out about the world and learn from sources other than his parents would lead Wes Craven to become the first member of his family to attend college, where he reacted against his upbringing with a vengeance. He studied literature and psychology at Wheaton College in Illinois, and took a Masters degree in philosophy at John Hopkins University in Baltimore. 'When I finally got out of it [his home life], there was a sense of having been cheated out of a great deal and of having been misled a great deal,' he remembers. 'I wouldn't be surprised if part of the energy and ferocity of my

Below: Dream master — at college, Craven developed the ability to remember and record his dreams.

films came out of that subconscious sense of having been shafted.'

While at college, Craven was exposed to works of literature that have resonated through much of his film work. 'I once had a professor who told me that the most powerful thing about Milton's *Paradise Lost* is that Lucifer is so attractive,' recalls Craven, creator of such magnetic villains as Krug Stillo, Freddy Krueger and Horace Pinker. 'That is always the key to powerful stories; the villain is always attractive and charismatic. So when I started working in popular genre films, I kept that in mind. First comes the villain.'

The nature of evil was a constant topic when Craven was living at home, and he found that it recurred again and again in the literature he was studying, giving him a very grounded view of the issue: 'It's part of our nature, part of our life and every religion comes to grips with that. In some form or another it's always there to deal with. Maybe it's at the very core of human beings having free will. If there was no possibility of evil, you wouldn't have any choice to make. The key to my films is not who or what you are, but what choice you make — that's how you define yourself.'

In his twenties, education was the driving force for Craven, and he seemed set for a successful teaching career, although during his college and university years he had been involved in various aspects of the arts: 'I had a long history of wanting to be a writer. I wrote prose and poetry throughout college. I had other artistic inclinations as well — I drew cartoons all through college and also had a lot of musical ability. I played guitar a lot of the time. There was a lot of talent floating around, but nothing really to do with photography or cinema whatsoever.

'I didn't see a great many films when I was young because I was restricted from seeing them by my family. The films I saw [in college] were [from] the European film-makers. I saw, almost exclusively, the films of Buñuel, Fellini, Bergman, Cocteau. I was immediately drawn to these sort

Left: *The young Wes Craven.*

of fantastic visions of dream-like things. I think if I had followed my natural course, I would be doing films much more on those lines. I learned about the horror genre as I became aware that was the only avenue I had. I became very interested in *fantastique* films. I'm standing on the shoulders, as we all do, of giants. I mean, I have the whole European film masters of the last generation behind me. I'm in complete awe of them.'

Other temptations at college were even harder to resist than the cinema, especially given Craven's sheltered upbringing and sudden exposure to a much freer environment. Sex and drugs were undoubtedly a large part of campus life, and recreational drugs were to give Craven an interesting take on the world, both at college and in his early film-making days in New York City: 'I feel that's the way I perceive consciousness, really. That it is, in many ways, a very carefully controlled dream of waking consciousness. That once you start to get into something like dreams, the mind becomes quite blurred. Certainly, during the time of my life when I was doing psychedelic drugs and so forth, I could see that suddenly reality all shimmers and it's transparent. You say, "My God, it's all just an illusion". You're putting your head over into an entirely different dimension. I'm fascinated by that, by what is out there, what is native to that and can operate in that and just pull itself into our little band of the world. I've never had bad trips — they've always been very interesting to me.'

Education itself, though, gave Craven an intellectual background which he later used to effective ends in his film work, drawing on themes and characters from the past greats of literature or cinema to inform his own work in the horror genre, which was often undervalued by critics and audiences alike. 'I think I had one great advantage in that I come from an academic background,' he asserts, 'where I was absolutely drenched in the best of literature and the best of cinema, whereas a lot of other film-makers come out of a very populist background, where they read comic books and at night they saw one-reelers. Because I used to teach and I went through a Masters degree in philosophy, I've read the best and I've seen the best, so I can't help but be influenced by it. I just take that and say how would that be in a popular film. Maybe I have a little bit of an advantage.'

By the mid-sixties, Craven was fulfilling parental expectations. He taught English and humanities up to college level, and by 1964 had met and married Bonnie Broecker. The couple had two children in quick succession, Jonathan and Jessica, while Craven continued his teaching career at an engineering school called Clarkson College in Potsdam (location of the original Elm Street), in New York state. Already, Craven felt a growing need to escape the confines of his career, and his general disillusionment with the academic world found an outlet in his first tentative film-making experience. Made with the help of Clarkson students in the first half of

1968, *The Searchers* was a 16mm, forty-five minute film apparently inspired by the TV adventure series *Mission: Impossible*. With very limited resources available on the campus, Craven and his students had to make do with whatever they could lay their hands on. The movie was shot on reversal stock, so the original film had to be run through a projector at each showing. Sound was recorded separately on a reel-to-reel tape machine and synched up with the projector during screenings. *The Searchers* went down well on campus, and Craven found himself looking for a more permanent way out of the life he had drifted into.

'I think at that point in my life I was still trying to please my parents, unconsciously trying to be the good boy that went off to school and then became a teacher,' he admits. 'This was an acceptable profession and very respectable. About four or five years into teaching... I was always in trouble because I was writing parodies of the power structures and mimeographing them out and writing all sorts of comedy. I was even making little home movies. I just realised I was profoundly bored and out of place. I didn't want to be going for my PhD, and that was the whole pressure: "Now, you must get your PhD". All my friends would say, "You have to get tenure". I was looking at their lives and, y'know, they were bored, everyone was drinking heavily and they were having affairs with each other's wives and husbands. It just wasn't me, and so I just made one of those big leaps. I said, "I'm gonna take a shot at doing something that I would really enjoy". So I just quit and went to New York.'

In reality, it wasn't quite as dramatic as that. Craven spent his summer 1968 vacation exploring the film-making opportunities in New York City. It was a useful summer for making contacts, although his time visiting documentary director D. A. Pennebaker, who was working on *Monterey Pop* at the time, which boasted Martin Scorsese as one of many editors, didn't lead to any work. Craven hung around the production offices of

Leacock-Pennebaker, met Norman Mailer and saw real-life film-makers at work. Having quit his job at Clarkson College, he was loathe to return with his tail between his legs as the summer drew to a close. The autumn of 1968 saw him return reluctantly to teaching, working for a year in a high school in order to make ends meet.

Craven took the next step towards the world of movies by making use of personal connections. Steve Chapin had been a student of Craven's at Clarkson College and got to know his professor very well through their common interest in music and work on the campus radio station, where Craven presented a late night show and Chapin played live with his band. They often saw each other after their Clarkson days as Craven, Bonnie and their two young children were living in the same Brooklyn Heights building as Chapin's mother. Aware of Craven's film-making ambitions, Chapin (whose uncle was Ricky Leacock of Leacock-Pennebaker) recommended that his ex-professor contact his brother Harry Chapin, who was then working as a film editor in New York City, to see what opportunities there might be. It wasn't until the summer of 1969, a year after his first attempts to start a film-making career, that Craven finally acted on this suggestion, after his additional year of teaching came to a close and it looked unlikely that he'd be able to return.

Above: Summer of love — in the late sixties, Craven became involved in music, playing guitar and presenting a college radio show.

Although he became known for his musical career, including the hits 'Taxi' and 'Cat's in the Cradle', Harry Chapin was then working as an editor on industrial films, television commercials and documentaries, while at the same time making award-winning films of his own, including *Legendary Champions*, a collaboration with Jim Jacobs which won the 1969 Oscar for Best Documentary. This was someone from whom Craven could learn much, even if Chapin couldn't actually offer him a job. 'It was a very intense year and a half of doing everything, from sweeping floors upwards,' recalls Craven. 'I started as a messenger, which was a pretty big jump from being a Professor, and I drove a cab in New York for about six months. I got robbed twice in Harlem.'

Craven was inspired by the creativity among the group of underground film-makers he'd fallen

Below: Proud father — Jonathan and Jessica Craven often visited the sets of their father's movies.

in with in New York. He admits that he learned much more during this short period than he ever could have by taking a more conventional route into film-making: 'It all helped immensely. It was a unique opportunity, because it was within a very wide open structure of people that were making documentaries, little feature films, industrials, everything. So I got exposed to a great amount of technique, and it wasn't within that rigid Hollywood structure where, for instance, if you're an apprentice editor in Hollywood, you must stay that way for eight years before you're even allowed to touch film. Within a year and a half I was doing everything. Even though I spent years learning some of the techniques that an apprentice might have learned in his more controlled way, I still had a chance to be making movies at the same time. It was a great way. I think if I had started in California, I would have had a much slower growth.'

Craven learned to edit film, a skill which was to stand him in good stead, and during this period he met director Peter Locke, who was later instrumental in launching Craven's *The Hills Have Eyes* films. Locke was working as a director on a series of low budget films, and gave Craven, along with three others, the chance to edit his early effort *You've Got to Walk It Like You Talk It or You'll Lose That Beat*, which featured Robert Downey Sr (who worked with Craven again on the 1985 revival of *The Twilight Zone* TV series), Richard Pryor, Allen Garfield, Zalman King and Liz Torres. The film was a satire about a young man who, in a New York City filled with absurdities, tries to find a purpose in life.

Although he was working, this wasn't quite the life that Craven or his family were hoping for: 'I can tell you, when I was getting robbed in Harlem when I was driving a cab, I thought: "This really is the end of a stupid man", because I'd quit teaching. I'd had all this comfort, summers off with pay, with a wife and two kids, two cars, two motorcycles, two dogs. It was a complete disaster. At the point I was driving the cab,

Left: *Family reunion — Craven with his mother Caroline, brother Paul and sister Carole.*

I just thought, "I've blown it", like it was some sort of foolish fantasy.'

Craven was willing to take any job in film simply to gain experience and learn how it all worked, but his endeavours weren't paying the bills or bringing in enough money to provide for his wife and two children. Making connections within the New York film-making community, he started getting odd jobs here and there on various underground film productions. 'I took sound on documentaries,' remembers Craven of one of his first jobs in film-making. 'I worked all around the clock, just going from one job to another, from day jobs managing post-production to synching up dailies [matching up the sound recorded to footage crudely assembled after shooting prior to a final edit] at night for various documentaries. It was very intense. My marriage collapsed. I lived on virtually nothing. I lost about 30lbs, falling to 135lbs once.'

About to be divorced from Bonnie due to the strain of their unpredictable existence, but with two children who still depended on his income, Craven came very close to calling it a day in the film business altogether. The insecurity the family now faced was very trying for them: 'I think I was switching everything. It was a real watershed in my life. I was dropping out, doing drugs, getting into film-making. Bonnie, to her credit, was perhaps more conventional than I wanted to be at that time. She was worried about the insecurity of the area of the arts in which I wanted to work, quite rightly, as the early seventies was not a successful time for me.'

A meeting with aspiring film producer Sean S. Cunningham changed the course of Craven's career, however: 'Within a few weeks I had this job synching up dailies on this little feature [*Together*], quit driving the cab and decided I was gonna try again. That job led directly in ten months to being offered a film to write, direct and cut.' That film was *The Last House on the Left.* ∎

The Cult Director

It had cost him his marriage to Bonnie Broecker, but thirty-one year-old Wes Craven was fulfilling his dream of working in the film industry as the seventies began. Over the next ten years he would only complete two films, but both marked out his future direction as an original, startling and unique film-maker.

As a result of his various assignments in the New York underground film-making community, Craven met many people involved in producing a wide variety of movies, and one of them was to prove key to Craven's first directorial work. Sean S. Cunningham was a vibrant, ambitious film producer two years younger than Craven. After working in theatre, Cunningham switched to movies, and his first feature was an underground film called *The Art of Marriage*.

Cunningham started working on his second movie in the spring of 1970. He had made some progress with his work when he asked Wes Craven to synch up the dailies, but Cunningham's cash ran out and he sub-let his facilities to other film-makers until he could resume production on the movie, now called *Together*, in September 1970. By that time, Craven was doing so much work on the feature, including synching, editing and co-ordinating the shooting, that he was billed as 'associate producer'.

Working under cinematographer, co-director and editor Roger Murphy, Craven was helping out with the editing much of the time, and, as Cunningham and Murphy had frequent disagreements, Craven was in the ideal position to carry on Murphy's work. Such was the flexibility of low-budget productions like *Together* that Cra-

ven even managed to cut his directorial teeth on the movie. During the cold winter months, Craven and Cunningham escaped for two days to Puerto Rico, where Craven enjoyed the chance to direct some 'sunny, romantic stuff' to

Opposite: Wes Craven (far right) with his The Hills Have Eyes *cast.*

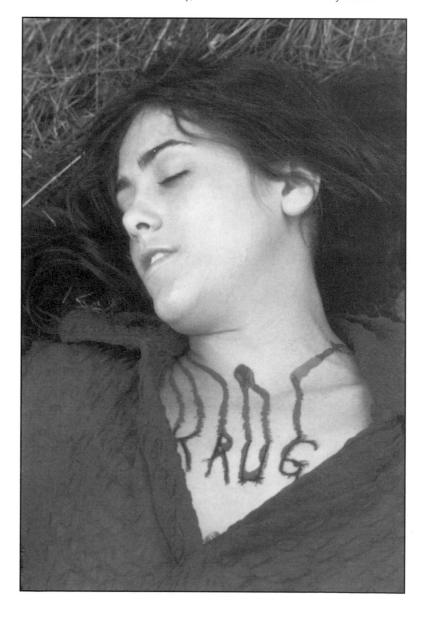

Previous page:
Mari
Collingwood
(Sandra Cassell)
in The Last
House on the
Left.
Right: The Last
House on the
Left's *Sadie*
(Jeramie Rain)
and Krug (David
Hess) prepare
for action.
Below: Dr
Collingwood
(Gaylord St
James) and Krug
(David Hess).

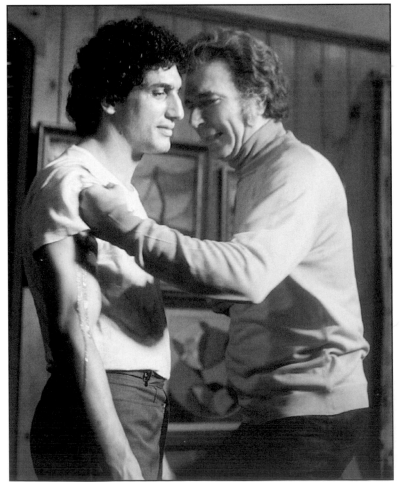

cut into the material Cunningham had already filmed.

Two more weeks of hard work on the final editing and sound mixing, and the film was ready to sell to a distributor. *Together* (also known as *Sensual Paradise*) featured an actress named Marilyn Briggs, who became better known as Marilyn Chambers, the Ivory Snow Girl, star of the Mitchell Brothers' film *Behind the Green Door* and David Cronenberg's chiller *Rabid*. Her co-stars included Maureen Cousins, Sally Cross, Jade Hagen, Kim Hoelter and Vic Monica.

The film was financed by a company called The Hallmark Releasing Corporation, film distributors whose parent company owned their own chain of cinemas and were always hungry for new material. While not a large outfit by any means, one skill that The Hallmark Releasing Corporation possessed in abundance was marketing and they produced an ingenious, teasing ad campaign.

The film, never released on video and now believed lost, made such a profit for Hallmark that they quickly came back to Cunningham and Craven and asked for another. This time Hallmark wanted to play up the violence. They needed some 'drive-in fodder', a 'no-holds barred horror movie'. Craven and Cunningham were only too ready to give it to them. It was what both men had dreamed of, the chance to make their own movie with a guaranteed release at the end of it. They were to be their own bosses and had the finance in place. The only question was, what kind of horror film could they make? According to Craven, Cunningham 'had been offered $90,000 as a whole budget for a scary movie, for a group of theatre owners in Boston. It was the result of having finished that first film [*Together*]. That film made money and he was offered by the distributor the chance to make another, if he would make a horror film. That's what they wanted for their programme. He asked me if I wanted to write it and direct it and cut it. I said, "sure", even though I had never thought of writing a scary movie before. And so I just decided that I would write it, and I did, and we shot it in 16mm. [That was] *The Last House on the Left* and it was picked up. So suddenly I was a horror director, though I'd never thought of doing that.'

'It was written in a weekend,' Craven says of

his first film script, which was actually sixty pages of close typed material not laid out in accepted screenplay format. 'I said, "Okay, what's a horror film?" I really didn't know what they were. I thought they had a lot of craziness and they scared people, so I went off and spent a weekend with friends in Long Island. I went and wrote something that I thought would scare people.'

The material Craven drafted over that weekend was later heavily revised and bore little relation to what eventually appeared on the screen. If censors in America and Britain thought that what they saw in *The Last House on the Left* was extreme, they are lucky that Craven's original screenplay, even more gruesome and sadistic and then entitled *Sex Crime of the Century*, never came anywhere near to being shot. Sean Cunningham acted as a script editor as well as producer on this ad-hoc project, cutting out impossible-to-film scenes and reworking others to make them more acceptable. Once they set out to film their script, Craven and Cunningham realised that they wanted to make a 'real' movie with a proper story. Craven dumped much of the sexual content of his scenario and reconceptualised the violence, inspired by an unlikely source.

An educated man, Craven was inspired by a

Left: Real terror — Sadie and Krug round on Phyllis (Lucy Grantham).

Above: Gun play — Krug takes aim at Mari.
Below: The Last House on the Left's bizarre criminal family.

Swedish film he'd seen the previous year, Ingmar Bergman's *The Virgin Spring*: 'When I saw *The Virgin Spring*, I thought, what an incredible story. It was very conscious and above board. I just thought it would be great to update [it] into something completely bizarre.'

Bergman's Oscar-winning film tells the story of the virginal daughter of a prosperous family who is abducted by a trio of shepherds when she gets lost after her family set off on a religious pil-

grimage. The girl is raped and murdered by two of the shepherds while a third, the youngest of the trio, watches in disgust. Later, the shepherds seek refuge at the home of the girl's parents and are found out when they try and sell a distinctive item of the daughter's clothing to the family. When the father's fears are confirmed by a witness, he takes bloody revenge on his three guests, pleading for divine forgiveness after the fact. The 'virgin spring' of the title appears on the spot where his daughter lost her life.

Using this template, Craven updated the tale of *The Virgin Spring* to modern Connecticut in a revision of his *Sex Crimes of the Century* script, which he now called *Night of Vengeance*, the film's shooting title. He replaced the virgin daughter with two hip teenagers, the innocent Mari (Sandra Cassell) and the street smart Phyllis (Lucy Grantham). The three shepherds became a quartet of escaped criminal psychopaths, led by Krug Stillo (would-be musician David Hess), who manipulates and torments his drug-addicted teenage son Junior (Marc Sheffler, later a children's television producer), the unwilling partici-

pant in the mayhem that was to come. Krug's bisexual, proto-feminist girlfriend Sadie (Jeramie Rain) and Fred 'Weasel' Padowski (porn star Fred Lincoln) made up the gruesome family.

The Last House on the Left sees the teenagers abducted, tortured, humiliated and then killed in long, drawn-out detail, well beyond what had been seen in cinema at the time, but no longer as shocking as some censorship bodies still seem to believe. After the murders, with the killers visibly repulsed and shocked by what they have done, the four arrive at Mari's home and are welcomed in as stranded travellers by her trusting parents, who are full of concern for their missing daughter. Putting various clues together — Mari's peace symbol necklace on one of the gang, bloodied clothes stuffed in a suitcase and an overheard conversation — John Collingwood (Gaylord St James), a doctor, and his wife Estelle (Cynthia Carr) find the body of their daughter. In their grief the pair plan a meticulous and deadly vengeance, the father booby trapping the house and attacking Krug with a chainsaw while the mother seduces and 'bobbits' Fred the Weasel

and slits Sadie's throat.

The violence of *The Last House on the Left*, although much of it happens off screen or has been so hacked about by various censorship bodies that it barely remains, is visceral and shocking. There is no looking away as the sordid drama unfolds. 'I felt it very strongly and I needed to get it out of my system,' admits Craven. 'I've never felt the need to go and have quite the same depictions in a film again. I went on to do films about

Above: Jeramie Rain as Sadie.
Below: *Chainsaw massacre — Dr John Collingwood lets rip.*

Above: *Mayhem — an out-take from the heavily censored scene where Krug stabs Phyllis.*

an initial stage in horror cinema, during which *The Last House on the Left* was made, where gore stood for everything that was hidden in society. Guts stood for issues that were being repressed, so the sight of a body being eviscerated was exhilarating to an audience, because they felt, "Thank God, it's finally out in the open and slopping around on the floor". But that gets very old very fast.'

Craven has never subscribed to the argument that what is seen on the screen can influence ordinary people to act out the scenario in real life: 'If you look at my films, it's the intensity rather than anything explicit that makes people think they're seeing a lot of gore. In *The Last House on the Left*, the disembowelling to which everyone refers isn't actually all that gory, but it is intense. On the other hand, I walked out of a screening of *Reservoir Dogs* because I felt at a certain point that the film-maker was just getting off on the violence and that it was being treated as something amusing, which it isn't to me.'

Craven and his crew set out to bring a documentary, hand-held realism to the depiction of violence and its aftermath. His influences were varied, but the newsreel footage of the American carnage in Vietnam playing on television every night provided a running commentary as he and Cunningham planned and executed their bloody little film: 'Films about violence at that time had become tremendously stylised. I was watching Peckinpah's films — violence becoming legitimised as balletic and almost beautiful. The critics were all swooning about how it could be handled so artistically. At the same time, Vietnam was going on, there was much there that was brutal and protracted and awful and ugly. So I set out to start a film that seemed to be a typical B-movie, with escaped convicts. There were all these jokes up front about how they'd killed a guard dog. It was standard B-movie fare, the villains walking down the street and bursting the balloon of a little boy.' That boy was, in fact, Craven's son Jonathan, who had accompanied

other things, [but] even though they may contain scenes of violence I never felt it was necessary to make that explicit statement about violence again. I mean, I could only watch that picture a few times. It's not a picture to be looked at over and over again and enjoyed.'

The impact of the violence in his début feature film was to affect the director throughout his career — the film has not been forgotten and interviewers never tire of asking him about it. For Craven, though, there is a moral justification for what he committed to celluloid: 'There was his father on the location shoot in Manhattan for the city scenes at the beginning of the film.

Craven wanted to play with audience expectations, to surprise and shock those whom he'd lulled into a false sense of seen-it-all-before security. 'I wanted to take that and stand it on its head,' he recalls. 'At the moment it gets violent, I wanted to make it very real, not swerving away, fading to black or dissolving or seeing a shadow do it, but just looking right at people at the moment they did it. That was very subversive and very threatening to people.'

After a quarter of a century, Craven has come to terms with the attention his notorious movie attracts: 'At this point, it is a film that is so far back in my past that it's more of an oddity than a sore point. I've thought about this a lot, and I see *The Last House on the Left* in a way as a protest film. It was made during the time of protest, the early seventies. It had, among other things, as well as attempting to be a popular film and a con-

troversial film, been an attempt to show violence the way I and the producer thought it really was, rather than the way it was typically depicted in films. In that sense, it had a real purpose to it and I think it has a legitimate artistic power.'

Craven deliberately set out to stretch the boundaries. It was his first film and, although still learning, he was determined to make an impact: 'We knew we were pulling out all the stops. There were many things in there that simply had not been shown in a film before. There was a level of reality and a length of time that things took that had never been done in any film that I knew of. That really went over the line of what people were expecting to see. You can call it discretion or you can call it squeamishness, but they had always either cut away or the camera would fade to black when certain things happen.'

Craven stands by the decisions he took in making *The Last House on the Left*, drawing on the

Below: *Striking back — Estelle Collingwood (Cynthia Carr) fighting with Sadie.*

Above: The end of the line — battered and bloody, Krug suffers at the hands of the vengeful father.

real lives of millions of people: 'I'm in my fifties, and I can remember growing up during World War Two and seeing newsreels of cities burning and things blowing up. That madness stayed with me. And it keeps happening. It happened in Bosnia — people who had been living together for years, suddenly they're cutting throats on the village bridge. And it happened again in Rwanda. It's quite chilling.'

Other influences were brought to bear on Craven's approach to the physical nature of filming *The Last House on the Left*. 'Perhaps it came out of my first year and a half of learning about

film-making,' he speculates. 'It was in a building in New York that was occupied by documentary film-makers. It was the core group which had come out of *Life* magazine and established the whole hand-held camera school of film and television. They were a very tough lot and they used to say to each other, "What if you were watching a mother dying on the sidewalk, would you go to help her?" They said, "No, keep filming". So the thing was that you do not blink, you do not look away, because then you become television, then you become American commercial movies. The notion was to have that sort of war correspondent's unblinking eye and show what happens after the camera fades to black.

'That, perhaps, is the most significant moment of all, because it's so overwhelming that we don't look at it and therefore you can continue to cause violence, because we really don't know from our films what it's like to drop a bomb on somebody, or to bayonet somebody. If we show them in our films at all, as we used to, it's very quick. So, for instance, in a war film, where they were being bayoneted, they would clutch themselves, fall down and die. Whereas, my feeling about it was that he would probably get stuck on the bayonet, and the guy would have to do it several times, and the person would be struggling to stay alive and probably they would not be killed by just one thrust.

'So, in *The Last House on the Left*, for instance, when Phyllis — who's the toughest one — is dying, she gets up and crawls away and they go after her. It actually becomes so terrible that the killers are repulsed. It's the whole turning point in the film, in that they can't look each other in the eye. They have to go change clothes. They become, in a sense, the most conservative, while the parents, in their revenge, become the most vicious. It was operating on a very, very intense level of confrontation with the audience.'

Craven deliberately set out to show sympathy for the devil, in this case his lead villain, Krug Stillo: 'I think that one of the most controversial things about *Last House* was that after the killers had done their worst — and they did really, they went right down to the bottom, to the nadir of the human capacity for cruelty and killing — they became human. They suddenly became aware that they were afraid. They were repulsed. They had love within their own strange, little family. The movie revolves around the coincidence of them stumbling into the parents' house for shelter after they have killed the teenagers, and they don't realise that these are the parents of one of them. The parents don't know that these are the murderers of their missing child. The killers are awkward at a table like this, they don't know what forks to use and they are aware that their clothes aren't that good. The audience got really angry that I was showing any sympathy to these people and at the end of the movie, the parents become the most brutal of killers when they take their revenge on [their daughter's] killers.'

This ambivalent approach to heroes and villains also coloured Craven's later work, from *A Nightmare on Elm Street* to *Scream*, where no one is ever entirely innocent: 'I continue to like doing that. I like not allowing the audience to be certain who is the villain and who is the hero.'

Above: *David Hess as Krug Stillo.*
Left: *The last supper — the killers dine with the Collingwoods.*

While Freddy Krueger is clearly a villain, tormenting and killing the Elm Street children, it was their parents who had murdered him in the first place, in a *Last House* style revenge.

The Last House on the Left was shot during October 1971 in and around Sean Cunningham's rented house in Westport, Connecticut. Although the film had been scripted after a fashion by Craven, many of the more memorable scenes were actually improvised as production progressed. Ideas came not only from Craven but from his actors, chief among them David Hess, who also wrote and sang on the film's featured songs. Several scenes, including Weasel's nightmare featuring Mari's parents as a pair of demonic dentists, Phyllis' death-defying struggle through the cemetery, Sadie's death in the swimming pool, Junior's coerced gunshot suicide and, most significantly, the killer's key moment of remorse, were all late additions improvised to some extent dur-

Below: Dream dentists — Weasel has Craven's first nightmare sequence, featuring Mari's parents.

ing shooting. Especially significant were the dream sequences, late additions to the film which effectively set the tone for Craven's future career as the master of movie nightmares.

There were some areas of *The Last House on the Left* that Craven would not return to again: 'I did a very difficult-to-watch rape scene in *Last House*. It's another thing that is very protracted and it's what ends up killing the central character. *Last House* revolves around this very shocking thing — the two central characters end up dead by the end of the second act. That's where she essentially commits suicide, but it's also where the villain completely loses his power. He never has power after that because she never gives herself to him and he knows it. I felt like that's enough, I've done it once and I don't want to ever be in any sense glamorising that and making it look like an interesting or dramatic device. It's such a touchy area, something that's been done so

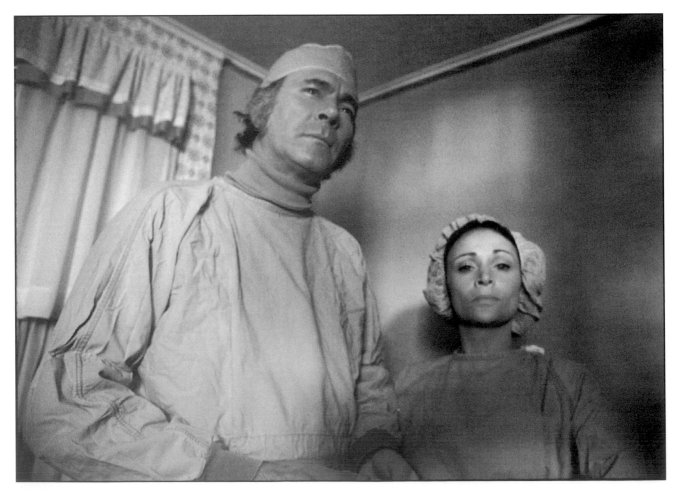

Left: Krug and company force Phyllis and Mari to strip.
Below: Marshall Anker and Martin Kove as the comic relief cops.

much in movies. I do shy away from that.' In making his films, Craven has been continually conscious of his own daughter Jessica and has claimed that Nancy in *A Nightmare on Elm Street* was intended as a positive role model for her.

One element of *The Last House on the Left* which makes many viewers uncomfortable is the comic relief, in the form of the bumbling sheriff (Marshall Anker) and his deputy (Martin Kove) who set out to track down the escaped criminals, only to have their car run out of gas and spend the rest of the film trying to hitch a lift to the Collingwood house. Naturally, the pair of buffoons arrive just in time to witness the carnage as the parents' revenge culminates in Krug's decapitation. The dumb cop character would later be reprised twenty-five years later by David Arquette in *Scream*. The comedic element in *Last House* was necessary, according to Craven, as a relief from the intensity of the murder scenes and as a natural extension of his own interests: 'Before I did my first horror film I was almost exclusively involved in comedy. Throughout high school and college I was known as the class wit, and I wrote parodies and comedies. Even after I got to Hollywood I wrote cabaret acts for several comedians. It always seemed odd to me that I ended up doing these horror films, and in a sense they have a very bizarre sense of humour. When we made them there was a great deal of laughter and giggling. The more grotesque the horror gets on the screen, the more you laugh and think it's some kind of naughty humour.'

Post-production on *The Last House on the Left*

was a shambolic nightmare for the neophyte film-makers. Continuity was an unknown to Cunningham and Craven, who simply tried to stitch together as coherent a narrative as they could with the footage they had. Shooting ate up in the region of $45,000, but by the time six months of post-production editing and sound work had taken place, the cost of *The Last House on the Left* had reached $100,000, well above Sean Cunningham's previous expenditure on a film. Most who worked on the movie, including production assistant Steve Miner (who later directed two sequels to Cunningham's *Friday the 13th*), agreed that it was Craven's professional editing skills that saved the film from disaster. Forced to cut many of the scenes tightly, Craven ended up with a feature film that fell a few minutes short of the typical hour and a half. Further trims were made by Cunningham in Craven's absence in an attempt to persuade the Motion Picture Association of America (the country's censorship body) to grant *Last House* an 'R' certificate, after Hallmark made

a deal with American International Pictures (AIP) for nationwide distribution.

'To me, aside from all the philosophical things behind it, it's an extremely crude film,' admits Craven readily, 'because I didn't know how to make a movie. It was literally the movie where I learned how to make a movie. It worked. A crude but effective device, as they say in the newspapers.'

His ultra-realistic morality tale outraged many, but Craven did win a couple of influential admirers for his courageous work. 'Well, Robin Wood was very good,' he remembers. 'He was key. Roger Ebert gave *Last House* a five star review, so he was very important to a young film-maker, because I can tell you that, with the exception of Ebert and one other in a magazine called *Creem*, a teenage music magazine, the rest treated me like the Creature from the Black Lagoon, like this reprehensible film-maker.' Ebert dubbed the film 'a sleeper... about four times better than you expect', while other reviewers reached for words like 'shameful',

Below: The psychotic Weasel (Fred Lincoln, centre), with Krug and Phyllis.

'morbid' and 'repugnant'.

It might be easy to suppose that because Cunningham and Craven were only starting out in the business that reviews wouldn't have mattered much to them. The truth was different, and Craven has taken critical responses to his work very seriously throughout his career: 'Reviews have a profound effect on artists. I've seen it with other people and you can't help but be influenced, as much as you try to say they mean nothing. Somebody told me of the famous response of, I think, George Bernard Shaw, who called up a critic and said, "I'm sitting in the smallest room in the house. I have your review before me and soon it will be behind me!" I can't tell you how many times I've got totally blasted or just sat in a room and wondered whether I should continue making films after reading a bad review. They are important. If they are good, they sustain you. It's been good over the years to watch my films be treated more and more seriously. At first, maybe I was seen as some sort of monstrosity, maybe I shouldn't have been making films.'

The film opened in Hallmark's cinemas in July 1972 under the title *Krug and Company*. There was also a single screening of a more complete print (perhaps the fabled ninety-one minute cut with all the gore intact) at Britain's National Film Theatre in London. Further screenings later in the summer in upstate New York saw the film retitled *Sex Crime of the Century*, the title on Craven's first draft screenplay. The combination of the final title of *The Last House on the Left*, released in August 1972, and the warning 'Not recommended for persons over thirty' sealed the lucrative fate of the film. Craven himself was never taken with the final title, although he has not stated a preferred option of his own: 'I still think it's a nothing title. There's no last house on the left in the picture. But it took off, and there were imitation titles like *The House at the Edge of the Park* and so on.'

Next was the remarkable slogan Hallmark

slapped on all the posters and advertising material: 'To avoid fainting, keep repeating, it's only a movie... only a movie... only a movie... only a movie...'. Hallmark had borrowed it from Herschell Gordon Lewis' *Color Me Blood Red* which claimed: 'You must keep reminding yourself, it's just a motion picture!'

While Hallmark's advertising campaign was re-used and similarly borrowed for years to come, both by themselves and by others, so too was the title. There was even a *Last House on the Left 2*, which has no connection with either Cunningham or Craven. It was a retitled re-release of Mario Bava's *Twitch of the Death Nerve*, aiming to capitalise on the publicity and notoriety Craven's film was generating. The director had his own idea for a sequel, which involved

Krug and company coming back from hell to continue their reign of terror, but he felt people weren't quite ready for that.

Censorship of *The Last House on the Left*, beyond the cuts imposed by the MPAA and carried out by Cunningham, was the work of local organisations, resulting in the circulation of various different prints of the film, some intact, some less so: '*Last House* was censored more or less *ad hoc* in the United States by local groups and by theatre managers and even by projectionists. Everybody had a snip at it, so it was not just the British film censors who have reacted to it. People either hated it or loved it. There were literally fist fights in the audiences, with people fainting and having heart attacks. It's always been a contro-

versial film and I'm not surprised it was banned in Britain. In the United States we have this joke about everything being banned in Boston — it usually means a film is going to be a success.'

The British release history of *The Last House on the Left* is complicated. It was submitted to the censors, the British Board of Film Censorship (later 'Classification') as *Krug and Company* in July 1974. This longer print, featuring an alternative take of the discovery of Mari's body by her parents in which she identifies the killers, was screened once at the National Film Theatre, rejected by the Board and banned. In a panel session in the summer of 1988, BBFC director James Ferman joined Craven and fellow genre writer and director Clive Barker, as well as *The*

CAN A MOVIE GO TOO FAR?
MARI, SEVENTEEN, IS DYING. EVEN FOR HER THE WORST IS YET TO COME!

TO AVOID FAINTING KEEP REPEATING, IT'S ONLY A MOVIE ..ONLY A MOVIE ..ONLY A MOVIE ..ONLY A MOVIE ..ONLY A MOVIE ONLY A MOVIE

LAST HOUSE ON THE LEFT

WARNING! NOT RECOMMENDED FOR PERSONS OVER 30!

...IT'S JUST ACROSS THE STREET FROM "JOE"!

SEAN S. CUNNINGHAM FILMS LTD. Presents "THE LAST HOUSE ON THE LEFT" Starring: DAVID HESS • LUCY GRANTHAM • SANDRA CASSEL • MARC SHEFFLER • and introducing ADA WASHINGTON • Produced by SEAN S. CUNNINGHAM Written and Directed by WES CRAVEN • COLOR BY MOVIELAB

R RESTRICTED Under 17 requires accompanying Parent or Adult Guardian

Guardian's film critic Derek Malcolm, to discuss issues of censorship. Naturally, *The Last House on the Left* was high on the agenda. Ferman explained his reasons for banning the film: '[It was] rejected because the violence was exploitative, unpleasant and it was felt that the film revelled in it. The film was never resubmitted, although the distributor told us he had cut some of the worst bits already. 104 courts in Britain have found the film obscene — it wasn't acquitted by one of them. In forty-four cases it went before a jury under Section Two of the Obscene Publications Act. Even if we wanted to classify it now, we can't take that view when so many juries have judged it obscene.'

The Last House on the Left was prime material for release by exploitative distributors, and for moral censure by jittery MPs, the National Viewers and Listeners Association and the predominantly right-wing tabloid press. In 1982, with the home video boom well underway, an apparently unauthorised Replay Video release of *Last House* hit the stores. Newspapers began highlighting the fact that videos of films such as *Cannibal Holocaust* and *I Spit on Your Grave* were legally available, uncertificated, for hire from video stores to anyone of any age. As the publicity increased, a BBFC sub-committee began looking into classification of video material in line with cinema releases, while campaigners urged prosecutions under the Obscene Publications Act. Police forces across the country began a series of apparently random raids, confiscating and destroying material. This resulted in the 1984 Video Recordings Act and BBFC classification of all video material and the maintenance of a list (subject to monthly review) of over sixty 'banned' videos (including *Last House*), the supply or distribution of which could result in prosecution. 'All that it means to me that it has been banned in Britain is that Britain is either not prepared for that sort of confrontation or does not want it,' says Craven. 'I think that's very much a cultural thing, and they're very much within

MOST MOVIES LIVE LESS THAN TWO HOURS! THIS IS THE ONE OF EVERLASTING TORMENT!

The windows look out on hell... a view that will take your breath away...permanently!

THE NEW HOUSE ON THE LEFT

Starring
KAY PATTY NORMA DELBERT
BEAL EDWARDS KNIGHT MOSS

SEAL of CONSUMER AWARENESS

EASTMAN COLOR

R RESTRICTED

Produced and Directed by EVANS ISLE
CENTRAL PARK DISTRIBUTING CORP.

Left: *One of the spurious* The Last House on the Left *'sequels'.*

their rights, within your own culture. You guys have to decide whether you want such things floating around in your cinema.'

The briefly available Replay label release of *The Last House on the Left* lacked end credits and a comic relief scene where the sheriff and his deputy try to hitch a lift on a wagon full of chickens (glimpsed briefly in the montage shots at the end, where the credits should have appeared). The Replay release also featured the original Mari death scene, lacking the accusatory dialogue seen in the NFT screening.

Although affected by the bad reviews, Craven was pleased that his film was something of a hit and earning a reputation. As the release rolled out across America in late 1972 and into 1973 the

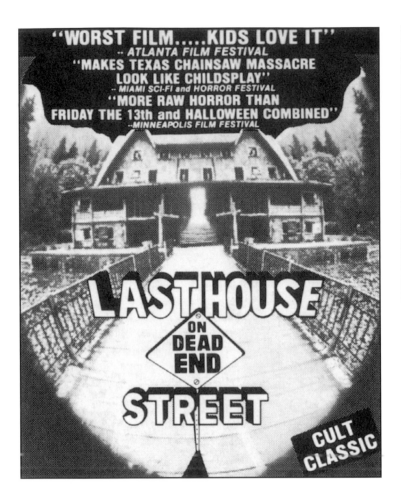

Above: Another attempt to cash in on the Last House *name.*

film continued to earn huge amounts in each city it played. Conversely, on a more personal level, Craven found friends and acquaintances changed their view of him after they discovered what he'd been working on: 'People literally wouldn't leave their children alone with me. They would get up and walk away from the table when I went out to have dinner. There was this powerful feeling that we had done something unspeakable.'

In 1973, six months or so after the film's release, Craven started to earn money from Hallmark. He made close to $100,000 from the film in the first year of release, almost ten times his salary as a teacher. It's difficult to establish how much money the film has actually made, but it has been claimed that by 1982, following various re-releases, foreign cinema distribution and video releases, that *The Last House on the Left* had

grossed around $18 million in total. Not bad for a $100,000 exploitation movie.

Immediately after completing post-production on *The Last House on the Left*, Craven went to California, trying to make some money while he waited for the returns from *The Last House on the Left* to come in and taking the opportunity to make contacts where it mattered. He had a job offer from director Peter Locke, who'd asked Craven to edit his movie *It Happened in Hollywood*. It was a comedy chronicling the rise of a telephone operator who becomes a star and wins the first X-rated acting Oscar for her role in the film *Samson and Delilah*.

Despite the slow build success of his first film and its immediate notoriety, *The Last House on the Left* didn't do Craven's nascent career any favours. 'In many ways it hampered me,' he recalls, 'because even in the United States I was considered such a bad boy that nobody would entrust me with anything but a horror film. After *Last House*, Sean Cunningham and I wrote about five films and nobody would talk to us. We had to go off and follow separate careers. I didn't want to be a horror film director, I just wanted to be a director. I just wanted to make films.'

Over the next three years Wes Craven tried to mount a variety of projects from his own scripts, but could find no one to back them. 'I wrote a very ambitious film called *Mustang*,' he recalls. 'It was based on the true-life story of a Colonel [Anthony Herbert] who was court-martialed for reporting American atrocities in Vietnam. All I wanted was $500,000, but nobody would listen.'

Other ideas Craven worked on during this time included a children's horror movie based around *Hansel and Gretel*, to be produced with Sean Cunningham, and a satire on American beauty contests. If any of these projects had come to fruition, Craven's subsequent film-making career may have taken a very different direction. As it was, forced to return to horror for his next film project, Craven spent much of the next twenty years engaged in a love-hate relationship with the genre he excelled at, but which he simultaneously resented for its limitations.

While Craven was struggling to escape his exploitation beginnings, Sean Cunningham gleefully stuck with his, producing a sex comedy called *The Case of the Smiling Stiffs* which mentions a character called 'Inspector Craven'. Steve Miner, production assistant on *The Last House on the Left*, worked on *Smiling Stiffs* and was later instrumental to the development of *A Nightmare on Elm Street*. Cunningham turned out a couple of kids' sports films at the end of the seventies, *Here Come the Tigers* and *Kick*, but it was only with a reluctant return to horror that both Craven and Cunningham got their careers back on track, with *The Hills Have Eyes* and *Friday the 13th* respectively.

Before tackling *The Hills Have Eyes*, Craven embarked on another film project as both actor and director. The almost unheard of *Tales That Will Tear Your Heart Out* was a horror anthology of the type popularised by Amicus in the seven-

ties, with films like *Tales From the Crypt* and *The Vault of Horror*. The segment Craven directed in 1976, written by Allan Pasternak, was a zombie-western which featured David Hess (*Last House*'s Krug) and Craven's friend Roy Frumkes (who was behind the project), as well as Craven himself, in acting roles. Sporting long hair and a beard at the time, Craven appeared in gruesome zombie make-up as an undead cowboy. Abandoned before it was finished, one section of the movie (not Craven's) surfaced as a prologue to the film *Dr Butcher M.D.*, an American release of the Italian movie *Zombi Holocaust*.

When production on *Tales That Will Tear Your Heart Out* collapsed, Craven once again found himself working for Peter Locke as an editor on *Car Hops*, a 1977 comedy sometimes known as *California Drive In Girls*. For the first and last time, he was credited as 'Wes "Hot Tracks" Craven'.

It was a direct request from Locke to produce another *The Last House on the Left* that finally got

Below: Tales That Will Tear Your Heart Out, *featuring Wes Craven.*

Craven back to working as a director. Craven claims that Locke had been asking him to do something in a similar vein since 1973, but he'd resisted, desperately hoping one of his other non-horror projects would get off the ground first. Finally, having run out of residual earnings

from *The Last House on the Left* and working on *Car Hops*, Craven began work on a script which became *The Hills Have Eyes*.

He created a simple story which could be made on a very restricted budget by hiring unknown actors and working largely on one out-

Right *Brenda Carter (Susan Lanier) is tormented in* The Hills Have Eyes.

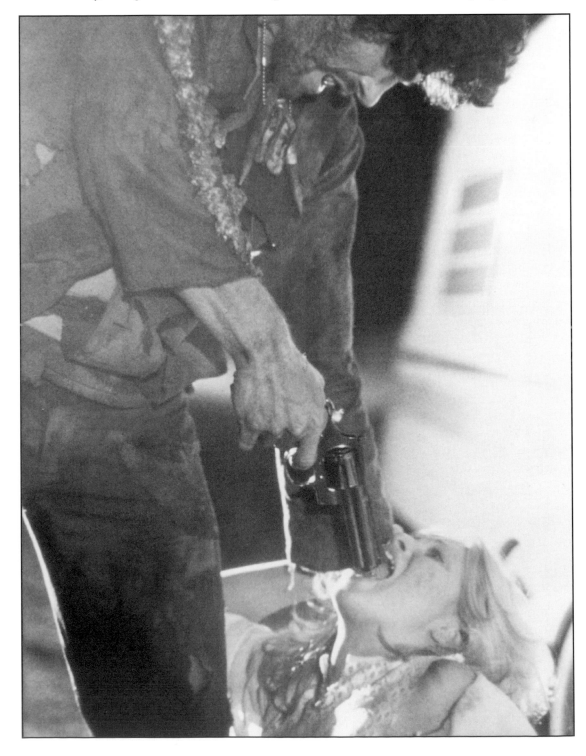

of-the-way location. The result was the tale of the happy-go-lucky Carter family, whose trailer home holiday is interrupted when they break down in the Californian desert. Drawing on the myth of a family of Scottish cannibals led by the murderous Sawney Bean, Craven has the Carters attacked by their evil opposites — a family of mutant, mountain-bred cannibals out for lunch. After one of the family is killed and another kidnapped, the Carters, in a none-too-subtle echo of *The Last House on the Left*, find that they have to strike back with the violence that was used against them. It was only his second completed film, but Craven was once more chronicling the destruction and deviance of the American family: 'Well, they say you write about what you're closest to. My deepest impressions come from my family, so a lot of that works its way out through my movies. I set out to have the two families in *The Hills Have Eyes* be mirror images of each other, so I could explore the different sides of the human personality — the two brothers being the [antithesis] of each other within the bounds of popular entertainment. I wanted something more sophisticated than *The Last House on the Left*. I didn't want to feel uncomfortable again about making a statement about

Above: *Michael Berryman (Pluto) and James Whitworth (Jupiter) on location.*
Left: *Wes Craven in the desert outside Los Angeles, filming* The Hills Have Eyes.

Opposite: James Whitworth in full make-up.
Below Brenda Carter in trouble again, at the hands of Jupiter.

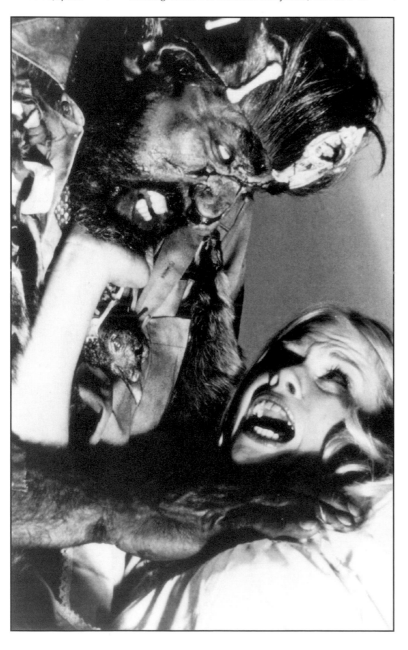

human depravity and then engaging in it to make the point.'

The process of making *The Last House on the Left* had taught Craven the basics of mounting a low-budget feature film, and he employed the same guerrilla film-making tactics on *The Hills Have Eyes*. Shot out in the California desert, Craven rounded up a cast of would-be actors for his new film. Among them was Michael Berryman, cast as a vil-

lain called Pluto, a pre-cursor of Freddy Krueger. Berryman had been born prematurely in 1948 to a medical family who could do nothing to correct their son's peculiar physical features. However, it was Berryman's extraordinary looks that secured him a movie career. Following a bit part in *Doc Savage*, Berryman won a role in Milos Foreman's *One Flew Over the Cuckoo's Nest* before signing up with Craven to play Pluto. 'That was the first time I'd shot out-of-doors,' said Berryman of the desert location shooting for *The Hills Have Eyes*. 'There were varying weather conditions and whatnot — it was a challenge.'

Craven intended *The Hills Have Eyes* to be a straightforward film in the style of a drive-in movie, but many people have seen the influence of comic book styles in his approach to the movie. It's an influence Craven himself denies: 'I don't think it was comic booky. I mean, I read comics when I was a kid, but only a few. It sort of came out of my own head. I didn't have any precedent for it. The only precedent that I mention is that the rough story was based on the Sawney Bean family. I ran across that in the New York Public Library. Once I'd read that basic story, I thought that would be a wonderful basic plot for a movie, brought up to date in a modern setting.'

The film's budget was only $230,000 — more than *Last House* certainly, but not really enough to provide a professional finish to the movie. Craven shot on 16mm film and blew the print up to 35mm for distribution. 'We couldn't afford a full union crew,' he remembers, 'and we were paying minimum to the actors. We shot in Victoriaville, outside Los Angeles, where it was alternately burning and freezing. We shot the trailer interior in a warehouse. *Hills* was technically much better than *Last House*, if not quite as profitable, but it resulted in a lot more offers of work.'

One of the more unusual reviews of *The Hills Have Eyes* was by Joe Bob Briggs, who recommended it as one of Ten Best Flicks to Get Nookie By: 'Of all the possible cannibal/dead-tourist classics, like *The Grim Reaper*, I think this Wes

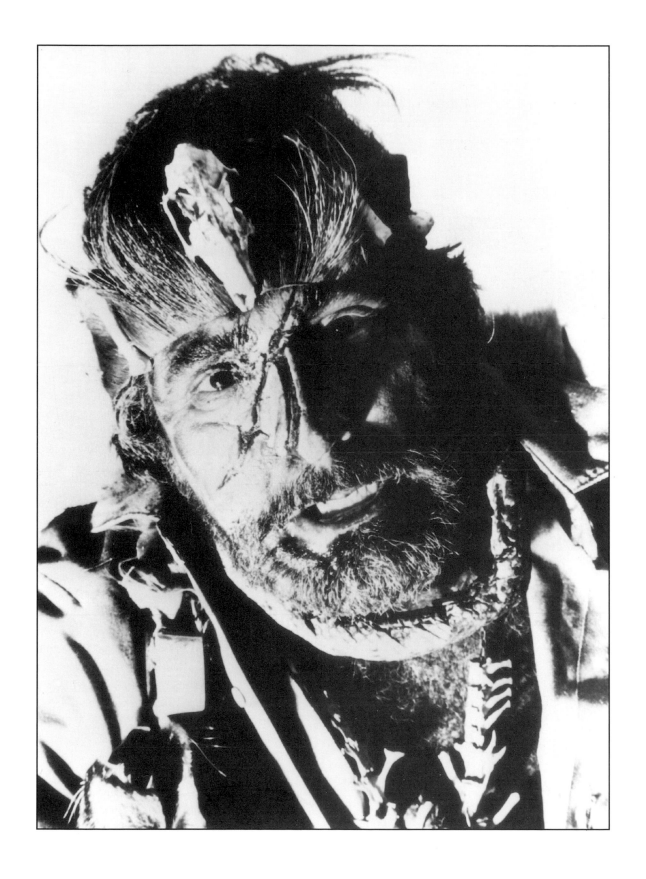

Craven stranded-Winnebago saga is the most terrifying to a female companion because it's the closest the movies have ever come to wasting a baby on-screen. It's one thing to see easygoing Papa Carter get crucified on a burning cactus, but when the nuclear-mutant desert family steals that baby and starts fighting over the dinner portions on their CB radios, girls have been known to vaporise and just leave a little slick spot on the upholstery.'

Dealing with cinematic violence again, Craven was faced with choices about what he would and wouldn't commit to celluloid. The baby scene that Briggs had cited was a particular concern. 'There's a great deal I wouldn't do and haven't done,' he claims. 'It would be hard to think of specific examples, but I continually monitor myself and say, "No, that's too far". *The Hills Have Eyes* is the closest I came to the line. For instance, where the baby was kidnapped and tossed back and forward. I could have killed that baby — that was one of the script options. I chose not to do that.'

That was a scene which *Hills* star Michael

Below: Doug Wood (Martin Speer), searching for his baby.

Berryman particularly remembers the audience reaction to. Watching the movie after doing an appearance in costume as Pluto for the *Detroit Free Press*, Berryman couldn't resist the theatrical lure of making his presence known to the unsuspecting audience. 'Right about the point where the heavies were threatening to kill the baby, this woman got up dragging her son out of the theatre, yelling, "This movie is sick",' he told *Fangoria*. 'The audience was screaming right back at her and her son looked like he was ready to deck the old lady. As she came up the aisle, I grabbed her by the arm and said, "Damn right, lady. This movie's horrible!" She went into hysterics and ran out into the street. Her son just said "Thanks" and went right back to watching the movie.'

The odd humorous incident aside, Craven takes his on-screen depictions of violence seriously: 'I don't like torture of animals. I'm softer on animals than I am on people! I've shied away

from protracted torture or suffering since *Last House*. I'm very careful of how I treat women in my films. They are victims, along with the men, but usually in my films they are the strongest. I have a daughter [Jessica] and I want her to have a very strong image of womanhood. I try not to do anything that isn't in some way intelligent — ultimately the central character is never a victim.'

Having a central, strong female character who could fight back against the villain of the piece was an idea that was to lurk at the back of Craven's mind for several years, before surfacing in *A Nightmare on Elm Street*. For the moment, Wes Craven had established himself to a point where he could be considered as a director for 'mainstream' Hollywood movies. ■

Dream Worlds

In the late seventies the horror movie was enjoying a new boom through the success of the stalk-and-slash movies popularised by John Carpenter's *Halloween*, giving Craven an opportunity to get back to work after *The Hills Have Eyes*. Although he'd been trying to work in the movie business for some years, Craven only had two films under his belt and was still something of a beginner.

He turned to television for the first time with the NBC TV movie *Stranger in Our House* (released in cinemas across Europe under the title *Summer of Fear*), not that he particularly wanted to work within the strict censorship of television, but he knew he needed the experience. 'They are not important works,' Craven has said. 'I used them for professional reasons and for getting into the Director's Guild. For example, *Stranger in Our House* was the first time I'd worked with any name stars with Linda Blair and Carol Lawrence. It was a great learning experience. It gave me some money and credibility, as well as residuals over the years.'

Craven still has reservations about his early television projects: 'To me, they were very much something to do either to make money to survive or else to learn techniques. *Stranger in Our House* was my first use of a dolly, first use of a crane, first shooting in 35mm, first time shooting with a full crew, and the first time with a decent schedule. Although it was a television schedule, it was longer than anything I'd ever had, so I learned a great deal of technical things on that. *The Last House on the Left* and *The Hills Have Eyes* had both been shot on 16mm film

stock, with very small crews. The whole crew on *Hills* was eleven people, and on *Last House* was about five. I knew nothing really of the techniques of film-making.'

Stranger in Our House was based on the novel *Summer of Fear* by Lois Duncan. Interestingly, another book by Duncan would provide source material for *Scream* writer Kevin Williamson's slasher hit *I Know What You Did Last Summer* twenty years later in 1997. Craven recognised in the novel a continuation of the thematic material he'd dealt with in his two previous films: the family under threat from within. The Bryants

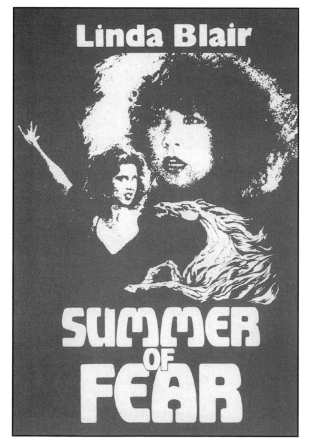

Opposite: The gang's all here — Michael Berryman returns, with Tamara Stafford and John Bloom in The Hills Have Eyes Part II. ***Left:*** *Summer of Fear — aka* Stranger in Our House.

TO THE VALLEY OF BEAUTY CAME THE SHADOW OF DEATH

DEADLY BLESSING X

Pray you're not blessed

PolyGram Pictures Presents An INTER PLANETARY PRODUCTION of a WES CRAVEN FILM "DEADLY BLESSING"
MAREN JENSEN SUSAN BUCKNER SHARON STONE JEFF EAST LISA HARTMAN LOIS NETTLETON and ERNEST BORGNINE
Screenplay by GLENN M BENEST & MATTHEW BARR And WES CRAVEN Story by GLENN M BENEST & MATTHEW BARR
Executive Producer WILLIAM GILMORE Music Composed by JAMES HORNER Executive in charge of Production JERE HENSHAW
Produced by MICHELINE And MAX KELLER PAT HERSAGUE Directed by WES CRAVEN
PolyGram Pictures   Copyright MCMLXXXI PolyGram Pictures Ltd All Rights Reserved
Released in the UK by Barber International Films Ltd.

open their home to their cousin Julia (Lee Purcell), a relative they have never met, after her parents are killed in a car crash. Julia has a hidden side to her personality, leading a double life as a witch and practising a form of Ozarkian black magic. Working her way through the family members, she manages to alienate the Bryant daughter Rachel (Linda Blair) from the rest of her family, wins away Rachel's boyfriend for herself, kills Rachel's favourite horse and threatens to replace Mrs Bryant (Carol Lawrence) as the 'mother' of the household by arranging an accident.

Craven deliberately cast Linda Blair, star of *The Exorcist*, against type as the threatened daughter of the family, Rachel. Blair plays the role in a winsome manner, emphasising the homespun normality of the Bryant household for all it's worth. Stifled by the strict code of conduct regulating what could be shown on network television, there was no way Craven was going to be able to recreate the visceral impact of his previous films: 'I wasn't allowed to have any violence, but the story didn't need it anyway.' The film relies on atmosphere and is more of a traditional ghost story than the cinematic

gorefests he had become known for, but Craven fails to shine as a director. It's a straightforward, competent work, but where it scores is in the editing. As the film builds towards its climax, it becomes clearer that the developing sense of tension depends on the pacing, and it's Craven's skilful editing that heightens the fear factor. It's a shame that *Stranger in Our House* opts for the standard 'back-from-the-dead' finale, which had become such a horror film cliché since Brian De Palma's *Carrie*. *Stranger in Our House* was the first of many of Craven's directorial efforts which could be classed under 'interesting but flawed'.

However, *Stranger in Our House* served Craven well in one particular respect — he lost the 'exploitation' tag and was seen by producers as a director capable of more than just spilling blood. Craven was approached by Italian producers who financed the development of two scripts which, ultimately, were never made, but served to occupy him for a while: 'I had written a script called *Marimba* about drug smuggling. Dirk Benedict and Tim McIntyre were cast, but the money I was promised never came through.' Craven was keen on the project, since it would have been a mainstream thriller, a move away from his horror beginnings, and he'd progressed quite far into pre-production. At the time of *The Serpent and the Rainbow*, shooting on location in Haiti reminded the director of his earlier struggles to mount his unmade script: 'I seem to have a thing for rough shoots. I spent years in the jungle in Colombia on this thing that never got made about cocaine smuggling, called *Marimba*. I've since turned down two more jungle things — one was a *Raiders of the Lost Ark* type movie; the other about a sniper in the jungles of Vietnam. I've no desire to get sick again and bitten by insects.'

When *Marimba* sank without a trace, the same producers asked Craven to draft a screenplay based on the Jim Jones mass suicide in Guyana, which was still big news at the time. On 29 November 1978, 913 members of the People's Temple religious cult were found dead, following the discovery of the bodies of American Congressman Leo Ryan and five others at a nearby campsite. The suicides, who lived on an agricultural community known as Jonestown, were followers of the Reverend Jim Jones, who'd induced them to drink a mixture of the soft drink Kool Aid and cyanide. A note, signed by Jones, explained the deaths as 'an act of revolutionary suicide'. The former Methodist preacher founded the cult in 1957 and relocated to Guyana with 1,000 followers in 1976. Jones' own body, with a bullet in the head, was found among the dead.

Although the topicality of the events would have ensured a lot of interest in the film, Craven was wary for two reasons — his experience over *Marimba* hadn't built his confidence in these particular producers, and he was worried about becoming trapped in another genre: 'I wrote it thinking "My God, I'm going from being a director of horror films to a director of horrifying true incidents". I was thankful when that was scrapped. I hadn't done a feature since *The Hills Have Eyes* and I began to think I would never work again.'

Craven's desire to work drove him to sign up for projects that were sometimes unsuitable: 'I quickly latched on to the first thing that I could. That turned out to be *Swamp Thing*, so I started work on that when the scriptwriters of *Stranger in Our House* asked me to do a rewrite on a script they had some interest in. It was called *Deadly Blessing*, and while the producers of *Swamp Thing* decided about the script I'd done for them, I did the rewrite [on *Deadly Blessing*] and from that moment on jumped between the two projects, until I filmed them virtually on top of each other.'

Initially, Craven was more excited by the prospect of directing the comic book horrors of *Swamp Thing*, perhaps because he knew George Romero was lining up to do *Creepshow* and there was a chance that horror cinema might be moving in the comic direction. *Deadly Blessing*, however, turned out to be the more interesting of the two: '*Deadly Blessing* had a very complex story. To my mind it was not a very good story, but the

money was there. The film would have a good distributor and it was a chance to work with some interesting people, so I did it.' First, Craven tried to tighten up the script, from the point of view of a storyteller and a director: 'I tried to minimise the problems in the script due to all those red herrings and I thought I clarified it as much as I could. I guessed the film would live or die on its images rather than rely on great storytelling coherence. I'm pleased with the film. It came off looking pretty good, as though it had cost a lot of money. In fact, it only cost $2.5 million. It made its money back in the first three weeks.'

As well as exploring once more his concern with deviant families, Craven tackled a subject very close to home for the first time — the effects of religious repression. *Deadly Blessing* explores a conflict within a fanatical religious settlement, modelled after the Amish (featured in the Harrison Ford cop thriller *Witness*), but more extreme in nature. Led by Ernest Borgnine at his mad-eyed, malevolent best, the order react to a young widow, Martha (Maren Jensen), and the arrival of her two college friends (one of whom is played by Sharon Stone). A series of bizarre mur-

Left: *Wes Craven with Sharon Stone on the set of* Deadly Blessing.

ders takes place which may or may not be occult in origin, and are attributed to their disruptive influence. By the end we discover responsibility lies with Faith (Lisa Hartman), a hermaphrodite, before a supernatural shock ending bursts on to the scene. Also among the cast was Craven's *The Hills Have Eyes* discovery Michael Berryman, playing clumsy handyman William Gluntz. Berryman was glad of the work: 'I had the opportunity to meet some great people, like Ernest Borgnine. I finally felt I had absorbed enough to consider myself somewhat of a professional.'

'It was an intriguing notion, to first of all look at the hypocrisy of the religion and then at the very end to say that it wasn't them [that were evil] either,' says Craven. 'It was a totally off-the-wall thing. I guess that I felt that the film was

Below: Maren Jensen as Martha Schmidt in the Deadly Blessing *bath scene, later revisited in* A Nightmare on Elm Street.

very complex in its plot. In a way it was almost too contrived. As a director, I was spending three quarters of the picture just setting up these red herrings. It took a long time to get down to the tension of the film, because you always had to spend another two scenes casting suspicion on somebody else, set up, set up, set up... finally, at the very end, I got it out.'

Directing the movie, Craven chose to steer clear of the gruesome 'look away' intensity of *The Last House on the Left* and also felt the horror-comedy mix and pace of *The Hills Have Eyes* was not suitable. He took his experiments in generating tension through atmosphere on his TV movie *Stranger in Our House* and applied them to the big screen production values and budget available to him. Despite featuring impressive visuals, coherent character development, a complex plot and an almost satisfying resolution, *Deadly Blessing* is not one of Craven's favourites among his own work: 'Interestingly enough, a lot of people really, really like that film. I have to take a step back from it and say there were certainly some things in it that were very successful. A lot of the scenes and images, just the sequences, were very powerful. I've had a lot of people tell me that the scene in the barn was one of the scariest things they ever saw, or the scene in the bathroom.'

Filming for *Deadly Blessing* took place on a wide variety of locations in Texas, in and around the city of Dallas and the town of Waxahachie. The principal set was an eighty acre farm, where the action was centred. An additional barn had to be built and aged by the construction crew, and a major facelift of the farmhouse was carried out, with the addition of a white picket fence, shutters around the windows and a new porch area complete with swing. Ernest Borgnine's living quarters were created in an old school, Red Vintage House in Waxahachie, which was owned by a Dallas hotel executive. Filming also took place at the farmer's market in the town of Bardwell and at a small town movie theatre in Ennis. A publicity photo shoot of the main cast

in their distinctive religious costumes took place at the Southern Methodist University in Dallas.

Dreams came into play for Craven during production of *Deadly Blessing*, just as they would in years to come, inspiring such films as *A Nightmare on Elm Street*, *The Serpent and the Rainbow* and *The People Under the Stairs*. Faced with a particularly difficult, not to say clichéd, scene, Craven dreamed the solution during the night then filmed it the next day: 'It was the classic Hitchcock shower scene — the heroine in the shower, the steam, the figure on the other side of the shower curtain, and I said, "I can't do this and hold my head up". So, the day before we were going to shoot it, I dreamed the entire scene as it appears in the movie, complete with fades, colours, everything. I woke up and wrote it all down, and we shot that version. It worked beautifully.'

Deadly Blessing shows a clear maturing of Craven's approach to the horror genre. It's much more grounded in a sense of reality and some of the scares rely on real-life sources for their effectiveness. The film showed just what Craven was capable of and laid some clear connections to his

later work, especially *A Nightmare on Elm Street*. As ever, though, the director saw the film as another stepping stone away from horror rather than a consolidation of the tricks he had learned over the years: 'It's almost a traditional whodunit. There was the suspense of the thriller there, you could have read that as a thriller rather than horror, both in the bath scene and in the barn. The end was added on — one of my famous added-on endings.'

In a precursor to the troubles he had over *A Nightmare of Elm Street* a couple of years later, Craven was faced with producers determined to end *Deadly Blessing* with much more of a bang than he intended. 'It was forced by the studio,' admits Craven of the bizarre shock ending. 'That was shot back in Hollywood, after the film was all cut together. The producers, Jon Peters and Peter Guber [later to produce Tim Burton's *Batman*], decided it needed a big, spectacular ending and they had this thing written.' The new climax to the movie featured a bizarre and barely seen incubus, feared by the religious community, erupt through the floorboards amid a spectacular light show to snatch Martha, the film's survivor,

Above left:
William Gluntz (Michael Berryman) meets a nasty end.
Above right:
Ernest Borgnine makes an impact as Isaiah Schmidt.

Above: Faith (Lisa Hartman) gets her come-uppance at the end of Deadly Blessing.

Right: Craven on set with Maren Jensen and Lisa Hartman.

off to hell. Special effects technician John Dykstra was approached to film the extra scenes, but he was unavailable due to other commitments, so the conclusion to *Deadly Blessing* was the work of Everett Alson and Ira Anderson. After a bad reaction by critics at a British press screening, the new ending was lopped off and the film released without it in the UK. It was a better version, and to this day Craven doesn't like the tacked-on ending: 'I preferred it without that. It used to end as the women said good-bye. If I'm not mistaken, I think there was a pan up into a window and something moved, I forget what. Even that I thought was a bit contrived. I think every major horror film of the past twenty years had been influenced by the end of *Carrie*, it was so successful. It was intriguing to the pro-

ducers to think that there was something striking the audience and hinting at a sequel at the same time. That's the dream, and I've had producers trying to impose that sort of ending on every film I've done ever since.'

A bigger budget, increased enthusiasm from the director and more extensive input from the producers couldn't save Craven's next film from being a disappointment. In retrospect, his ill-fated cinema version of Bernie Wrightson and Len Wein's DC Comics creation Swamp Thing seems to have been doomed from the start, despite his intentions: 'I wasn't aware of *Swamp Thing*. I certainly felt once I'd taken it on that I had the responsibility to do [it] as best I could, because by the time I had absorbed it all and realised what a following it had and how important it was to people, I wanted to capture the spirit of [the comic].'

With a $3 million budget, his biggest so far, and permission to alter the comic book story in any way to make it suitable for the big screen, Craven had everything in place to produce a decent film version: 'In actual fact, I changed very little apart from peripheral characters. The stories were in some ways so visually fantastic as to be impossible, at that time, to put into the film that I had a budget for. So, many of those fantastic little creatures that *Swamp Thing* has, little hands running around

and everything, we simply didn't have the capacity to do. It had to be modified.'

The *Swamp Thing* story concerns the fate of Dr Alec Holland (Ray Wise, later of *Twin Peaks*), a brilliant scientist who has discovered a formula which stimulates plant growth. Realising that this could solve the world hunger problem, he

sets about developing it. However, a madman named Arcane (Louis Jourdan) wants to use Holland's discovery to rule the world by controlling the food supply. In a battle with Arcane's henchmen, who attempt to steal the formula, Holland is splashed with the solution and set alight. He escapes into the swamp lands surrounding his laboratory, only to have the chemical react with the swamp waters and turn him into Swamp Thing (stunt man Dick Durock), a hideous half-man/half-plant creature able to take nourishment through roots and regrow severed limbs. Naturally, revenge is on his mind, not only for his own fate but also for the death of his sister at Arcane's hands.

'I changed the character of Cable (Adrienne Barbeau), who is obsessed with finding out who the Swamp Thing is, into a woman, so I could add a more romantic element,' explains Craven. 'Then I realised I would have to change Holland's murdered wife into his sister, as I didn't think it was valid that three days after losing his wife he would be running around after Cable. There is also an Arcane character in the original story that was a magician, but here he's just an international villain. In fact, I combined all of *Swamp Thing*'s villains into just one, which is where Arcane gets transformed into a monster. I was intrigued by making it into a Beauty and the Beast tale, seeing again that ambivalence of the monster where really, inside, there is this handsome, young, witty scientist, full of tenderness and love. Then

we have Louis Jourdan as Arcane, who on the outside is the most beautiful person in the world, [so] sophisticated, and he is the real monster. At the very end when he takes the potion, that is the real monstrosity coming out. That was the intriguing thing about it, it being a template for a beautiful old myth.'

Craven's ambitions were not realised, unfortunately, and the finished film failed to live up to expectations, although it has since become a cult favourite. When the budget turned out to be inadequate for the look he really wanted, Craven became acutely aware of the problems he faced. Interference from the producers, Benjamin Melniker and Michael E. Uslan, removed much of the power from the director: 'They fired my cinematographer and the production manager. They kept asking me why I needed this shot and that shot and why I needed all the coverage I was shooting. The film was being done on the cheap and they were under a completion bond. The film couldn't and doesn't rely on its special effects — [but] as the producers went for the person who did the effects on the basis of the lowest quote, you can understand why I had to make the film more of a human experience.'

Handling the creature effects on *Swamp Thing* was thirty-two year-old Bill Munns, who'd offered to do the job for only $80,000, the lowest bid received by the producers. They took him on enthusiastically, looking forward to some successful, if cheap, monster suits and make-ups. It was a fatal mistake and the silly costumes used for *Swamp Thing* undermined the film's credibility to such an extent that there was little Craven could do to hide the problems. Even worse, Munns' cheap rubber suits proved susceptible to acid in the swamp waters on location in Charleston, South Carolina. Although lightweight and comfortable for the stunt men, the suits began to rot, so Munns had to constantly dose them with an antacid. There was one of Munns' creations which Craven did like — the creature which Arcane transforms into, with the mane of a lion,

the face of a boar, complete with tusks, and a reptilian body: 'It [the creature] came together looking quite nice, even though the special effects and make-ups aren't what it was about.' Overall, though, Craven knew he was fighting an uphill battle trying to realise the complexity of the comic book with the budget he had: 'For the quote we were given, I just knew we would never be able to pull it off. There was even talk of fully motorised heads, but I knew it would never work. The money [promised] was all there, but it was an inadequate amount for the picture.'

Other problems arose, some of them hopelessly amateurish. Inexperienced set builders hired locally were commissioned to construct the laboratory set for the film. This they duly did, in a warehouse, but they built the set in one enormous, solid piece instead of several interlocking sections which could be transported. The set had to be chainsawed apart, touched up and recreated on location.

'It was like being in jungle combat,' says Craven of his experiences in South Carolina. 'We had to cut our own roads into the swamps, which were infested with caterpillars and snakes. We wore rubber bands around our shirt and pant cuffs to keep out the bugs, and some of the crew were armed with rifles to protect us from the snakes. Everyone was supplied with a daily ration of bug spray, and I think we exhausted every store in a twenty mile radius.' Charleston was chosen after Craven had scouted other possible filming bases in Florida, Louisiana and Georgia. It was the only city where the architecture was not dominated by steel and glass towers, and it was surrounded by the mansions, plantations and swamps needed for the film. One scene required a dungeon, where Swamp Thing and Cable were chained up. The city of Charleston boasted the second oldest jail in the United States in the 1867 Exchange Building, which made an ideal location. Other city buildings used included the Hibernian Hall, built in 1839 and packed with ancient Greek artefacts.

Craven was happy with the finished film, taking into account the circumstances of the production and the problems he'd encountered: 'My limitation was that we ran out of money

Left: The creature Arcane turned into was the one Swamp Thing *costume Craven was satisfied with.* **Below:** *The make-up team at work on* Swamp Thing.

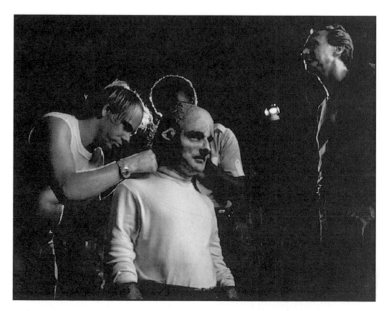

towards the end. We had to cut about a week of shooting, so the ending of the film [where Swamp Thing and the Arcane-creature battle in the swamps] was not technically what I would have liked. Aesthetically, yes, I thought it was successful. I've run into a lot of people who liked it. In my experience, about three out of four really liked it rather than thought it was a let-down compared to the comic.'

Critic Vincent Canby liked some aspects of *Swamp Thing* enough to highlight them in his *New York Times* review in July 1982: 'It does have the virtue of being single-mindedly hokey. Parodying the style of Vincent Price at his most grandly second rate, [Louis] Jourdan appears to be having fun with the character. When the two creatures slug it out in the swamp, it looks as if two guests at a costume party were fighting over the last hors-d'œuvre, which, of course, is Miss Barbeau.'

The burst of activity on *Deadly Blessing* and *Swamp Thing* had kept Craven active from 1980 through to 1982. While planning ahead for his next project, he married actress and model

Millicent Meyer, thereafter known as Mimi Meyer-Craven (and who appears in *Swamp Thing* as Arcane's secretary). They met when Craven was flying back and forth to scout the locations for *Swamp Thing* and she was working as an air hostess. 'We all thought she was so pretty,'

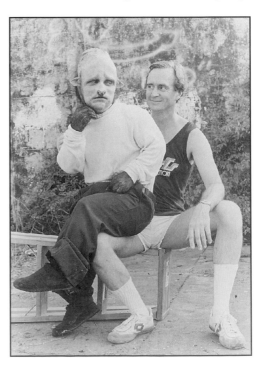

remembers Craven. 'I gave her my card and asked her to audition for a part [in *Swamp Thing*].' They dated for a year before marrying in 1984, and over the next few years Mimi Meyer-Craven took a variety of small roles in her husband's film and television ventures. The liaison lasted until 1987, ending in an acrimonious divorce.

The ultimate test of *Swamp Thing*'s success or failure was at the box office. Unfortunately, the film flopped — a temporary setback to Craven's nascent movie-making career. It wasn't until 1984, while developing *A Nightmare on Elm Street*, that he was given the chance to return to one of his previous successes: '*The Hills Have Eyes Part II* I did because, after *Swamp Thing* I had a difficult time finding another job, quite frankly. It was the first of my films that really didn't make its money back right away. There was an attitude about in Hollywood at the time to horror films in general — they were considered evil.' Craven discovered that, as a reaction to the success of some of his movies, as well as Sean Cunningham's *Friday the*

13th series, John Carpenter's *Halloween* and their countless imitators, horror films were falling back out of vogue. Hysteria was beginning to grow about the possible effects on audiences, culminating in the 'video nasties' debate in Britain which ensnared Craven's *The Last House on the Left*.

'I saw a studio's list of what films they were interested in and what films they were not interested in,' recalls Craven of the sea change that affected his career. 'They wanted films about ordinary people doing interesting things, stories about love and wacky couples in strange adventures. They were not interested in films about World War Two, Vietnam, Central America — and they had no interest at all in horror. The movement was towards small films, like *Terms of Endearment*, and nice films about nice people doing nice things, like *E.T.*'

As a result of the ever more derivative and bloody imitations of the successful slasher movies, the genre had become devalued, regarded as not just bad but dangerous: 'Horror films were out and horror film directors were out. I

Opposite

above: Craven directs John Laughlin in his The Hills Have Eyes *sequel.*

Opposite

below: John Bloom as Reaper, a new addition to the tribe.

had gone, I think, about two and a half years without a job and had come to the end of my resources. After *Swamp Thing*, I had written *A Nightmare on Elm Street*. In the months following it was rejected by everyone in town, until Bob Shaye [president of New Line Cinema] took it. He went to raise the money, which took about two years. During that period I wrote about twelve different full-length treatments for various projects; re-writes for people; script doctoring and several things of my own.' It was around this time that Craven took his first crack at adapting Virginia Andrews' *Flowers in the Attic*, although another project came along first.

Peter Locke and Barry Cahn, the producers of

the original *The Hills Have Eyes* movie, felt that a sequel was worth doing. 'A friend of mine [Locke] said, "I can always get the money to do a sequel, if you want to do it",' remembers Craven. Out of work and running out of money, he opted to take the job, even though he was none too keen on bringing back these particular characters, fearing that he'd said all he could about them in the first film.

Craven's decision to tackle the *Hills* sequel was purely a business one: 'We had a budget of $1 million, which was really marginal, but it got me working again and I went right from that... Once you're doing a film, there is a lot more heat around your name, so once people heard I was doing a sequel, we got the money to do *A Nightmare on Elm Street*, which obviously turned my career around.' The money raised by Peter Locke for *The Hills Have Eyes Part II* came largely from the British distributor New Realm, who'd released *The Hills Have Eyes* in 1978, and British video company VTC (Video Tape Centre), who had enjoyed a huge hit with it in the early days of home video.

At the thirty-sixth Cannes Film Festival in May 1983, Adrienne Fancey of New Realm and Guy Collins of VTC used a promo reel for the sequel made up of clips from the original movie to drum up interest and further investment, while Craven began work on the scenario. Craven's screenplay, originally called *The Night of Jupiter*, had to resolve the problems he'd set for himself by killing off his key villains Jupiter and Pluto. He also had to find a way of bringing back both young Bobby Carter and Ruby. The tag-line Craven worked to was modelled after the one used on the *Jaws* sequel: 'Just when Bobby thought it was safe to go back into the desert...'

'It was a much better script, I think, than the movie turned out to be,' notes Craven. 'It was an important film for me to do, just to get the momentum going again, but it was very underfunded. The movie was originally budgeted on the first draft of the script, and the producers said they thought it should be expanded, so I wrote a much better and bigger script, but the budget stayed the same. It was a real nightmare to shoot.'

With his then-unproduced screenplay for *A Nightmare on Elm Street* on his mind, Craven replaced the middle-class family of the original movie with a group of teenagers, led by Cass (Tamara Stafford), who is blind but has the gift of prophecy. *The Hills Have Eyes Part II* sees Pluto's sister Ruby (Janus Blythe), now known as Rachel, married to her original would-be lunch, Bobby (Robert Houston), and running a Yamaha dealership. While Bobby remains behind, she sets off with a bus load of teenagers into the desert to test hubby's new formula for a supercharged motorbike racing fuel. Straying into the one-time domain of Papa Jupe, Rachel begins to suffer flashbacks to the events of the previous film.

The new cannibal characters created for the sequel included Reaper, played by John Bloom, a 7'2" ex-dock worker from San Pedro who had landed parts in *The Incredible Two-Headed Transplant*, *Dracula vs Frankenstein* and other exploitation fare. Reaper is a mutant, like Pluto, so Craven turned to make-up to create the right formidable visage for the character. Make-up man Ken Horn returned from the first film to handle the new look monsters: 'Wes didn't want a gimmicky make-up requiring endless appliances. Reaper had to be simple, believable, yet durable enough to move around aggressively on the set and ride a motorbike. I managed to get by with one appliance, false teeth, some extra wig hair and standard make-up. The entire process required about two hours.'

The Hills Have Eyes Part II saw Craven cast his first black roles. Actor Willard Pugh won a part in the film after he met Craven under less than happy circumstances. '*Hills* was really a lot of fun, because Wes wrote me into the movie,' he told *Starburst*. 'Originally, there was no black character in it. I was doing a movie called *Toy Soldiers...* [and] Wes came down to do a rewrite, to help them save that script. There really wasn't much he could do! While he was there, I got to

Above: *Axed — Willard Pugh suffers at the hands of Craven and producer Barry Cahn.*

meet him and he saw some of my work. Later, he came back and wrote me into *The Hills Have Eyes Part II*. Wes is the one director that over the years I'm buddy-buddy with. He called me up once and asked me if I wanted to work, [when] he was directing an episode of *The Twilight Zone*. Wes is a great guy and a good friend — when I left California to move to South Dakota, [he] came to my going away party.'

No sequel to *The Hills Have Eyes* would have been complete without the return of Michael Berryman as Pluto, even though he'd apparently died in the first movie. 'I've had eight years to heal, and I still have a slight limp,' he joked in an interview with *Fangoria* magazine during production. 'There have been some major changes in the hill tribe. Our traps, our techniques and even our costumes are much more elaborate and advanced.' Berryman felt the time was right for the new *Hills* movie, just as the horror boom of the late seventies and early eighties was fading away: 'The whole run-of-the mill genre of imitation splatter films has played out, and a lot of

sequels to the more routine gore films have come and gone. That leaves plenty of room for this to be a classic in its own right.'

Berryman was being overly optimistic if he genuinely believed that *The Hills Have Eyes Part II* had the makings of a classic. Relying heavily on flashbacks to the original film, including one from a dog's point of view, it turned out to be simply more of the same, lacking the budget to do justice to some of the concepts in Craven's script. Somewhat higher production values and an increasing sense of black comedy replaced the relentless menace of the original. The film was true to its origins as a piece Craven agreed to direct because he needed to be working. Years later he realised the absurdity of some of the scenes he'd shot: 'We ended up with this 7'2" villain [John Bloom] on a motorcycle, and he made it look like a tricycle. It was the most ridiculous sight in the world when he actually got on this thing and his feet were hanging off... I'm sorry about *The Hills Have Eyes Part II*. The reason I did that film was that I was dead broke and needed to do any film. I would have done *Godzilla Goes to Paris*. It does have the first flashback from the point of view of a dog, so that's something!'

Although Craven was not too proud of his work on *The Hills Have Eyes Part II*, it led directly to the chance to make another TV movie, *Invitation to Hell*, and to finally get his cherished *A Nightmare on Elm Street* screenplay into production. Craven remembers how he came to work on three movies in one year: 'We were a few days away from doing the sound mix on *Hills II* when the TV movie offer came through. Negotiations on *A Nightmare on Elm Street* were dragging on and on, and my agent felt we weren't being taken very seriously, so I decided that I would do [*Invitation to Hell*].'

The ABC TV movie *Invitation to Hell* was based on a preposterous storyline, but Craven was happy to shepherd it to the screen in order to pay some bills: 'It had Robert Urich, Joanna Cassidy and Susan Lucci. The premise was that

Susan Lucci was a woman who ran a country club that was attracting all the executives from these high-tech agencies, but she was really the Devil and the steam room was the entrance to hell, if you can believe that...'

Invited by the producers to an interview on a Friday, Craven accepted the job that weekend and began two weeks pre-production on the film the following Monday morning: 'I was in pre-production on *Invitation to Hell* during the day, while we were still mixing the sound for *Hills 2* at night. At the same time I was doing a major re-write on *A Nightmare on Elm Street*. I wasn't sleeping much, but it was a very ecstatic kind of energy, after not having worked for so long, to be doing three pictures back-to-back.'

Undistinguished though *Invitation to Hell* was, it is nevertheless an entertaining potboiler which takes effective shots at the growing range of glossy soaps on American television, from *Dallas* to *Falcon Crest*. Urich played a technical engineer hired to work on a spacesuit designed to allow explorers to withstand the temperatures on the bright side of Venus. When his wife (Joanna Cassidy) and their children join an exclusive

Above: *Pluto's revenge — the return of Michael Berryman.*
Left: *Rachel, aka Ruby (Janus Blythe), is back as that Craven favourite, the resourceful female.*

The last few years had proved a trying time for Craven. His TV movies were little more than wage earners, while his reluctantly undertaken *Hills* sequel had been doomed from the start to be a pale imitation of his ground-breaking earlier work. His major disappointment was *Swamp Thing*, which Craven had hoped would allow him to move in another direction, away from horror altogether. Only *Deadly Blessing*, which Craven himself did not rate too highly, was a really successful and mature examination of the concerns central to his best work. His next project would be his biggest yet, but Wes Craven may have thought twice about exploring the fantasy dreamscape of *A Nightmare on Elm Street* had he known where it was to lead. ∎

Opposite:
Pluto. Leaner, meaner and back from the dead.
Left: *Roy (Kevin Blair) takes on the cannibal family.*

country club, they begin to act strangely. Urich discovers that they have fallen under the sway of Satan (Susan Lucci) and in the special effects-driven climax, he dons the experimental suit and invades hell itself to rescue his family. According to the critic John J. O'Connor, *Invitation to Hell* 'managed to whip up a respectable share of scary moments as there unfolds a morality play about decent wives and kids being threatened by the temptresses of this world.'

As on *Stranger in Our House*, television restrictions became a concern: 'This little girl was supposed to be possessed. I had her in the living room stabbing this doll with a kitchen knife, and it ended up she had to use a golf club or a crowbar because the network censors thought it was too upsetting. I made TV movies to pay the bills and keep the lights on in my office — they don't represent my body of work.'

So you think you're lucky to be alive . . .

THE HILLS HAVE EYES part 2

Starring MICHAEL BERRYMAN, JOHN LAUGHLIN and introducing TAMARA STAFFORD as Cass
Produced by BARRY CAHN and PETER LOCKE
Written and Directed by WES CRAVEN

THORN EMI
Screen Entertainment

The Nightmares Begin

Craven's cult audience had grown following his return to a past triumph in *The Hills Have Eyes Part II*, but he'd been unhappy with much of the film. 'I'd had enough,' he remembers. 'I had done two pictures back-to-back and I had some money in the bank. I decided I could afford to write for six months. It was the first time in my life that I'd had time for that, because I'd always had two children to support, so I had to continue to generate income. Now that I had some money, I wrote my first script totally for myself. It was completely experimental work and it took me several years to find the money to get the film made. That became *A Nightmare on Elm Street*.'

The idea for the film that finally propelled Wes Craven into the big league originated in discussions Craven had with Steve Miner. Miner had been a production assistant on Craven's début film and had followed Sean Cunningham into the *Friday the 13th* series. The pair met casually at a coffee shop in Santa Monica and discussed a series of local newspaper reports. 'There was a series of unrelated articles I'd clipped out of the *Los Angeles Times* in about 1981, perhaps even earlier,' recalls Craven of the genesis of his dream killer story. 'Over a period of about a year and a half, there were incidents of people having severe nightmares, telling their families about them, about how these dreams were worse than anything they'd ever had before. All of them had a similar reaction — they didn't want to sleep again. They were afraid of going back to the dreams. They tried, one way or another, to stay awake. The next time these people fell asleep, they died.

'This guy managed to stay awake for three or four days. His family said he was having a nervous breakdown, should take some warm milk and some sleeping tablets — exactly what he didn't want to do. He finally fell asleep and they heard screams and thrashing about. They went to his

Opposite:

Freddy Krueger — the man of your dreams.

Above: One, two, Freddy's coming for you...

room and he was dead. An autopsy revealed he hadn't had a heart attack or anything — he was just dead. They happened so far apart, the newspapers never connected them.'

Recognising the potential of this material, Craven became intrigued by the idea of a dream killer who reached his victims as they slept: 'I thought, "There has to be a movie in it. What if somebody were trying to kill you in your dreams? Nobody you told would ever take you seriously". Then it was a matter of writing it down, plotting it out. Who would this killer be?'

Craven developed two movie ideas — one about a dream killer and the other about a dream lover, settling on a story involving a killer from a nightmare and a resourceful teenager who stays awake as a defence against the stalker who is killing her friends: 'The real problem of the script and the turning point in solving the story was: if you have a character like that how do you eventually get to him? How do you combat somebody who has such tremendous powers? The light at the end of the tunnel was that you must get him outside your dream and into your own world, get him on your territory.'

Taking his time to develop the story, Craven was determined to explore one of his obsessions — the nature of dreams: 'The dream world premise had interested me for a very long time. In some of my earlier films [*The Last House on the Left* and *Deadly Blessing*] I'd played with dream sequences where you weren't sure whether the person was dreaming or not. I found that idea intrigued me so much that I wanted to build a whole film around it.'

In fact, Craven's interest in dreams pre-dates his film-making days. While in college he wrote a research paper on dreaming and as part of the project he was required to keep a record of his own dream experiences. He became quite adept at recalling them, and it stood him in good stead when it came to developing *A Nightmare on Elm Street*. Craven claims to have based some of the scenes in his movies on his own dream experiences, mainly in *The Hills Have Eyes*, *Deadly Blessing*, *The Serpent and the Rainbow* and *The People Under the Stairs*:

'I've been developing a natural skill in using dreams over the years. I find that there is natural progression if you write them down. After a while, you start to have dreams which correspond to your work. It happened first with *The Hills Have Eyes*, where I dreamed the structure of the two families that were the antipathy of each other. At the Brussels Film Festival in 1989 this culminated with me dreaming the entire film of

The People Under the Stairs. I was aware that I was Wes Craven, a film-maker, dreaming. I woke up and wrote it all down. That's a skill I've developed after reading several books about dreams and dreaming.'

For Craven, film is a very dream-like medium: 'I'm interested in expanding the forms of consciousness within film because I think, with the exception of certain European directors, film is quite limited in the areas of consciousness it deals with. I think it's a limiting of the art itself, because film is very dream-like. It's able to distort time, to contract it. It's able to go back and forth in time. It's not like a stage play — you can have optical tricks at your beck and call, you can have strange soundtracks, and everything else that you can do with film.'

Having developed the idea of a killer who claims his victims while they sleep, Craven next had to decide what form his dream monster should take. The villain of the piece, Freddy Krueger, was to be a horror anti-hero, capable of the most vicious acts, but still someone the audience could identify with. 'Freddy is vicious, but he has a sense of humour. He has a humanity to him,' explains Craven. 'American films especially are trapped in a very strong dualistic nature. In Western slang, you have a guy in a white hat and a guy in a black hat, one's the good guy, the other's the bad guy. We have to be aware that within the purest hero is the potential to be a real villain and within any villain there is the capacity for, or even elements of, humour, tenderness, vulnerability and love.'

Craven then turned his attention to the nature of the weapon his new dream killer would use. He had one clear concern — it would not be a knife. The weapons of the 'stalk 'n' slash' genre had become horror clichés. Whatever his dream killer used, it would be original.

Craven worked his way through various knife-like implements for his villain, including scythes and sickles. It wasn't until he reached the third rewrite of his speculative screenplay that

Below: *Under the covers — Freddy's reign of terror on Elm Street continues.*

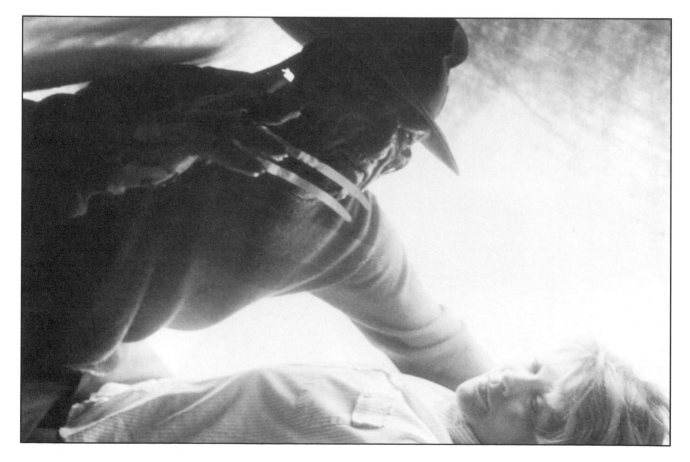

Freddy's trademark razor-fingered gardening glove appeared in the script. Craven's invention had the added spine-tingling advantage of the sound that could be inflicted on the audience as Freddy scraped the blades along a wall or pipe.

A Nightmare on Elm Street meant a good deal more to Craven than most of the projects he had worked on — this was an idea he had originated himself. 'It was one from the heart,' says Craven. 'It had a good, solid story, it was totally original and it worked. The finished script had a really high success rate with the studio executives who read it, but I couldn't get anybody to put their money where their mouths were. That was my

Right: *Defying gravity — Tina's death throes.*

first indication that I was onto a real winner. The second was realising that I was actually able to put ninety-five per cent of what people were reading on screen.'

A Nightmare on Elm Street opens with four teenagers, led by Nancy Thompson (Heather Langenkamp), sharing an identical nightmare about a dead child murderer who has returned to haunt their dreams. Nancy's best friend, Tina (Amanda Wyss), is killed in her bedroom when the figure from their dreams begins to affect reality. Tina's boyfriend (Nick Corri) is strangled with a sheet, while Nancy's own boyfriend Glen (Johnny Depp) also meets a nasty end. Nancy discovers from her alcoholic mother (Ronee Blakley) that Freddy Krueger (Robert Englund), a real-life local child killer who got off on a technicality, was hunted down and burned to death by the town's parents (shades of *The Last House on the Left* here), including Nancy's policeman father (John Saxon). Now, Freddy has returned to torment the children of his old enemies through their nightmares. Nancy realises that the only way to end the deaths is to draw Freddy into her reality and confront him on her own terms, with a little help from a booby trapped house.

'That was a tongue-in-cheek quote of the last scenes in *The Last House on the Left*,' says Craven of *A Nightmare on Elm Street*'s climax. 'In *The Last House on the Left*, the father of the girl who's been killed does that. It came from a series of books that I'd ordered in the United States. They have these survivalist bookstores and they have all these army manuals and there was a whole manual on booby traps. I always thought we'd get sued by some kid blowing up his living room, because all those things can be done. You can file a light bulb and put gunpowder in...'

Despite its obvious attractions, the script was rejected by all the major studios that Craven submitted it to and the process nearly bankrupted him: 'While I was trying to get funding for *A Nightmare on Elm Street*, I had to earn a living by rewriting other people's scripts. I lost all my sav-

ings and I lost my house, which I thought would be my ultimate investment in old age. I'd had to sell that at a loss. It's a long, sad story, ending with me not being able to pay any bills. I had to borrow money from Sean Cunningham to pay off my taxes.'

The problem the studios encountered was that the script was difficult to categorise. It wasn't a straight slasher movie, it wasn't a monster movie in the old fashioned sense and it wasn't in the style of the films Craven was particularly known for up to that point. Although fantastic in nature,

Below: *Wes Craven and Amanda Wyss in the remarkable revolving room set.*

much of the film was rooted in the realities of suburban America. They simply didn't know what to make of it, and rather than take the risk, studio after studio passed on the project — despite claiming to be impressed with the script. It was a disheartening time for Craven, who had put so much effort into his dream screenplay.

Right: Tina comes back to haunt her best friend Nancy.
Below: The dream demon in action, stalking Tina.

However, there was serious interest in *A Nightmare on Elm Street* from one very unlikely source — Disney. Their take on the film was for a kiddie frightener, a toned down version of the tale which could have a short theatrical release and then run every Halloween on the Disney Channel. Another studio, Paramount, turned down the script because of its similarity to a science fiction

film they were distributing. *Dreamscape* had been scripted by Chuck (later Charles) Russell, who made his directorial début with *A Nightmare on Elm Street 3: Dream Warriors*, and won acclaim for *The Mask*. Craven is adamant that *Dreamscape* at least 'drew inspiration' from ideas in his script for *A Nightmare on Elm Street*. Directed by Joseph Ruben on a budget of $6 million, *Dreamscape* starred Dennis Quaid as a psychic able to enter another's dreams via scientist Max Von Sydow's dreamscape device. The finale of the film takes place within the post-apocalyptic nightmares of the President of the United States.

'Everybody in the industry knew about *A Nightmare on Elm Street* three years before we made the movie, because I'd talked about it... The script itself had been submitted to virtually every studio in Hollywood,' remembers Craven. '*Dreamscape* featured a guy with claws on his fingers, a kid who was frightened to go to sleep and

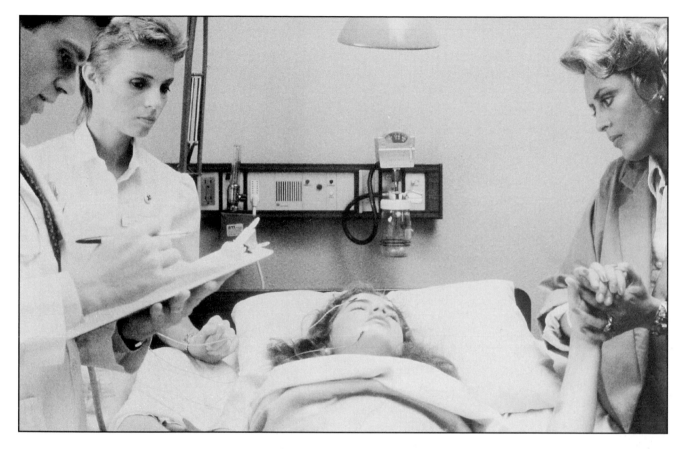

the basic premise was suspiciously coincidental. That film hurt me a lot, mentally and financially. Paramount had been about to pick up *Nightmare* when they saw *Dreamscape* and felt it was too similar.'

Eventually, Craven took his script to the independent sector, which was just beginning to blossom again. Only one person, New Line Cinema's Robert Shaye, had enough faith in *A Nightmare on Elm Street* to set about raising the funds required.

Before forming New Line Cinema in 1967, Robert Shaye had been something of a one-man industry, writing, producing, directing and editing a number of short films, trailers and TV commercials. He produced and directed two award-winning shorts, *Image* and *On Flying Witches*. Both films have been acquired for the permanent collections of the Museum of Modern Art and the British Film Institute. With New Line, Shaye had

been responsible for distributing around 150 films, including the 1978 Oscar winner for Best Foreign Language Film, *Get Out Your Handkerchiefs*. He'd also picked up the cult horror films *The Texas Chain Saw Massacre* and *The Evil Dead* for American distribution, the latter after it had been championed by critics at the London Film Festival. Shaye executive produced a handful of films, including Jack Sholder's *Alone in the Dark*, and, after the success of the *Nightmare* series, several John Waters films. He saw the enormous potential in Wes Craven's dream killer script, and once taken up by New Line, production on *A Nightmare on Elm Street* could begin. Casting was the first priority, and Craven brought together a group of unknowns, many of whom have gone on to much bigger things. Heather Langenkamp was cast in the central role of heroine Nancy, having failed to make the final cut of Francis Ford Coppola's *Rumble Fish*: 'When we screen tested

Above: Nancy Thompson (Heather Langenkamp) under observation, with Wes Craven's wife Mimi Meyer-Craven (left) as a nurse.

her I really liked her looks. She put across a very real, strong image. Those were primarily the qualities I wanted. She had to work very hard, mainly because she's in almost every scene.'

The casting of veteran actor John Saxon was Craven's only nod to the horror genre. Saxon's past credits included a variety of low budget horror films, amongst them *Beyond Evil* and *Tenebrae*. The veteran B-movie actor would return to the *Elm Street* fold twice, in the third movie *Dream Warriors* and Craven's own post-modern *New Nightmare*.

The only one of the original teen victims to become a genuine star is Johnny Depp, the heart-throb who grew into a much respected actor in films like *Ed Wood* and *Donnie Brasco*. Depp was twenty-one and just divorced from singer Lori Ann Allison, with whom he'd tried to kick start a rock career. Lori soon began dating a young actor

Below: *'I'm your boyfriend now' — Freddy makes a move on Nancy.*

named Nicolas Cage, nephew of *The Godfather* director Francis Ford Coppola. Oddly enough, it was Depp and Cage who struck up a lasting friendship. Cage suggested Depp should try acting, put him in touch with an agent, and as a result Depp found himself heading along to an audition for *A Nightmare on Elm Street*. For two nights before the audition Depp and Cage stayed up all night, running through the lines to make sure the would-be actor was prepared. As he explained to *Fangoria*, the character in the script bore little relation to Depp himself:

'I was not what Wes had written for the story. He had written the part of a big, blond, beach jock, football player guy and I was sort of emaciated, with old hairspray and spiky hair, earrings, a little catacomb dweller — and then five hours later my agent called and said: "You're an actor".'

Depp may have been surprised to win the role so easily, but Craven had listened to the counsel of his teenage daughter Jessica who'd sat in on the auditions. 'He had a quiet charisma which none of the other actors had,' notes Craven. 'Johnny really had that sort of James Dean attraction, a very powerful, yet very subtle personality. My teenage daughter and her friends were at the reading and they absolutely flipped over him. He's got real sex appeal for women.'

Once production got underway there was a feeling among the cast and crew that this was no ordinary horror film. 'Everyone worked very hard on the picture,' says Craven. 'There was an atmosphere on the set relating to the potential everyone thought the finished product would have. It was a watershed film in many ways and has made stars out of a lot of people.'

Producer Robert Shaye was clear about the attraction the unusual project had for him. 'This is not a killer-on-the-loose film,' he explained to *Cinefantastique*. 'It's an archetypal movie monster in a dream who happens to have the ability to keep you from waking while he gets you. There is none of that slasher gore-for-gore's sake in this film. This has some very unique fantasy-

thriller moments.'

Craven hoped this would be the film that changed the industry perception of him as a slasher director. 'This isn't horror really,' he claimed at the time, echoing his thoughts on *Deadly Blessing* and even *Swamp Thing*. 'It's more of a fantasy, an impressionistic thriller. It's really a departure for me. I really feel this will be a landmark film for me, my watershed film.'

Developing the unique look of Craven's phantom killer for *A Nightmare on Elm Street* was one of the first problems facing the production crew. Three people played key roles in the process: Craven himself, make-up designer David Miller and the man who has donned the Freddy mask in all seven *Nightmare* movies, Robert Englund. The description of Fred Krueger in Craven's script called for 'a truly hideous face,

pus-filled and heavily scarred'. Originally, Craven only intended for half of Freddy's face to be burned, but when New Line started production, Shaye and co-producer Sara Risher insisted that the movie's monster should be just that — monstrous, not merely a scarred human being.

Make-up man David Miller had previously worked on *Dreamscape* and was involved with the rock band KISS when he became aware of Craven's project. The film's special effects supervisor Jim Doyle had invited him to submit a budget for the main monster make-up.

Miller had eight weeks on the film with a very tight budget, and the amount available for the film's many make-up applications was in the region of $20,000. The make-up effects consisted mainly of basic prosthetics to create Freddy's face, mechanical techniques and a minimal amount of

Above: *(l-r) Nick Corri, Heather Langenkamp, Amanda Wyss and Johnny Depp join Robert Englund for a drive.*

optical work. Miller developed a look that took between four and six hours to apply, which he could afford to use only eleven times during the shoot. As time went on, however, Craven began squeezing in more 'Freddy days', and Miller ended up applying the make-up twenty-five times over the thirty-two day shoot.

The shooting schedule had been the subject of much tough negotiation between Craven and Shaye. Craven wanted thirty-six days to shoot his script, but Shaye argued that the budget only allowed for thirty days filming. As it was, over-runs allowed Craven to spend thirty-two days getting the film in the can, which was a luxury compared to some of his earlier films. He'd had only twenty days on *The Last House on the Left* and twenty-five on *The Hills Have Eyes Part II*.

As the schedule was so tight and the crew

Right and below: Robert Englund begins the arduous make-up process.

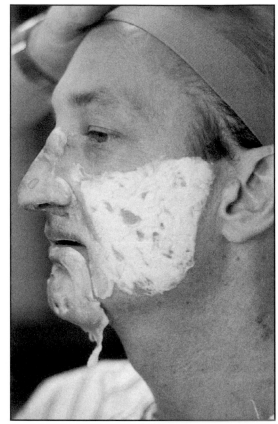

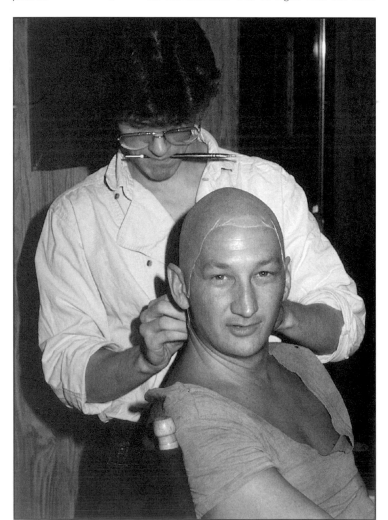

couldn't afford to fall too far behind, Miller repeatedly worked through the night manufacturing the make-up appliances for the next day's shooting. In ten days, he claimed to have lost fifteen pounds in weight.

'In the script Freddy was described somewhat vaguely,' Miller told *Fangoria*. 'At first, New Line and Craven were hoping to have David Warner play the role and I did a sculpture based on David's face. It was basically the same as the final version, but was more charred. Then David had to bail out for various reasons.'

Actor David Warner was concerned about typecasting when Wes Craven approached him to play the villain. 'Producers tend to see me that way,' he claimed. Having played the bad guy in *Time After Time* and *Time Bandits*, Warner was not ready to play another villain so soon. Besides, he had a very specific way of choosing his roles: 'Have I been to that part of the world, and how many days off do I get? If you're fortunate enough to be in that position, it's nice to be flip about it. Work is all out of one's hands.'

The subsequent casting of Robert Englund as Craven's dream killer was something of a coup, both for the film and for the actor. Craven was immediately taken with Englund's approach to the part: 'He was the only one whom I thought really had it. I looked at very many guys. With all my characters I go through a progression. I used to look for very big guys, like in *The Hills Have Eyes*. I found out they were never as powerful as a very good actor who could play evil. It has to do with someone who's not embarrassed to play really evil and get into it. A lot of people will step back from it and become camp and joke with it.'

Englund had been a television bit part actor, turning up as the villain of the week on long running shows like *Charlie's Angels*. He had appeared in a variety of films throughout the seventies, such as *Stay Hungry*, all in fairly minor roles. When he was cast as Freddy Krueger, Englund was best known for his portrayal of friendly alien Willie in the two *V* TV mini-series of 1984. Englund accepted the role because he had an ambition to play a movie monster. 'Fred Krueger is the perfect contrast to my sympathetic, cuddly character in *V*,' Englund said during production of the original *Nightmare* movie. 'Krueger relishes the chase, the torture and the predicament. The actor in me wants to talk a lot more intellectually about the part, but what it really comes down to is I just wanted to be a monster. I mean, I've done a Western, a space movie, a youth movie, a Vietnam movie — this is my monster movie.'

Below: *The finishing touches.*

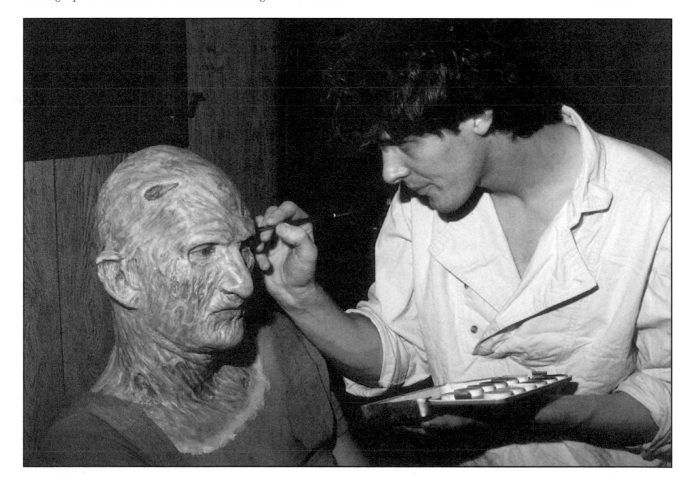

Right: Freddy Krueger's original, darker incarnation is still a fan favourite.

Englund's own common sense and the continuing financial inducements kept him attached to the series right up to the seventh and final instalment, *Wes Craven's New Nightmare*, in 1994. 'The series is a hit and I'd be a fool not to go where I'm wanted,' he says.

It was his appearance in *National Lampoon's Class Reunion* that won him an audition: 'They originally wanted a big man, a sort of Glenn Strange type, for the part. When the casting director saw how physical and ready to go down to the wire I was in *Class Reunion*, she brought me to the attention of Wes.' Englund took a unique approach to securing the role: 'I liked the script — all I had to do was convince the director that I was right for it. When I went to meet Wes, I was all punked out — I wore black, pencilled circles under my eyes and greased my hair straight back. I played a staring game with him. I got the part.'

Despite Englund's attempts at DIY make-up, it was David Miller who was ultimately responsible for turning him into a monster: 'After David Warner dropped out, they'd chosen Robert Englund, and he showed up with this incredibly friendly face. I did four sculptures based on a burns unit photo I got from the UCLA medical centre. Instead of using regular foam I made the mask out of Glastzan, a plastic material that's translucent. You can paint veins on the inside and still see through it. It's usually used in films to make bald caps. Wes thought that it looked too real and at the same time wasn't horrific enough. So I did little variations on what is now the Freddy face, and Wes chose a little bit from each one to create what we finally used.'

Early make-up test photos from *A Nightmare on Elm Street* show Freddy's make-up to be a lot less human than that eventually used. The face is more skull-like — skin peeled from bone, rather than the more familiar Freddy scar tissue, with the mouth a wide-set toothy grin. With the casting of Robert Englund, the make-up was redesigned to follow the actor's features much more closely than had been originally intended. Miller had no doubt that his make-ups contributed greatly to the film's ultimate success: 'I really think the first one stands alone — it's very scary. The make-up effects weren't done to stand out. Now they've become major effects films and that's what's popular.'

As well as the Freddy make-up, Miller was also responsible for a variety of other effects on the first movie: 'The easiest was Freddy cutting open his own chest, while the hardest effect to achieve was the cuts appearing through the girl's chest. At one point we were going to sever Johnny Depp's head, but the idea was dropped somewhere along the line.'

Jim Doyle was the special effects supervisor on *A Nightmare on Elm Street* and had worked with Miller on a variety of projects. Doyle's previous film credits included *One From the Heart*, *WarGames* and *The Sword and the Sorcerer*. In dra-

matic contrast to the later *Nightmare* films, the first boasted only five major special effects set ups, supervised by Doyle: 'It was brilliant the way Wes had written the story. He starts giving you indications of what's real and what is not and then twists those around on you and makes you very uncertain.'

Doyle had to tackle these set pieces with a mixture of imagination and ingenuity, with the film's rather limited effects budget in mind: 'In one scene, Nancy falls asleep in the bathtub and Krueger's clawed hand creeps out of the water. Then the mother knocks on the door, waking Nancy up. The hand disappears and you see bubbles. She falls asleep again and she's hauled under water as if the bathtub is bottomless. We had to shoot the interior of that from the bottom of a swimming pool, looking up.'

The death of Johnny Depp's character, Glen, who is swallowed whole by his bed only to be spat out in a stream of blood, presented a major challenge for the effects team. Craven decided to film the complicated sequence using a rotating set. The cameraman and director were strapped into a pair of Datsun car seats, mounted along with the camera rig on one wall of the revolving set. Depp performed his death throes while the room rotated and 110 gallons of substitute blood (made from water mixed with starch and colouring agents) was pumped out of the bed, appearing to climb up the walls against the force of gravity.

'I love this stuff,' said Depp to *Fangoria* magazine after shooting his scene. 'The kid falls asleep and it's all over. He's sucked right into the bed and spat out as blood. I heard some talk about having a dummy, but I said, "Hey, I want to do this. It'll be fun. Lemme do it".' It was reported that a TV version was shot with a skeleton being ejected from the bed, but this scene didn't make

Above: *Nancy and Freddy in one of* A Nightmare on Elm Street*'s enduring images.*

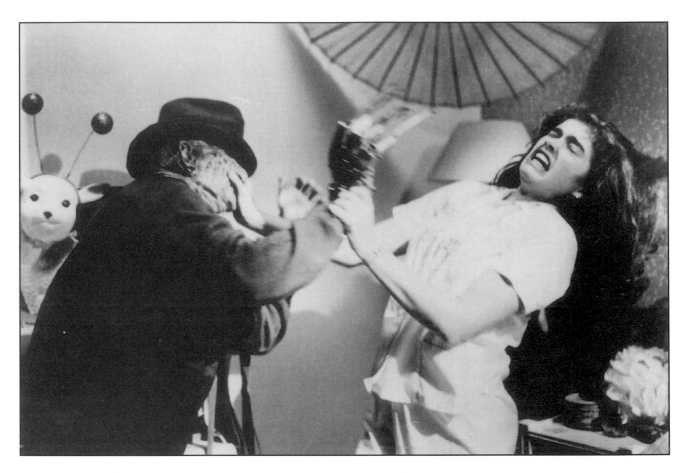

Above: Fighting back — Nancy stands up to Freddy in the second half of the film.

it into any released version of the film.

Although it was his first film role and he was paid the princely sum of $1,200 a week, Depp didn't let his tussle with Freddy Krueger give him unreal delusions of stardom: 'I got sucked into the bed. What kind of reviews can you get opposite Freddy Krueger? "Johnny Depp was good as the boy who died"?' Craven was glad to note that Depp did become a huge star later in his career. '[He] has gone onto better things, and I'm gratified by that,' says the director.

Production on *A Nightmare on Elm Street* wrapped in July 1984, with the producers aiming for a Halloween release later that year in the United States. At the time, Shaye admitted that the film was 'literally being edited as it's being shot.' The ending, however, was to become a bone of contention between the director and the producer, resulting in a falling out which lasted for the best part of a decade.

At the climax of *A Nightmare on Elm Street*, Freddy reappears to claim Nancy's mother as a final victim, while the surviving Elm Street kids drive off into the fog in a car with a red and green striped retractable top. Craven says he had no intention of ending the film that way: 'New Line put a lot of pressure on me to have an ending that would lend itself to a sequel. I didn't particularly want to do that.'

Craven was convinced the film should end as in the script, with the defeat of Freddy by Nancy. Nothing more was needed: 'I felt the first film was complete in itself. If they wanted a sequel they could always invent a way for things to go on. In my version the film ended with Nancy turning her back on Freddy and telling him he was nothing. It showed that evil can be confronted and diminished in the sense that Nancy had become as tough as Freddy and was able to turn away from him. Once you've confronted the evil, shrugged it off in a way, the next step is to turn away from it. That ending was very carefully thought through and had to do with a world view of my own.'

Craven had deliberately set out to avoid a clichéd horror movie climax: 'I don't like horror films that end with general massacres, a survivor crawling out at the end and the bad guy jumping on him for the very last scare. I read so many horror scripts that have that kind of bleak ending. They say villains will win out and the most brutally powerful survive. In my work I'm continually fighting that.' Craven says he fought for his proposed ending to be retained, but was up against concerns about long term returns and franchise possibilities should the film prove commercially successful. 'Bob Shaye was the only person willing to back the film and raise the money,' admits Craven. 'He was saying to me, "This is a partnership. Give me this one thing, a hook to

hang a sequel on. That and some jump at the end". It was a compromise. I felt I owed him that because he had seen the value of the film. Sometimes you make a compromise and years later you say you were sorry you did it. On the other hand, there might not have been any *A Nightmare on Elm Street* at all if I hadn't done that.'

Craven was driven to a compromise, but not all the way. Shaye had wanted Freddy to be driving the car at the end of the film, but Craven refused: 'The end of my compromise was that I would not have Freddy sitting in the front seat. I would not have him driving that car.' To Craven, that image would signify a victory for evil. The idea was later used in the opening scenes of the first sequel, in which Freddy drives a school bus into the depths of hell.

New Line personnel had a slightly different take on the saga of *A Nightmare on Elm Street*'s original ending. '*A Nightmare on Elm Street* was a collaborative effort,' Sara Risher told *Cinefantastique*, explaining that Craven spent a whole year

Below: *Don't fear the reaper — to defeat evil, Nancy must turn her back on it.*

Right: A key moment — Ronee Blakley, as Nancy's mother, admits her involvement in the Freddy story.
Below: Freddy takes revenge on Mrs Thompson for helping to burn him alive.

rewriting the script with input from executives at New Line. Risher also claimed that she and Robert Shaye spent days in the editing room cutting the film together while Craven finished off the job of shooting the script, apparently due to the tight production schedule and the looming October release window, not because Craven had abandoned creative control of his film.

As for the script's original ending, Risher explained: 'There never was an ending. The sky turned black. Lots of birds came out. It was very apocalyptic. Wes came up with the ending that's on the film and he shot it. He also shot the ending Bob wanted, with Freddy driving the car. Both of them looked at the footage and it was agreed to use Craven's ending, Freddy pulling Nancy's mom through the door. Bob's ending isn't there.'

Despite the production problems and the wrangles over the ending, *A Nightmare on Elm Street* was well received upon its American

release. The *New York Times* noted that Wes Craven specialises in 'graphically depicted mayhem and gore', and David Edelstein in the *Village Voice* said, 'Craven's movie drills for fresh nerves... the first murder is one of the most convulsive and (literally) stomach churning I've ever seen because there's an implicit contract between a horror film director and his audience that dreams don't kill.' Despite criticising Craven's script and describing the ending as one of the most irritating he'd seen, Edelstein hailed the film as a 'minor masterpiece'.

Released in Britain almost a year later in September 1985, *A Nightmare on Elm Street* received several similarly enthusiastic notices. The *Daily Express* called it 'a shocker, a 100 per cent nerve tingler', while the *Telegraph* dubbed the film 'an admirably crafted piece of horrific nonsense, calculated to make even the most blasé viewer hold on to his seat.' Writing in the *New Statesman*, Francis Wheen thought it 'most refreshing to see a chiller in which the strongest character by far is female'. *Starburst* saw the movie as a valuable contribution to the genre: 'Craven expertly layers nightmare within nightmare within dreams... delivering the wildest moments to be had in the horror cinema for ages. Craven's visual free reign upturns conventional expectations... it is a film that lingers in the memory.'

The critical reception was not entirely positive, however. Clancy Sigal, film critic of the BBC's now defunct *Listener* magazine, called it 'a nauseating slasher film' and 'a bad dream'. Sigal went on: 'Nothing is left to the imagination as Fred, the nightmare figure with razor blade fingernails, springs out of the collective dreams of some American high school kids to maim, rip, rape and eviscerate.'

When the film was later released on video in Britain (in a coffin shaped video box), newly launched film magazine *Empire* commented that *A Nightmare on Elm Street* was 'the first in the cult series, and the only really scary one. Wes Craven damps down the humour that has since overtaken the films and goes all out for shivers. There are several memorably surreal horror sequences involving tongued telephones and bottomless baths and Craven's unhealthy imagination runs riot.'

With *A Nightmare on Elm Street*, Craven achieved what he'd set out to do — produce a film from his own script which was a commercial and critical success. Following *A Nightmare on Elm Street*, Craven harboured serious hopes that its success would allow him to develop films outside the genre. However, the spirit of Freddy Krueger was set to haunt him for many years to come. ∎

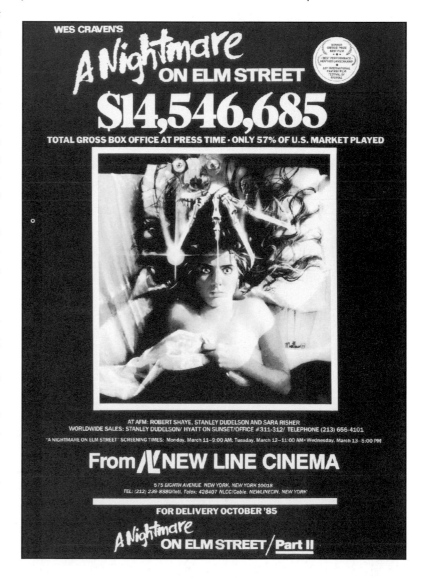

The Wit & Wisdom of Freddy Krueger

Robert Englund brought Wes Craven's dream killer Freddy Krueger to life in the original *A Nightmare on Elm Street* and continued to develop the character right up to the final episode, *Wes Craven's New Nightmare*, in 1994. Englund has seen Freddy go from an unspeakable monster to the comic character of later films, as well as something of a cultural and merchandising phenomenon.

Englund first seriously considered acting as a career at the age of twelve. He enrolled in a children's theatre programme at California State University and appeared in a variety of productions, including *Peter Pan*, *Hansel and Gretel* and *Pinocchio*. 'I remember being in the eighth grade after that experience, studying pre-algebra and missing the smell of the greasepaint,' says Englund. 'It's the oldest cliché in the book, but it's true.'

By the time he reached high school, Englund had taken every drama class he could find and won ten acting awards in the teenage drama workshop at Cal State. He continued to pursue his ambition by studying drama at UCLA, and was accepted by the prestigious Royal Academy of Dramatic Arts, enrolling at their school in Rochester, Michigan after gaining a scholarship award. Studying all day, Englund put his learning and theory to practical use at night, appearing at the Meadowbank Theatre, one of America's longest established and most prestigious repertory theatres.

It was a part in the 1972 Cleveland production of *Godspell* that Englund considers to have been his big break. He followed it with many roles in regional theatres across the United States, gaining

experience as a classical actor: 'In theatre I did exclusively comedy. I did every Shakespearean clown, with the exception of Touchstone and the Fool in *King Lear*, professionally before I was twenty-five.'

Englund made the often difficult switch to Hollywood and lucrative film and television roles relatively easily. While in Detroit in 1973, a student who had admired Englund's work intro-

duced him to the art director of the Terrence Malick film *Badlands*, which was in pre-production. Englund set off for Los Angeles to audition for the film. 'I didn't get the part,' remembers Englund, who lost out to Martin Sheen, 'but I was hooked and decided to stay.'

Before long, Englund was cast in his first feature film, *Buster and Billie*, alongside Jan-Michael Vincent. In 1975, he achieved notoriety as the small-time hood who shoots Burt Reynolds at the climax of *Hustle* and, as a result of his growing presence in Hollywood, was cast alongside Arnold Schwarzenegger, Jeff Bridges and Sally Field in *Stay Hungry*. Quickly establishing himself as a character actor, Englund continued to win small roles in mainstream films like *A Star is Born*, *Big Wednesday* and *Bloodbrothers*. In Tobe Hooper's *Eaten Alive*, Englund makes his entrance with the unforgettable line: 'I'm Buck and I'm ready to fuck.' He also won guest parts in lots of TV movies, one-off pilots and episodes of popular series: 'I've done countless bad per-

formances as bad guy number three chasing Charlie's Angels down the street. I'm embarrassing myself on cable and reruns all the time. Some of the early films I appeared in have been rediscovered now that people know who I am.'

These roles led to a part in the sci-fi double bill *V* and *V: The Final Battle*, top-rated TV mini-series about an alien invasion of Earth which first aired in 1984. In the resulting short-lived weekly series, Englund continued to play Willie, an alien friendly with the Earth resistance, which brought him wider attention than any previous role.

Cast as Freddy Krueger, Englund's first task was to come to terms with the process of putting on the Freddy face each day: 'Three hours in the make-up chair can make anybody pretty fierce. That's not fair on my make-up man! To get into character on the first film, I used my jealousy of all these eighteen year-old actors like Johnny Depp [and] Heather Langenkamp, fresh to Hollywood, being pampered. I'm sitting there, jaded and a bit bitter, getting all this make-up put on me, and it itches. So I used my envy of their youth and freshness, my doubts as to whether this film would be any good or not. I used that — Freddy hates youth and beauty because he has no

place in the future. That worked for me.'

Englund recalls an incident during filming of the original movie which brought home just how powerful the image he was creating could be: 'I had a small make-up trailer. You sleep against one wall, there's a make-up mirror along the other wall and the toilet in the corner that's impossible to sit on. We were not worried about losing the light when shooting that picture, but of losing the night. It was coming up for dawn and we were desperately trying to finish some shots. I went back to the dressing room in full Freddy gear and fell asleep, then there was a knock on the door and I woke up with a start. I wheeled around and there, in the half light of dawn, in the mirror opposite me was this old, bald, disfigured man. It scared the bejezus out of me — I completely forgot that I was in the Freddy make-up.'

Freddy Krueger's success with movie audiences lies in a combination of unique factors. He can stand alongside the great cinematic monsters of the past, but unlike Frankenstein's lumbering creation, Freddy has a voice, and unlike Bela Lugosi's classic interpretation of Dracula, a wicked sense of humour. As a fully developed, rounded and, as the series developed, a changing personality, Freddy is unique in the annals of movie monsterdom.

The nearest the earlier classic horror films came to producing a monster with character was Lon Chaney Jr's interpretation of the Wolf Man. Larry Talbot was a human with the unfortunate curse of lycanthropy, and Chaney's performance expressed the tortured nature of Talbot's character. Unlike his contemporary film fiends Jason Vorhees in *Friday the 13th* and Michael Myers in *Halloween*, Freddy's face was not hidden under a blank mask. He could speak, grimace and crack his trademark bad-taste jokes. 'Freddy's not just a one-dimensional splatter-film killer. He's your classic bogeyman and a Freudian kind of nightmare. He's the physical incarnation of some of our deepest fears,' says Englund.

Thanks to New Line's clever marketing, Freddy Krueger became an amazing success. The studio took the original subversive character, whom Craven calls, 'the most evil being you can imagine, someone who goes after children', softened him and made him acceptable by rewriting his past, turning Freddy into a mainstream hero and a money spinner.

The character seen in the later films was far removed from the one Craven outlined in his

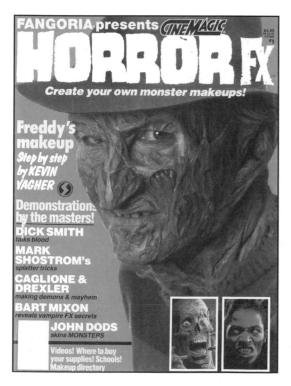

Left: Cover star — Freddy quickly became a monster pin-up.

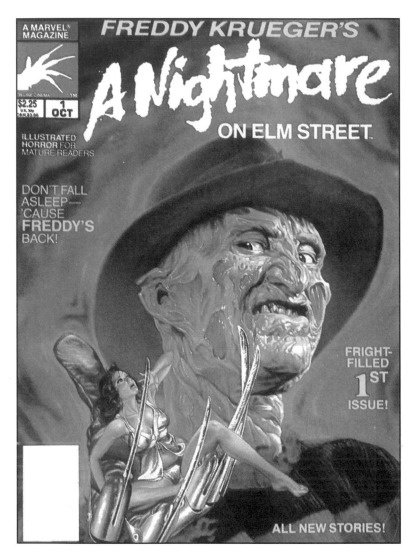

any of the publicity that surrounded later instalments. The marketing consisted of a movie poster and some half-hearted TV and press promotion. The film took off by itself, word of mouth drawing in the audiences who ensured that a long-running series followed. Craven remembers sitting in on screenings in movie houses across America: 'All the teenagers loved it, but each group responded in a different way. I think horror movies are a form of catharsis. The genre attracts a very young and vital audience that's intolerant of boredom. If you do something that's fresh and new, they really let you know.'

By the time the sequel, *Freddy's Revenge*, was being developed, Freddy had become a much more marketable commodity. Craven watched the process with a kind of grudging respect for Shaye's commercial savvy: 'Bob Shaye's genius in marketing was to soften Freddy and make him a little bit more of a buffoon. Now, he's embraced by younger kids and they can make fun of him. In a way he's dangerous and in a way he's a joke. It's probably safer to deal with him that way.'

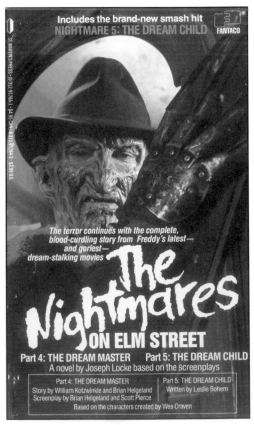

Above and right: *From comic books to novelisations, it was impossible to avoid Freddy fever.*

original *A Nightmare on Elm Street* script. Robert Englund recalls: 'Wes wrote the most evil, corrupt thing he could think of. Originally, that meant Freddy was a child molester. Right while we were shooting the first *Nightmare*, there was a huge scandal based around an area of single parent yuppies in California known as South Bay. Child molesters had descended on this unsupervised flotsam of seventies leftover Me-generation American children. On the spot we changed the script from child molester to child murderer, mainly so that Wes wouldn't be accused of exploiting the South Bay case.'

The first film was a sleeper success, without

New Line's director of licensing and promotions at the time, Kevin Benson, agreed that a deliberate change of style for Freddy was adopted on the second film: 'We decided that with *Nightmare 2* we should market Freddy as if he was a rock'n'roll band. We did these great posters and then we did this trendy black T-shirt, like rock bands have. I knew it would be incredibly popular, and I was right because we sold hundreds of thousands of them.'

Robert Shaye was heavily involved in the new direction taken by the Freddy character. '*Nightmare 2* caught on in a big way with the non-gross out teen and young adult audience,' he said to *Cinefantastique* at the time. 'We're not out to alienate the horror audience, but we do want to broaden the film's potential audiences.'

Craven could see that the dramatic repositioning of Freddy Krueger was a calculated process: 'I know Bob Shaye always had the feeling that there should be more humour in the movies. He thought the first one was too dark a vision. His idea is that kids want to have a laugh and a good time. It's no secret that he talks about the movies as a "good cheeseburger". You determine a formula and then you crank them out like fast food. I don't think that way. Bob Shaye would call that darker and less humorous — I would call it more important and serious.'

Shaye didn't agree with Craven's analysis of the New Line attitude, but he did admit that his Freddy was a different beast altogether: 'I do think the films should be "date movies" and that they should be entertaining. I may have talked at some juncture about the idea of popular entertainment being more a "fast food" kind of entertainment, as opposed to film as "art".'

The man in the mask, Robert Englund, had his own take on events: 'Some of the purists have criticised us for abandoning the way of gore and violence, just as people have criticised us for the gore and violence. We've taken a new path, exploiting the special effects as a means of showing the dreamscape and the nightmares.'

It's always been the case that the bad guys get the best lines, and the anticipation for Freddy's first appearance in each subsequent *Nightmare* movie became a ritual for young audiences. Anything and everything was used to promote the Freddy movies. There were books, T-shirts, masks, hats, jumpers, gloves (complete with plastic finger knives, supposedly only for sale to those aged ten and over), key rings, hologram wristwatches, bubblegum, *A Nightmare on Elm Street* board game, a talking Freddy doll which threatened its owner, a build-him-yourself plastic Freddy model kit, an alarm clock, mugs, Christmas tree ornaments(!), even a *Freddy's Greatest Hits* album. An Elm Street road sign was promoted with the slogan: 'Why steal a sign and get into trouble? Buy one today and tell everyone you stole it!' The list is endless. At one stage, Freddy even had his own comic book, written by the creator of cult hero Howard the Duck, Steve Gerber.

Kevin Benson was particularly proud of the talking doll: 'It's insane! You press a button and he says: "Hello. Welcome to Elm Street. I'm

Left: *Don't try this at home, kids — the Freddy mask, hat and glove set, only for sale to those aged ten and over.*

©1984, 1994 New Line Productions, Inc. All Rights Reserved. Freddy, Freddy Krueger and A Nightmare On Elm Street are registered trademarks

Right: Back from the dead — the New Nightmare *calling card.*

Freddy. I want you!" We had to keep it fairly clean for the kids, so unfortunately I couldn't let him say the original line I had in mind, which was: "Welcome to prime time, bitch!".'

Benson was adamant that all this merchandise could do no harm. 'Kids have always loved monsters,' he told *Empire* magazine. 'My aim is to keep those kids happy by giving them a bang for their buck.' Those bucks were particularly big. By the beginning of the nineties, New Line had made well over $10 million in profit from merchandising and licensing deals in the United States alone.

Freddy was like a virus that spread through the culture. Seven amusement parks across America boasted of featuring Freddy rides, while fans wore Freddy costumes to all-night screenings of the *Nightmare* movies. Other films made references to Freddy. In the big screen version of the TV cop show *Dragnet*, star Tom Hanks made Freddy jokes and impersonated him. In *The Prince of Pennsylvania*, Amy Madigan sported a Freddy mask during a kidnapping, while in *Critters 2* (a New Line movie) a shape-shifting alien adopted Freddy's image, copying the look from a poster.

Robert Englund himself, whose image was used on all the merchandising, is ambivalent about the subject. 'I'm two-faced about that, actually,' he said just before embarking on another Freddy sequel. 'I finally have a piece of that action, a small piece, in my contract for *Nightmare 4*. I think it was necessary to make the glove, the sweater and the hat and the mask — you have no idea the number of requests we got for those things. I get a little embarrassed when I see the bubblegum cards, the decals and the little Freddy troll dolls that hang on rear view mirrors. There's also an inflatable stress doll in the form of Freddy which you box with. The Freddy toilet paper is a little embarrassing.' Englund even appeared in a pop promo for The Fat Boys rap single 'Are You Ready for Freddy?' in full Freddy regalia.

One of the most surprising spin-offs from the *Nightmare* phenomenon was the not-very-successful television version, *Freddy's Nightmares*, which ran for two seasons between 1988 and

1990. The potential problems of having a child killer as the star of a prime time television show were circumvented by having Robert Englund's Freddy character as the host of a series of *The Twilight Zone* style chilling tales. Freddy introduced, and occasionally appeared in, mild tales of terror suitable for television. The series was kicked off by a two hour *A Nightmare on Elm Street* 'prequel' directed by Tobe Hooper, which rewrote the story of Freddy's origins for television. It was broadcast in October 1988, two months after the American release of the fourth film, *The Dream Master*.

'I was seduced into *Freddy's Nightmares* for a couple of reasons,' remembers Englund. 'Firstly, we wanted to do something like *The Twilight Zone* or *Alfred Hitchcock Presents*. Secondly, we were going to get a lot of movie directors in to do episodes and I'd be directing some. The problem was a lot of these directors didn't know how to handle episodic television in six days on a budget of $450,000. So the last two or three days of the shoot would be incredibly rushed. Out of the twenty-two in the first series, I think there are probably twelve that are very good and out of those twelve, five that are classics. There are some

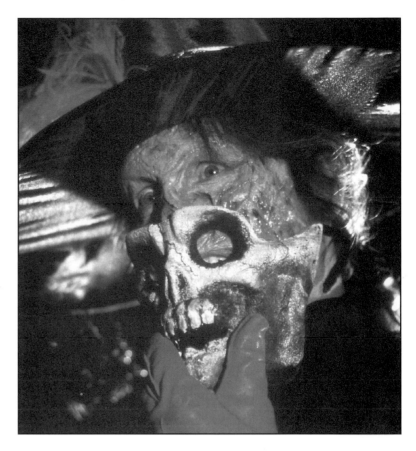

clinkers in there, too. Tobe Hooper, of *The Texas Chain Saw Massacre*, directed the first one and he had problems because he thought he had eight days as it was a pilot, but they only gave him six. We know how to do episodic television very well in the States, and there are these crack crew who can do amazing things in six or seven days, but they've never done special effects. They can do car chases, but they don't know how to budget for the extra time effects take. We really got into trouble on a couple of shows where we ran out of time.'

Freddy's Nightmares started production during the 1988 writers' strike, which also affected *A Nightmare on Elm Street 4*, so the first batch of episodes were written by non-Writer's Guild authors. The scripts were selected from hundreds submitted, according to Englund: 'I wouldn't have gone near it with a ten foot pole if it was just a commercially exploitative idea.'

Although the series was made directly for syn-

Above and left: The success of Freddy Krueger led to Robert Englund's rise as a horror star in The Phantom of the Opera *(above) and Tobe Hooper's* The Mangler.

Right: Reaping the rewards — Wes Craven and Robert Englund in 1993 at a film festival in Milan.

dication by Lorimar, thereby avoiding network restrictions on sex and violence, *Freddy's Nightmares* was always intended to be very different from the feature films. 'With the television show, the yucky side was held to a minimum,' remembers Robert Shaye, one of the series' three executive producers. 'We believe the fun is in the suspense and the twists. We don't feel the programme should mimic the feature films.'

The first series was a mixed bag, a situation not helped by the writers' strike. 'We had some problems,' admitted producer Scott Stone in *Fangoria*. 'It was twenty-two episodes of just learning what we were doing. We found that people were not really identifying with the characters in the show. I think we did a good job of giving a look to the show, but we often confused the audience as to where the story was going. We got so wrapped up in the idea of the dreams. In the second series, Freddy was to be the puppetmaster, the guy who comments on the story and makes things happen.'

Englund was in favour of an overhaul for the series: 'A major problem was that we rushed into a formula and a set of rules that nobody really believed in. It was determined that the *Freddy's Nightmares* audience had to centre on the teen market. We fell into that trap early on.'

The series managed a second and final season when the three producing companies, Warner Brothers, Lorimar and New Line, were persuaded that there was enough life in the concept to produce a further run of episodes. This time, Robert Englund had to be persuaded to return to the role: 'The only carrot in the second series for me was the opportunity to direct a couple of episodes. I wouldn't have done it if they hadn't let me direct.'

So determined were New Line to keep Englund tied to the *Nightmare* movie series, they were willing to indulge him in the TV show. Overly familiar with the part of Freddy by this stage, Englund no longer approached it in the same way. 'I don't do any preparation to play Freddy now,' he candidly admitted at the time.

'That makes playing the character more fun. I'm much more open to the immediacy of the moment. I'm making Freddy a bit goofier.'

Producer Bill Froehlich, who also wrote and directed several episodes of *Freddy's Nightmares*, saw the second season as a chance to take the Freddy TV show concept one step further. 'We're trying to bring a lot more sophistication to the stories this year,' he told *Fangoria*. 'Freddy and his nightmare world are still at the core of it, but we're trying to make the terror more psychologically frightening.' Despite the efforts of the production team to make the second season more adult in nature, inconsistent programming, a tight schedule and the feeling that Freddy was already over-exposed, led to the series' cancellation after a second batch of twenty-two episodes.

With a fifth *Nightmare* on the way, the reinvention of Freddy as a kiddie-friendly bogeyman had worked for New Line, but the whole process had soured Wes Craven to his original creation. 'I'm sure they'll make seven or eight movies,' he said at the time of the third film in the series, somewhat presciently. 'They'll make as many as they can. As business people, why not? That's obviously allowed New Line to expand the company and make other movies. That's the business

side of making movies — it's called a franchise.'

As Freddy hit television, Craven was keen to distance himself from the commercial creature New Line had produced. 'I didn't create a Freddy like that,' he said. 'I've seen New Line's internal notes, and it's very much towards taking the edge off the films and making them more popular. They want to make Freddy cute. I think it's an interesting phenomenon, but it's not something I feel attached to.'

Although he'd left it behind, Craven was to find that the *A Nightmare on Elm Street* franchise would become his concern yet again, contributing story ideas and a script for the third film and reinventing the whole concept afresh in the post-modern *Wes Craven's New Nightmare*. ■

Above: Robert Englund, entering into the spirit of his most memorable role.

VUELVE EL HOMBRE DE TUS SUEÑOS!

ORION
FILMS DISTRIBUCIÓN, S. A.

NEW LINE CINEMA, HERO COMUNICATIONS INC. Y SMART EGG PICTURES PRESENTAN

Pesadilla
EN ELM STREET · 2
LA VENGANZA DE FREDDY

A ROBERT SHAYE Production "A NIGHTMARE ON ELM STREET, PART 2: FREDDY'S REVENGE" Starring MARK PATTON · KIM MYERS
ROBERT RUSLER · Special Appearances by CLU GULAGER and HOPE LANGE and ROBERT ENGLUND as FREDDY KRUEGER
Music by CHRISTOPHER YOUNG · Director of Photography JACQUES HAITKIN · Executive Producers STEPHEN DIENER and STANLEY DUDELSON
Line Producers MICHAEL MURPHEY and JOEL SOISSON · Co-Producer SARA RISHER · Written by DAVID CHASKIN
Produced by ROBERT SHAYE · Directed by JACK SHOLDER
FROM NEW LINE CINEMA

R RESTRICTED
UNDER 17 REQUIRES ACCOMPANYING
PARENT OR ADULT GUARDIAN

© 1985 NEW LINE CINEMA CORP.

The Nightmares Never End

Despite his reluctance to be involved, Wes Craven found it almost impossible to escape Freddy Krueger and the *A Nightmare on Elm Street* films. In order to solve his pressing financial problems, Craven had entered into a deal with New Line Cinema which meant the creator of the characters sold his ownership rights to any sequels: 'By the time I made *A Nightmare on Elm Street*, I was virtually broke... They bought it outright and owned the whole thing.'

Although under no obligation to do so, Robert Shaye at New Line had tried to tempt Craven back to direct the second film in what looked like becoming an on-going series, but he turned the offer down: 'I told them that if they came up with a script that I found intriguing, I would consider it, but the script for *Nightmare 2* had certain problems, and I felt it was not in my best interests to direct.

'They didn't intend to change it [the script] at all. It brought Freddy out into the waking world a great deal, and scenes like the pool scene where he's running around amok — he's not really that big a guy and they were putting him in scenes with these six foot tall kids. I said, he's going to be diminished, he's going to be ridiculous.'

Craven felt that some of the story elements and concepts in the proposed sequel script did not hold true to his original creation: 'I had a real confusion with Freddy coming out of the central character. I had some structural problems with it. There were things in there that were just patently ridiculous, like the scene where the parrot attacks. What does that mean? To me, it had no philosophical thread which I could follow, so

I just bowed out.'

With Craven sidelined, it fell to others to perpetuate Freddy's reign of terror. The script he had been so scathing about had been drafted by David Chaskin, a Long Island, New York native who'd begun working at New Line in 1978 as a part-time film inspector. He'd risen through the company, working on the marketing and distribution of such releases as *The Evil Dead* and *The Texas Chain Saw Massacre*. Shaye felt that Chaskin would be ideal to develop Freddy as he knew about the current horror film market. What

Opposite: *The Spanish poster for* A Nightmare on Elm Street Part 2: Freddy's Revenge.
Left: *Freddy Krueger — out for revenge.*

Above:

Newcomers Kim Meyers and Mark Patton in the uneven A Nightmare on Elm Street Part 2.

Shaye and Chaskin both failed to take into account was the unique nature of Craven's original dream demon.

By turning to the sales side of the business for story concepts, Shaye ran the risk of allowing the marketing of the movies to assume paramount importance. Within three days Chaskin had hammered out a fifteen page treatment, and was quickly commissioned to produce the full script. He spent a month sitting in front of his word processor, producing the first draft of *A Nightmare on Elm Street Part 2: Freddy's Revenge.*

Chaskin was realistic about the restrictions he faced working for an independent outfit like New Line. 'I think low budget film-making is more exciting,' he told *Fangoria*. 'It puts more pressure on creative people when you don't have a big studio behind you, but you have to make as good a project for less. You're forced to use your imagination a little more.'

The thirty-one year-old faced a daunting task figuring out a way to follow Craven's original frightfest: 'I sat down and thought about what scares me, what makes me feel creepy and tried to wrap that around the already frightening Freddy Krueger character that Wes created in the first film.'

Craven's comments on the script did prove valuable to Chaskin, but the writer didn't implement them all. 'Wes made some suggestions,' remembered Chaskin, 'some of which we used and some of which we didn't, mainly location changes. I had the finale in a more open space and he wanted it in a more closed, confined area. I think it was a good idea to close it in. He also suggested that we shift the focus from Jesse, the male lead. In the script the focus was on him ninety per cent of the time, then suddenly it shifted to Lisa, his girlfriend.'

Taking over from Craven as director was Jack Sholder, who'd previously made the thriller *Alone in the Dark* for New Line. 'I went into this film knowing I had no choice but to top the original,' said Sholder of the $3 million, seven-week shoot in Los Angeles. He'd been directing since 1964, with a series of award-winning shorts and a host of TV work to his name, and was tapped to helm the *Nightmare* sequel only six weeks before shooting was due to begin. 'This is one of those movies that has an appeal beyond the hard-core splatter film audience,' he claimed.

Sholder set out to lighten up the *A Nightmare on Elm Street* universe, aiming to deliver the franchise that Robert Shaye hoped would support a market for *Nightmare* movie merchandise. Humour was to be the key to making Freddy palatable. 'Our picture is lighter,' Sholder explained to *Fangoria*. 'Wes is a very serious guy and his film was very dark, very oppressive, very serious and fairly unrelenting. There wasn't much intentional humour in it. We, on the other hand, leavened ours with humour. It got filtered through writer David Chaskin and Bob Shaye's sensibilities. The pair of them developed the script on their own without Wes, and then I added my own two cents' worth.'

Chaskin agreed that the philosophy was to play Freddy for fun: 'I think horror should be tempered with humour. I think they work hand in hand. The idea is to catch the audience off guard with a gag and suddenly have the gag turn around on them. Some humorous things start building into a terror situation.'

Robert Englund was back on board, and at the time he saw the humorous route the production was taking as a virtue. 'Most of the fun element was cut out of the first film,' notes Englund, 'because the people involved wanted to emphasise the absolute evil. The writer of the second film instinctively picked up on the humorous side, and he put into it a certain sense of intimacy and sly perversion. It's these elements that I

found the most attractive.'

Freddy's Revenge is set five years after the original film and features a new family who have taken up residence in the house once occupied by Nancy Thompson. The lead character of Jesse Walsh was played by Mark Patton. His girlfriend Lisa Poletti, who has to save Jesse from the attentions of Freddy, was played by Kim Meyers, making her feature film début. The roles of Jesse's parents were filled by Clu Gulager and Hope Lange. The relatively unknown cast was another indication of the limited budget allotted to the production.

Below: Shower scene — Freddy Krueger emerges from the steam.

Right: Jesse Walsh (Mark Patton) faces up to the killer inside him.

In between romancing his girlfriend and fighting at school, Jesse begins to uncover the history of Freddy as he appears more and more in the boy's nightmares. Freddy wants to take over Jesse's body to continue his mission to revenge himself on the Elm Street parents. After assorted confrontations and the death of the school's coach Schneider, Freddy is apparently defeated through the power of love. Jesse and Lisa ride off into the sunset in the school bus — until they discover who the driver is...

'The capper was that Bob Shaye, who had always wanted me to have Freddy at the wheel of the car at the end of the first film, put it in *Nightmare 2*,' says Craven. 'Sure enough, Freddy's driving the bus'.

As they developed, the *A Nightmare on Elm Street* films drove the Hollywood special effects industry, and *Freddy's Revenge* was the first to be structured around the set pieces. 'We tried to keep the human element in there,' said Sholder. 'I see the picture as a love story. It's Beauty and the

Beast after the hero turns into Freddy. His girlfriend has to win him back, and she does it through the power of love. It's kind of touching, not the usual horror film. It has human values. Everyone says the money is in the special effects, but really, for me, the money was in having those effects relate to and come out of real characters.'

David Miller was originally slated to return to supervise the make-up for *Freddy's Revenge*, but he dropped out to take up a more lucrative offer when it became clear that Craven's involvement would be marginal. He was replaced by twenty-three year-old Kevin Yagher, who'd previously worked on *Dreamscape* with Miller as well as the fourth instalment in Sean Cunningham's *Friday the 13th* series. *Freddy's Revenge* was his first solo assignment. Jack Sholder instructed Yagher to simplify the make-up process, complaining that Miller's original dark design featured 'too much pizza'. 'I did some research and got some books on burn victims,' said Yagher of his revision of Miller's Freddy concept. 'The producers wanted

Left: The Freddy's Revenge *make-up —* *'real shiny'.*

Freddy's face to look wet, so I put glistening KY Jelly on it. They wanted it real shiny, and kept telling me, "more goop"!'

Yagher got the application process down to nine separate pieces, including a shoulder piece used in the sequence where Freddy stabs himself in the chest. Yagher had once worked as an actor and sympathised with Englund's request for make-up which was quicker and easier to apply and remove: 'I tried to make the make-up less bulky and as thin as possible, so it would move naturally with Robert's face.' Yagher also added burns to Freddy's non-gloved hand and developed some new soft contact lenses to give Englund's eyes a more demonic look.

Budget limitations had made the job difficult for Yagher and Mark Shostrom, who was handling all the Freddy transformations, but neither were prepared for the shock they got on watching the finished film. Jack Sholder had decided at the last minute to play down the special effects sequences, aware that he had not concentrated

on the characters sufficiently. The result was a film that appealed neither to those who loved the first for the characters nor those who were looking for a special effects led scarefest.

'I didn't know what the hell I was looking at,' admitted Yagher to *Fangoria*, after the first screening of *Freddy's Revenge*. 'I was looking at the screen and saying, "What is that?"' Yagher was particularly disappointed by the climactic meltdown for Freddy: 'The whole scene doesn't work. This is supposed to be the film's dramatic climax, and instead, Freddy dies just like that. You're left wondering, "What the heck just happened?"'

Aiming to play up mood, atmosphere and character, Sholder's dark lighting scheme and attempts to edit down the special effects sequence left *Freddy's Revenge* an emasculated horror film, lacking bite. 'They took the hide-the-monster approach,' explained Yagher. 'That was okay at the beginning, but it was disappointing towards the end because they kept the

Right: A second bite at the box office — Nightmare 2 boosted New Line's hopes for a successful franchise.

film so dark. It's upsetting that after all that work, none of it shows.'

The climax was only one of the casualties. Many sequences shot by Yagher and Shostrom were trimmed or deleted altogether, or were lit so badly that the detail carefully built into the make-up effects is all but invisible. A giant tongue created for the Jesse character by Shostrom, plus a group of demonic nightmarish creatures designed by Rick Lazzarini, were built and shot, but hardly visible in the film.

Yagher understood that Sholder had viewed the full meltdown sequence many times, only to decide that it would dominate the film at the expense of the confrontation between the two lead actors. 'He cut it down to nothing,' said Yagher. Sholder claimed he had a specific aim in mind: 'I wanted to go for the "ah" rather than the "ugh", to amaze people rather than disgust them. The film is not big on gore. I hope it's big on imagination.'

The star of the show was as disappointed as Yagher by the finished article. 'We all worked hard on *Freddy's Revenge*,' says Robert Englund,

'but Jack Sholder's experience came mainly from the editing room, and although I quite like the beginning and end, I hated the clumsy swimming pool scene.' None of this seemed to be a problem for mainstream audiences, who were just beginning to catch onto the Freddy phenomenon. With a meagre budget of $3 million, *Freddy's Revenge* grossed over $30 million, ensuring that New Line quickly thought of ways to prolong the Freddy franchise.

When the dust settled from *Freddy's Revenge*, Wes Craven was happy he hadn't been involved in what many saw as a misguided sequel. 'There was not a clear cut hero who remained intact,' says Craven in a critique of the movie. 'There were a lot of events in that picture that I thought were disconnected and had no real reason for being there.'

It seems likely that Robert Shaye realised *Freddy's Revenge* had been a misjudgement, albeit a commercially successful one. Keen as ever to build a series on the back of the Freddy character, and with signs that he was becoming a cult figure despite the poor reception of the second film among hard-core horror fans, Shaye determined to revive Freddy one more time. Despite the problems on the original and his refusal to take on the sequel, Wes Craven was the person Shaye and Sara Risher approached to help get the series back on track. 'I always go to Wes first each time,' admitted Risher.

No one was more surprised at the approach from New Line than Craven himself: 'They came back to me for number three and asked me if I wanted to direct. I was just completing *Deadly Friend*, so I wasn't available, but I mentioned an idea they liked, so I wrote the script.' Craven wasn't coming back aboard the *Nightmare* train just for the hell of it — he had other aims in mind: 'I wanted to do *Nightmare 3* because I felt compelled to come back and expand on the original concept. I like taking that one more step... It was important for me in a business sense that I was able to negotiate a percentage point in the

sequels I didn't have from the original film.'

Craven's concept for the third movie was the creation of the Dream Warriors, a group of variously skilled teens who found that together they had the power to take on Freddy in the dream world. It was an intriguing development of the ideas Craven had introduced in the first film and it grounded each of the subsequent movies. Despite this, the journey of *A Nightmare on Elm Street 3: Dream Warriors* to the screen was not an easy one.

Craven co-wrote the screenplay with Bruce Wagner, later to create the Oliver Stone sci-fi

Below: A Nightmare on Elm Street 3: Dream Warriors.

thriller mini-series *Wild Palms*. 'We decided that it could no longer be one person fighting Freddy. It had to be a group, because the souls of his victims have made Freddy stronger,' Craven explains.

The screenplay Craven and Wagner wrote was faithful to the first film's original concept — that good can overcome evil, rather than the negative evil-defeats-good climax of *Freddy's Revenge*. It featured seven of the remaining Elm Street kids, who meet in a psychiatric ward. They are united by Nancy Thompson (Heather Langenkamp), the survivor of the first movie, now a doctor specialising in dream disorders, to tackle Krueger on his own terms.

'I took an executive producing credit,' says Craven of his involvement in the film. 'My understanding was that I would be asked about

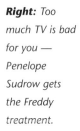

Right: Too much TV is bad for you — Penelope Sudrow gets the Freddy treatment.

things all along. I would be brought into casting and have a real creative part in the picture. The reality was that New Line Cinema never really contacted me again after they had the script.' It was a familiar story for Craven: 'They changed it quite drastically in some ways. The director and a friend of his rewrote it and changed the names of all the characters, and included several key scenes of their own. They changed a lot of things they thought were too expensive to attempt, and they added some things I thought were not as good. A lot of the reasons [why] I had agreed to do the picture were taken away.'

Not surprisingly, Shaye and Risher had their own view of the development of the script. 'They thought they had it nailed,' claimed Shaye of Craven and Wagner's final draft screenplay. 'We thought it needed more work. There was never any acrimony as far as I know. I think the tremendous success of the film speaks for itself.'

As Risher explained to *Cinefantastique* magazine, 'Chuck Russell made the script work. I give Wes the complete credit for the terrific idea of these kids, the Dream Warriors, I'm not faulting that. But Chuck Russell and Frank Darabont turned that script around. We wouldn't have made it with what we had. They rewrote seventy per cent of it.'

To Craven, New Line's motivation was straightforward: 'They were interested in having my name on another *Nightmare* film.' Craven's initial idea for a prequel chronicling Freddy's origins had been rejected, but the idea of bringing back Nancy and teaming her with the psychic teens who take on Freddy was seen as a winner.

Craven was now faced with an uncomfortable situation. New Line hired Chuck Russell to direct — the man who'd scripted *Dreamscape*, the film which Craven has always felt was a thinly disguised reworking of his then-unproduced *A Nightmare on Elm Street* script. Freddy actor Robert Englund thought that might have been the source of tension behind the scenes: 'It was strange. If you think about it, Wes has always blamed *Dreamscape* for ripping him off and suddenly the writer of that is the director.'

Russell brought in Frank Darabont to rewrite the original screenplay. 'I didn't really know who Freddy was at the time,' Darabon admitted to *Fangoria*. 'I knew of the character, but I hadn't seen the first two films. I know that Craven and Wagner had done four drafts of this thing, but we only saw the final draft, and that's what Chuck and I worked from. We locked ourselves away in Big Bear to get away from the phones and wrote it in eleven days. Three weeks after we were hired, Chuck jumped in and started directing.' After working as a writer-for-hire on various projects, Frank Darabont hit the big time writing and directing *The Shawshank Redemption* from a short story by Stephen King.

The matter ended up in arbitration at the Writer's Guild, and all four writers (Craven, Wagner, Russell and Darabont) were credited on screen. 'I had this idea that New Line and I could patch up old differences with this film,' said Craven at the time. 'They didn't inform me

when they had rewritten the script, and it wasn't until I made a stink that I got to see the final version. I was not even informed when filming was supposed to start.'

For Englund, the entire production process was something of a real-life nightmare, given the accelerated shooting schedule. It was the money and profit participation on offer that locked him into the third film, before he'd even read the script: 'I told New Line I hadn't done the previous two films for money, but I felt I was an important part of their success. They agreed and I got a small percentage of the picture.' For a first time director, Chuck Russell must have had sec-

Below: A major operation — Freddy adopts the guise of a nubile nurse to trap Joey (Rodney Eastman).

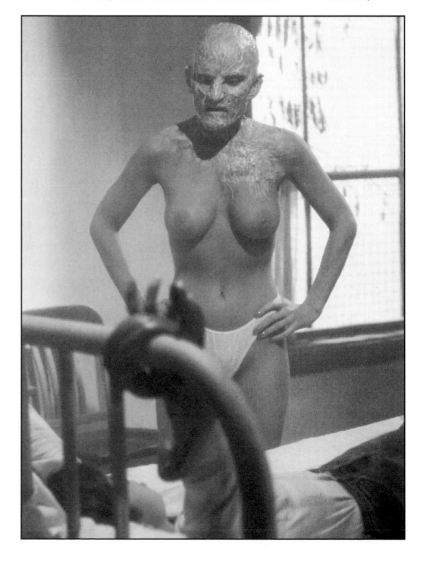

ond thoughts, faced with a six week shooting schedule to December 1986, followed by additional make-up shots in January the following year, with the film due to be released in America in the middle of February 1987. 'Chuck didn't sleep for weeks,' says Englund.

For Russell, *Dream Warriors* was his big chance to make an impression as a director. It was his criticisms of the second film in the series that had persuaded Shaye to hire him for the third. 'With the first two films, the nightmares were based in the real world,' noted Russell in a *Fangoria* interview. 'People would fall asleep and Freddy would appear. In this picture, we go deeper into Freddy's territory. The characters are lured into the dream world where Freddy forces them to confront their deepest fears.'

Chuck Russell saw it as his job to continue to broaden the potential audience for the developing Freddy franchise. Although *Freddy's Revenge* had been a critical failure with horror fans, it had proved to be a surprise commercial success, attracting new audiences to the genre and making an

icon out of Freddy. Nonetheless, Russell wanted to correct what he saw as the mistakes of the second film. 'We have gone to great lengths to make the fantasy deaths much more interesting than the literal slasher deaths,' he said of the more imaginative approach evident in *Dream Warriors*. 'We have also done more with the characterisation than has been done in the previous *Nightmare* films. The bottom line for me is that the magic of Freddy is there. I felt that he lost some of that in the last film because he came into the real world so often. There were times in *Nightmare 2* where Freddy was just another mad slasher.'

The formula that emerged from *Dream Warriors* set the course for most of the following films. Instalments three, four and five make up a discrete trilogy, sharing the same basic concepts and settings, making the *Nightmare* movies a production designer's dream. For Robert Englund, it was art directors Mick and C. J. Strawn, a brother and sister team, who did the most to create the distinctive world of the Dream Warriors: 'For every $100 you give Mick and C. J. you get

Right: Heather Langenkamp joined the cast of Dream Warriors, *led by Patricia Arquette.*

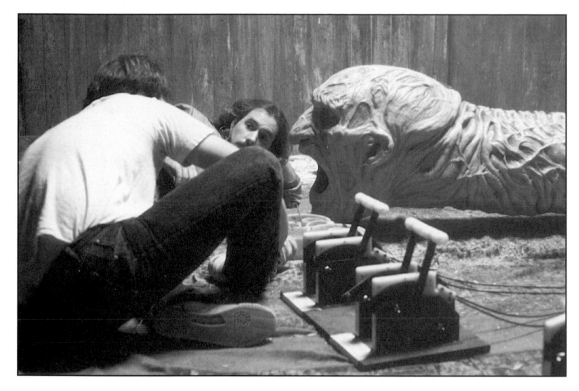

Left: Preparing the enormous Freddy snake.
Below: Kristen (Patricia Arquette) almost meets a sticky end.

$1,000 on the screen. They're truly amazing.'

With a $4 million budget, Russell and his production designers faced a major challenge in bringing Freddy's dream world to the screen. Three months before shooting began, construction was underway on an eerie, rotting version of the original Elm Street house, a blood-splattered tunnel, rooms with collapsing walls and a 'Freddy Hell' for the climactic final battle. The compressed shoot took place in and around Los Angeles, with location work in a car scrap yard north of the city and a graveyard in east LA.

Returning to the Elm Street fold was actress Heather Langenkamp. Twenty-two at the time, she was now the most adult character taking on Freddy this time out. It was the challenge of playing Nancy as a grown woman rather than as a screaming teen that brought Langenkamp back. 'The nature of many horror movies is that the adult figures are very stiff,' she says. 'In that movie, I was the only adult who really understood the kids. Nancy is strong and smart, and in *Nightmare 3* she's a little more careful, too.'

The cast of Dream Warriors who team up against Freddy featured a couple of actors who went onto bigger and better things, like Johnny Depp before them. Patricia Arquette, sister of Rosanna, was cast as Kristen, who holds the key to defeating Freddy. 'I knew it was a lot better than most horror movies,' says Arquette, later

the star of *True Romance*.

Also among the cast was Larry Fishburne, who'd featured in Francis Ford Coppola's *Apocalypse Now* as a teenager and would later call himself Laurence Fishburne. John Saxon returned as Nancy's father, with Rodney Eastman, Bradley Gregg, Ira Heiden, Jennifer Rubin, Ken Sagoes and Penelope Sudrow making up the rest of the team. Having cost $4 million to make, *A Nightmare on Elm Street 3: Dream Warriors* took $45 million at the American box office alone.

Craven and Englund found themselves caught up in controversy when suicides among American teens in New Jersey were wrongly linked to the release of *Dream Warriors*. The film features Freddy inducing his victims to kill themselves, in what Craven calls a legitimate attempt to tackle a tricky subject: 'That was one of the points of the film. We were aware of teenage sui-

cide, and the notion was to show that it's not just some drug or something that's making them do it, it's a real perception of evil. A real teenager committing suicide doesn't want to do it, he wants somebody to know what's going on inside of him, so he can be understood and not seen as just sick.'

Having approached the subject in what he felt was a responsible and adult manner, Craven was surprised to be the subject of newspaper attacks in Britain, claiming the movie had sparked off a wave of copy-cat suicides: 'It was with some astonishment that we saw that connection being drawn. It was just the opposite of what we intended. I don't think from the kids that I talked to that there was any reception of it that way in the United States. There was a story about a little boy of five who'd killed his three year-old sister; he'd said he was Freddy and killed her. We paid for an investigation and found the entire thing to be fabricated. There was no such case whatsoever. There is a continuous, insidious attempt on behalf of certain members of the press to draw parallels [between horror films and real life violence].'

For Englund, there was no question that the film could have had any responsibility for teen suicides: 'No correlation has been proved. It was just one questionable press item blown out of all proportion [and] nothing to do with *Dream Warriors*. The cynical popular press seemed to go out of their way to glibly hunt down a story where none existed. Timing meant *Dream Warriors* became the scapegoat, whereas we all know it could have been any other horror film released at the time.'

Far from being pleased by the publicity such controversies generate, Craven is disturbed by them: 'They scare me. I've been sued once. I'm always fearing that at any moment I could face that ruinous law suit or accusation that would end my career. One of the reasons why it's not attractive to continue to make horror films is because the controversy can get very nasty and very dangerous, and at certain points I just feel like I'm pushing my luck to continue to make horror films.'

For all the disappointment and aggravation involved, Craven still had too much personal investment in the *Nightmare on Elm Street* name to want to see the series fail. 'I would definitely like to see a fourth one,' he told horror film magazine *Fangoria* after *Dream Warriors*. 'I feel overall that *Nightmare 3* does a good job of expanding the boundaries of Freddy and the dream world. It opens things up to new areas that can be explored in future films. There is a certain sense of fun in trying to think up new twists and it should be done, as long as the quality is good.'

New Line Cinema plunged straight into production on a fourth *Nightmare* movie, and, in time honoured tradition, Shaye and Risher approached Craven yet again, despite the frosty relations between them. 'Initially, I approached Wes about the fourth film,' Risher told *Cinefantastique*. 'His idea was illogical. It was about time travel within dreams that broke all the rules of dreams. We decided not to go with that.' Robert Shaye felt that New Line had given Craven a fair chance to pitch his preferred development of the *Nightmare* universe: 'He, Sara and I had a conference call together. I told him I thought it [Craven's time travel idea] was kind of interesting and that I'd get back to him. After a lot of discussion, it was decided the idea didn't really have the impact we were looking for. Ultimately, we felt it wasn't workable. We had to make a producer's decision about whether we wanted to go ahead with his idea, and we decided not to.'

Producer Rachel Talalay took a central role in guiding *Nightmare 4* to the screen. She'd risen through the ranks at New Line, having worked as a production accountant and location manager on the original *A Nightmare on Elm Street*, and was ideally placed to have an overview of the series' development. Talalay would later direct

the sixth entry in the series. 'I knew there was something special about the original *A Nightmare on Elm Street* because just reading the script scared me,' she told *Fangoria*. 'You never think a film is going to be as successful as that one was. It was a big surprise.'

The problem was, where next for Freddy? The third movie, with its team of teen heroes, surreal dream world settings and fast-paced Freddy wisecracks, had broadened the *Elm Street* audience well beyond the hardcore horror fans. 'We debated a long time on how to do *Nightmare 4*,' recalled Talalay. 'Did we want to do a small, really scary film and go back to the film's roots, or

Below: *The Spanish* Dream Warriors *poster.*

Above: A Nightmare on Elm Street 4: The Dream Master.

did we want to continue to do a roller-coaster ride laced with comedy? Originally, we decided that to try and make it scary was most important, but we ultimately felt that since the wider audience was so familiar with Freddy, it would be harder to scare [them], [so] it would be better to go with the same feel that the third had.'

Ditching Craven's time travel notion, the producers decided to work on a script written by William Kotzwinkle, entitled *The Dream Master*, which developed much of its plot and settings directly from Craven's concepts in the third movie. Risher confirmed that she then approached Craven again, with a view to having him rewrite Kotzwinkle's script: 'We decided to go with Kotzwinkle's *Dream Master* idea, which we thought was terrific. I told Wes we were doing that. When the script we had didn't work, I went

to Wes and Bruce Wagner to see about rewriting it and directing it.'

Craven feared a repeat of the *Dream Warriors* experience, with New Line determined to get his name on the script to give the film the continued seal of authenticity. As it happened, he was busy working on reshoots for his Universal film *The Serpent and the Rainbow* and didn't have the time to get involved. Once bitten, twice shy was Craven's motto this time out: 'The script I saw was written by William Kotzwinkle. He's obviously a gifted writer, but when they had problems with the script they came to me and my partner Bruce Wagner to rewrite it. Bruce and I thought if we were going to be approached, we should be approached as artists of the original material. So, New Line went off to do some more work with the script they had. They never really contacted us again. That's their way — they come and they go. I was not really interested in participating any more.'

Craven's decision to cut off all ties to his creation was never going to stop the progress of the series. As far as Shaye and Risher were concerned, there was life in Freddy Krueger yet. 'Freddy Krueger is the man audiences love to hate,' says Shaye. '[He] has become a great anti-hero. The world was ready for a character like him. He struck a chord in a large number of people.' The ever increasing box office returns for each film were proof enough of this assertion. The original film took $23 million in the States in 1984, the second over $30 million and the third chapter $45 million in the spring of 1987.

Taking the Dream Master concept devised by Kotzwinkle, New Line hired writer Brian Helgeland (later to work on *L.A. Confidential*) to beef up the story after Craven declined. He worked up a screenplay with Scott Pierce which introduced the character of Alice (Lisa Wilcox, in her first film role), a shy and introverted teenager who feels helpless as Freddy picks off her friends one-

Left: *The Dream Master — introducing Alice (Lisa Wilcox), Freddy's nemesis.*

Above: Kristen mark two — Tuesday Knight takes over the role in Nightmare 4.

by-one, including the survivors of *Dream Warriors*. Realising she can control her dreams like Kristen in the previous film, Alice absorbs her friends' good qualities and uses them to become the Dream Master and tackle Freddy face to face.

Always on the look out for new talent, Shaye decided to pursue Finnish director Renny Harlin, whose first American film, the low-budget chiller *Prison*, had demonstrated his ability to deliver visceral thrills on a limited budget — exactly what was needed.

Harlin was determined to learn from past mistakes, particularly those made on *Freddy's Revenge*. He felt Russell's *Dream Warriors* had provided a perfect template to take the series forward, and chose to work within the same parameters, further developing the surviving characters: 'To make a great sequel, you've got to do everything a little better with more originality.

Left: Nightmare 4's team of dream warriors. **Below:** Tuesday Knight and Robert Englund relax on the set of Kristen's fatal beach dream.

For this film, I wanted to develop stronger characters and relationships. A film can have all the special effects, but if the audience doesn't care about the characters, you are lost. Great films need great characters.'

Harlin was the first to face the possibility of having to do a *Nightmare* picture without Robert Englund. The actor was growing tired of the role and felt that he'd reached a creative dead end. With nowhere left for Freddy to go, Englund saw no reason to play him again. 'I was a little weary of the whole thing,' recalls Englund. 'I did not come onto the fourth picture real excited.' A meeting with Harlin convinced him otherwise, along with commitments from New Line to offer Englund opportunities on other projects. 'We'd reached a point where the audience saw Freddy as the hero,' notes Harlin. 'They came to these movies to hear his funny lines and to see him do those amazing things.'

Shooting began on the fourth *Nightmare* movie in April 1988 and the film was in cinemas just twenty-two weeks later, in time to catch the end of the summer movie season. The character was becoming more popular than ever, and shooting was brought to a halt when thousands of people mobbed a San Pedro location where the crew were preparing to film a beach scene. The local police had to be called out to clear the area and escort Robert Englund, in full Freddy regalia.

Five special effects houses worked simultaneously on *The Dream Master*, speeding the production process up exponentially. The usual roster of over-the-top effects sequences were lined up for the $6 million film, including trapped souls appearing in Freddy's chest, the air being sucked

Right:
Metamorphosis
— Brooke Theiss
tries out her
new limbs.
Below: *'Wanna*
suck face?' —
Sheila (Toy
Newkirk) is
picked on in
class.

out of an asthmatic character, a cockroach transformation, a pizza from hell complete with the faces of tortured teens and a weight-lifting scene which gave new meaning to the phrase 'no pain, no gain'. Although he was not associated with the film, Craven nevertheless found he put in an

appearance, in spirit at least, as a restaurant scene between Freddy and Alice took place in the Crave Inn, where 'if the food doesn't kill you, the service will'.

'I shot for forty-two days,' noted Harlin as his film was prepared for release. 'I finished the film

on schedule and delivered my cut two days later. In post-production we were under the agreed two week schedule, which meant the release was brought forward from 25 August 1988 to the nineteenth. I feel I broke some sort of world record.' The highest budgeted of the four *Nightmare* movies enjoyed a $13 million opening weekend and went on to take over $50 million at the American box office.

An unexpected fan of the fourth film turned out to be Wes Craven, at least according to director Renny Harlin: 'Wes loved it. It was important to base the film in images the audience loved and would remember from the first film. Wes came to the first screening and sent me a letter saying how much he liked it. I thought that was a nice compliment.'

Shaye's timing on *The Dream Master* was good, with the $13 million opening weekend making it the most successful independent production, knocking *Halloween* from the position it had held for ten years. *The Dream Master*'s success resulted in the instant go-ahead for a fifth film with a larger budget.

A longer break between the fourth and fifth movies was anticipated as Robert Englund was committed to working on the *Freddy's Nightmares* TV series and there was a danger that the popular character would be over-exposed. 'I don't believe the character is being spread too thin,'

Above: Freddy dines out at the aptly-named Crave Inn.

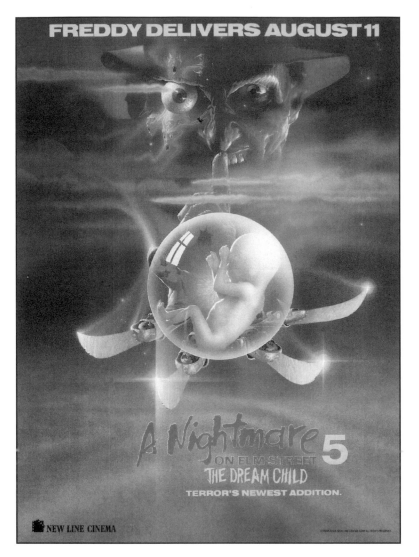

enforced a clause in his contract which committed him to the film. 'I had no choice,' complained Englund while making *Nightmare 5*. 'When I agreed to do *Nightmare 4*, I guaranteed to do *Nightmare 5*. It seems like we never get to start fresh. We finished the last one in July [1988]; here it is April [1989] and I'm starting again. That's a little too close.'

With Wes Craven attempting to develop another horror franchise based around *Shocker's* Horace Pinker, there was little point in New Line approaching him about the new *Nightmare* movie. Craven's concepts for *Dream Warriors* had sustained the series through two instalments and looked likely to provide the basis for the fifth.

New Line commissioned two sets of writers to work on a script based around the birth of Alice's child, who was to be the focus for Freddy's revenge. In December 1988, horror novelists John Skipp and Craig Spector were set to work, as was California-based writer and former musician Leslie Bohem. 'I think there's an operating philosophy with the *Nightmare* movies of employing as many writers as possible,' noted Spector in *Fangoria*. He and Skipp lost out in the unconventional scripting contest, with New Line opting to go with Bohem's first draft, commissioning him to produce two more. Some of the concepts in *Nightmare 5* came from work Bohem had done at the time of *Nightmare 2*, when he'd developed storylines for the first sequel. 'The idea of Freddy controlling an unborn child dates from then,' recalls Bohem, 'but New Line passed on it because Sara Risher was pregnant at the time and I understand the idea upset her.' Bohem was given the Skipp and Spector script to use as a source for his revised screenplay.

By the time Bohem was hard at work on his third draft, Shaye had found a director to handle the latest Freddy film — Stephen Hopkins. Hopkins had been a designer on pop promos directed by Russell Mulcahy. When Mulcahy agreed to direct *Highlander*, he brought Hopkins with him as the second unit director. Convinced

contended Englund in a *Fangoria* interview at the time. 'As long as storylines and new nightmares can be created that are consistent with Freddy's cruelty. I think the films should continue, but now might be the time to put the *Nightmare* series on hold for a couple of years.' On the other hand, he was quite happy to consider the possibility that *A Nightmare on Elm Street 4: The Dream Master* could be the end of the series: 'There is a sort of completeness, a release at the end of this movie that could be considered an absolution and a finish.'

It wasn't to be, and Englund was back in the Freddy make-up for a fifth movie when New Line that he could direct his own film, Hopkins went to Australia to shoot the B-movie *A Dangerous Game*. Ever on the look-out for young and cheap talent, Shaye was quick to offer Hopkins the latest in his ever expanding series.

'I very quickly discovered that the *Nightmare* films were all very last minute,' Hopkins told *GoreZone*. 'They were already a week into pre-production without a script when I signed.' Leslie Bohem finished the fourth draft of his script before leaving the production in March 1989 to fulfil a previous commitment. Hopkins brought in his writing pal Bill Wisher, who'd worked on *The Terminator* with James Cameron, to revise the existing screenplay, incorporating many of Hopkins' ideas and a few from Shaye.

Finally, horror novelist David J. Schow took a crack at combining key elements from all the previous drafts to produce a working script. He was revising the dialogue throughout the shooting process. 'It was clear there were structural problems with the sequences that link the Freddy gags,' he told *Fangoria*. 'The only way to fix them was to buttress the gags by boosting the dialogue. The

Left: The dream child and an unwelcome guest.
Below: You are what you eat, as Greta (Erika Anderson) discovers in A Nightmare on Elm Street: The Dream Child.

time factor was so tight, the schedule so demanding, that they had to go with what they had.'

The mix was the same as the previous two films, with Hopkins attempting to downplay the gore in favour of an atmospheric ghost story that

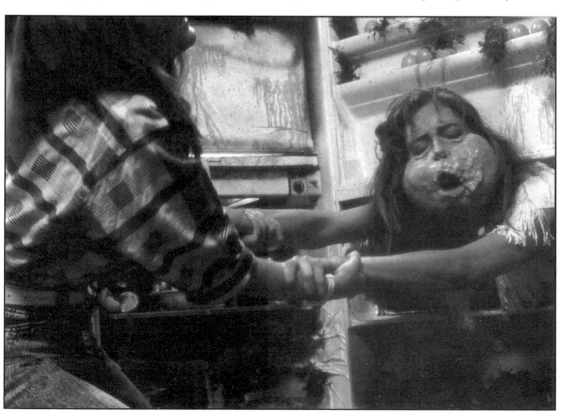

returned to the roots of the Freddy character. In keeping with this thematic concern, original make-up artist David Miller returned to revise the Krueger look once more. He decided to make this Freddy more of a burnt-out, world-weary spook than before. 'We aged Freddy quite a bit,' confirmed Miller, who agreed with New Line that he would only return if he could make Freddy look more like his original 1984 design.

The August 1989 release of *A Nightmare on Elm Street: The Dream Child* saw Freddy face up to his slasher rival Jason in *Friday the 13th Part VIII: Jason Takes Manhattan* at the box office, where it opened the week before. 'I don't fear Jason,' claimed Englund at the time. 'I know how good *Nightmare 5* is, whether or not there's going to be competition between the two films.' Any notion of a box office battle between Freddy and Jason

was simply a publicist's dream, as the *Nightmare* series had a far wider popular appeal than Jason ever achieved. As the decade drew to a close, so interest in the sequels waned. Enjoying a similar production budget to the previous movie, *The Dream Child* only grossed around $22 million on its American release (on a par with the original

Below: Freddy poses with a grotesque model of himself as a baby for The Dream Child.

film's $23 million take), suggesting the appeal of Freddy had peaked. The box office performance of *Nightmare 5* proved disappointing to New Line and Robert Englund. 'We hit our peak Stateside with *Nightmare 4*,' the actor recalls. '[The fifth film] wasn't a huge hit and I thought, "Oh, well, that's it". But it proved successful in Europe.'

For New Line executive Michael DeLuca, Freddy Krueger was coming to the end of his useful life. 'We became realistic about the limitations of the genre,' he told *Cinefantastique*. 'It's not James Bond. I always thought sequels were cheesy to begin with. You have an original idea that works, then you spend the next ten years ripping it off. What I've always liked about the *Elm Street* movies is that, even when they're incoherent, they're ambitious.'

DeLuca, Englund and Rachel Talalay decided to give Freddy a stylish send off, proposing to Robert Shaye that they produce a final Freddy movie entirely in-house featuring the things the fans of the series had been asking for over the years. Two years after the fifth movie, New Line decided *Freddy's Dead* would be Krueger's swan song. 'The *Final Nightmare* plot, such as it is, was an accumulation of all the ideas and scenes we wanted to see in one wrap-it-all-up movie,' explains Englund.

The production was handled by *Elm Street* veterans, with executive DeLuca working on the script and Talalay bagging the director's role following an initial request she'd made to handle *Nightmare 5*. 'I wanted to get away from the gothic feeling of the last few *Nightmare* films,'

Above: Robert Englund as the human Freddy Krueger, before he was burned alive, in Freddy's Dead: The Final Nightmare.

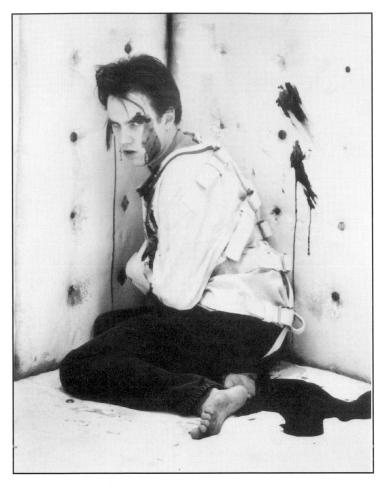

she told *Fangoria*. 'I wanted this movie to have a more gritty and urban feel and a distinct visual style to it.' Spiking an early idea to resurrect some of the deceased Dream Warriors, Talalay left behind the mythology and characters from the previous three films and launched Freddy on a new and supposedly final adventure.

Talalay was also determined to learn from New Line's past mistakes and avoid the manic production process of the most recent movies. DeLuca took his time with the script and Talalay scheduled a relatively leisurely production process that was not tied to a specific release date. 'I think there are flaws in all of them, except maybe the original,' said Talalay of the fading franchise. '*Nightmare 4* had no story, we wrote the effects [first] and we were patching the story together during the production process. *Nightmare 5* had too convoluted a story. Freddy wasn't integrated into it enough. There were a lot of mistakes — I think New Line were too greedy. Right after *Nightmare 4* they put out the television series and went into the next feature. What I tried to bring to *The Final Nightmare* was a real story.'

Freddy's Dead: The Final Nightmare saw Krueger

move to an urban environment in search of new blood, only to be forced back to Elm Street to confront his own past. Cast alongside Englund were Lisa Zane and Shon Greenblatt, with Yaphet Kotto in support. Fearful that the audience who had deserted *Nightmare 5* might not return on the basis of Freddy's death alone, New Line hedged their bets, packing the film with cameos from the likes of Johnny Depp (a nod to the original film), Alice Cooper as Freddy's stepdad and sitcom star Roseanne. The capper was an extraordinary 3D climax which featured a journey through Freddy's brain to explore his past. The 3D idea was not a new one and Talalay found herself forced to use it: 'New Line had always talked about it. We tried to talk them out of it, but marketing was into it, and it was a big deal for selling it internationally, so we were strapped into it.'

Released on Friday 13 September 1991, *Freddy's Dead: The Final Nightmare* was promised to be Freddy's final fling. 'The whole *Nightmare on Elm Street* character and mythos are gone and over with,' claimed Michael DeLuca. A twist ending in which the dream demons who had tormented Freddy Krueger settled on a new child to corrupt was dropped at the last minute in an effort to convince sceptical critics and audiences alike that this was really the end. The trick worked and audiences flocked to see Freddy do his stuff one last time. The film grossed $13 million in its first three days — not blockbuster territory, but very respectable for the last in a decade-old horror series which cost only $5 million to produce. It finally made around $35 million in America alone. 'We were definitely surprised,' admitted DeLuca of the audience response. 'The fact that it was the last part and we'd had a two year gap helped a lot.'

It had been a phenomenal ride for Wes Craven, New Line Cinema and Robert Englund. Without Freddy Krueger, New Line might never have risen to become one of the mini-majors of modern Hollywood. The extreme profitability of each of the *Nightmare* movies, produced as Robert Shaye

told Craven like 'a good cheeseburger', meant the series continued as long as there was an audience for it, although following Craven's departure the films lacked a creative guiding hand.

The best of the films, the original *A Nightmare on Elm Street* and *Dream Warriors*, the third outing, reflect Craven's aims and aspirations for Freddy. Despite cutting all his ties with New Line and with Freddy after the second sequel, Craven would nevertheless find himself drawn back to his creation yet again, to hammer the final nail into Freddy's coffin. ∎

Director's Choice

For Wes Craven, *A Nightmare on Elm Street* had not provided the immediate boost to his filmmaking career he might have expected. 'When I get my profit share from *A Nightmare on Elm Street*,' he commented at the time, 'I'll actually be able to open a savings account again. My fee for the movie was Director's Guild minimum.' While weighing up possible future film projects, Craven was tempted to take part in the revival of Rod Serling's *The Twilight Zone* series for television in 1985: 'I was called in as a director for *The Twilight Zone* specifically by name, which I really considered to be an honour. One of the strongest backers of *The Last House on the Left* turned out years and years later to be Phil DeGuere, the executive producer of *The Twilight Zone*. He still thinks *The Last House on the Left* is my best film. He gave me a stack of scripts that they were planning on doing in the first year and said, "Direct any ones you want". I had time to do seven, so it was a great gift and a great entrustment.'

DeGuere had encouraged Craven to stay in the film industry after *The Last House on the Left* and been instrumental in having him relocate to Los Angeles, introducing him to his first agent. When DeGuere was producing the TV series *Simon and Simon* he'd invited Craven to get involved, but Craven had declined due to feature film commitments.

Craven began immediately on the three episodes which opened the series, 'Shatterday', 'A Little Peace and Quiet' and 'Word Play', drawn from material by Harlan Ellison, among others: 'They were really good stories, very gratifying. They were all written by very talented people.

They were cast superbly and they had people who were not only big names but really fine actors. I got the chance to work with actors like Bruce Willis, Robert Kline and Annie Potts. Everything about *The Twilight Zone* was well produced. It had a great cinematographer, Brad May, who I'd love to work with again, really superb crews, stages and everything. It was a real dream.'

Nostalgia was another driving force behind Craven's participation in the new *Twilight Zone* series. He'd watched the originals during the sixties and felt a loyalty to the show that meant he couldn't turn down the chance to get involved. It

Opposite: Zombie queen — Kristy Swanson made her film début as Samantha in Deadly Friend. ***Below:*** *Family man — Wes Craven with his children.*

Right: Dealing with the Devil — Morgan Freeman (far right) enters The Twilight Zone.

was also an opportunity to direct material which, due to television censorship, didn't involve much violence. Craven was behind the camera for four more episodes — 'Chameleon' with Terry O'Quinn; 'Dealer's Choice' with Dan Hedaya, M. Emmet Walsh and Morgan Freeman; the acclaimed 'Her Pilgrim Soul'; and 'The Road Less Travelled'. His opening segment, 'Shatterday', and 'The Road Less Travelled' turned out to be mirror images, with a benign ('Shatterday') or evil ('Road') doppelgänger turning up to haunt the lead character. 'A Little Peace and Quiet' saw Melinda Dillon find a way to freeze space and time, giving her the break indicated in the title, while 'Word Play' revolved around an over-worked salesman who loses the ability to understand those around him. In 'Chameleon', a space shuttle returns from a mission with something on board that wasn't there on take-off, and in

'Dealer's Choice' the Devil himself sits in on a friendly poker game in New Jersey.

Craven also took the opportunity to try his hand at acting in an episode directed by Robert Downey Sr called 'Children's Zoo': 'I made my acting début in a *Twilight Zone* segment because I agreed to put Robert Downey in one of my episodes if he'd put me in his. I got my SAG [Screen Actor's Guild, the actor's union] card because of that, which was quite historic. I've not been inundated with offers.' Craven may have thought little of it at the time, but his experiences before the camera, including small cameos in his own films, were great preparation for *Wes Craven's New Nightmare*, where he effectively played himself on screen.

In 'Children's Zoo', a withdrawn little girl, caught between her battling parents, receives an invitation to a most unusual zoo. 'I played this father who was locked up in a zoo for parents,' says Craven. 'They cut my favourite line, which I ad-libbed, where I threatened the little girl by saying, "I know where your teddy bear sleeps". I thought that was genius, but it was cut out.'

Craven's remaining *The Twilight Zone* episodes were 'Her Pilgrim Soul', about a scientist experimenting with computer holography who captures the image of an infant which then takes on a life of its own, and 'The Road Less Travelled', in which a Vietnam draft-dodging family man has to face the spectre of the man he would have been if he'd fought.

Following *A Nightmare on Elm Street*, Craven's creative frustrations with horror films began to come to a head. It was a theme he never tired of returning to — how to escape the genre: 'I had really grown tired, very limited by it. *The Twilight Zone*s were outside the horror genre. It was a great opportunity for me when no one else in town was giving me that chance. I wanted to do other sorts of things. I wanted to educate the world that I wasn't just an assault-and-slash guru of gore. I felt really restricted by that label.'

To that end, Craven built on the relationship he had with the Disney studio, dating from their interest in *A Nightmare on Elm Street*. The result was a television movie Craven directed for ABC TV that started life as *Crimebusters*, but was retitled *Casebusters* for transmission in 1986. 'It's not for the money,' protested Craven at the time, accused of selling out. 'It's a way to show Wes Craven doing comedy, with cute young kids and a loveable grandfather. How can you fit that into horror? You can't. You must look at me in a bigger framework. *The Twilight Zone* gave me a chance to do science fiction, comedy and family things that I don't normally get the chance to do. The Disney project was a logical extension of that. It's the story of two grandchildren helping their grandfather, who owns a struggling security agency, solve a crime.'

The TV special, which was only an hour long, starred Pat Hingle as the grandfather, with *Battlestar Galactica* child actor Noah Hathaway as one of the grandchildren. The film was produced by Erwin Stoff, Keanu Reeves' manager, and Paul Aaron, Reeves' film director stepfather.

Craven had pitched various ideas to Disney for other possible TV movies, including one called *Circus Gang*, a script he'd written himself relating the adventures of a group of circus children. He'd

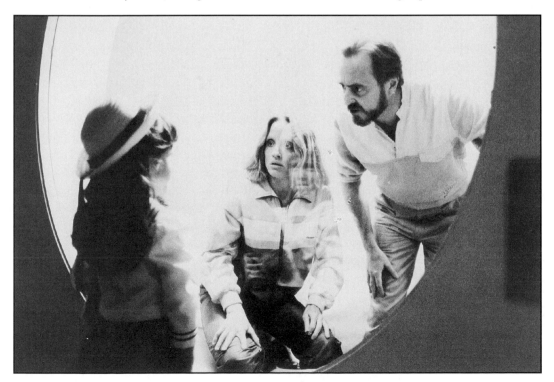

Left: *Craven earns his Screen Actor's Guild card in 'Children's Zoo'.*

completed the first draft before making *A Nightmare on Elm Street*: 'I'm trying very hard to expand my horizons. There are projects I have in development that will be horror, but I plan to expand beyond that narrow genre.' *Circus Gang*, however, remains unmade.

For a major movie director, Craven has never entirely ruled out opportunities to work in television, despite being acutely aware of the limitations of the medium. 'If I were to do it again, I certainly wouldn't do any more "Movies of the Week",' he has said. 'I've been offered plenty of those and turned them down. I would do more TV if it could be very particular, pure Wes Craven TV. If I got the chance to do something out of the genre, that'd be fine.' With Freddy enjoying his own show, Craven was interested in branding a

series himself, along the lines of *Alfred Hitchcock Presents*, something he thought could be called *Wes Craven's House of Horror*: 'I've been trying to think up a format for that for years. I pitched one to Fox Television, but they passed on it as being too intense.' The series outlined to Fox was called *Dream Stalker*, and aimed to create a new Freddy Krueger-type character for television. Although the series didn't progress very far, the concepts Craven developed formed the basis of his 1989 film *Shocker*.

Craven made more progress with *Chiller*, a TV movie. It started life under the title *Frozen Man*, and was one of the reasons Craven backed out of any involvement in *Freddy's Revenge*: '*Chiller* was about a man frozen cryogenically ten years ago. He's now brought back to life entirely restored, except he has no soul. It's not horror in the sense of a maniac stalking people. *Chiller* was a kind of interesting thing. Of the three TV movies that I've done, that was the most interesting. Along with *The Twilight Zone*, I found it to be a totally different thing.' He even found room in *Chiller* for his wife Mimi, who played the role of Nurse Cooper.

Although Craven enjoyed making *Chiller*, critics were not as impressed by his workmanlike efforts. *New York Times* reviewer Walter Goodman described it as 'directed by Wes Craven as though he was following the commands of a computer, with a collection of scare tactics that ought to be frozen, wrapped in aluminium foil and placed in a cryogenic chamber for at least a couple of generations. There's scarcely a chill in *Chiller*.'

At the beginning of 1986, Craven was faced with a choice about his return to feature films. He'd written a script for Roger Corman's reworking of *Frankenstein*, but Corman himself was planning to direct: 'It was a futuristic horror story, a new version of the myth updated to the twenty-first century. It was a very bizarre examination of the barriers between organic life and machine life, about the frontiers of human evolutionary barriers.' In the end, Corman ditched Craven's screenplay, opting instead to film Brian

Aldiss's *Frankenstein Unbound*, with John Hurt, Bridget Fonda and the late INXS rocker Michael Hutchence in the cast.

Craven also had other film projects in development. *Working Class Bride* was a comedy which Craven was lukewarm about. Three that interested him were *Old Fears*, *Haunted* and a film version of Virginia Andrews' *Flowers in the Attic*, which he'd been attempting to script for some time: 'Old Fears was based on a book about a town where everybody's worst childhood memories and fears begin to take shape. *Haunted* was based on a book by Tom Ropelweski, a love story about an eternal triangle between a young man and two eighteen year-old girls. The girls were locked in a competition for his affections that goes beyond the grave when one of them dies. It wasn't bizarre so much as strange and haunting, a teen comedy with an off-centre love story.'

Flowers in the Attic was a best-selling novel which could make a good mainstream film. 'I would not classify *Flowers in the Attic* as a horror film,' claimed Craven of his proposed adaptation. 'It's a good old-fashioned escape story, *Hansel and Gretel* on a big scale, with children with mean parents who have to follow their own resources to gain freedom. I wrote the script, and the ending used portions of the book's sequel, *Petals in the Wind*, so you actually would have seen the grandmother and mother get their comeuppance, which doesn't happen in the first book. I had to add extra drama and make it more visual as the book was very cerebral.'

Craven's plans to film the book came to nothing when the Charles Fries Organisation and New World Pictures, who owned the rights, failed to raise the finance for the project. The film later resurfaced in 1988, written and directed by Jeffrey Bloom, who rejected Craven's original screenplay in favour of his own adaptation. 'I never got a strong feeling that the people had a handle on the material,' says Craven of those who took over the *Flowers in the Attic* project. 'In the event, I was right. It came out as a TV movie

type thing, much too cheap and bland.'

When *Flowers in the Attic* collapsed, Craven turned his attention to his next potential project — a film version of a teen novel called *Friend*, written by Diane Henstell. 'Deadly Friend came about as a direct consequence of my agent saying to me, "You should do a studio film, because otherwise you'll be stuck doing small films for the rest of your life",' remembers Craven. 'It turned out to be a real nightmare. When I started on it, it was called *Artificial Intelligence*, then *A. I.*, before we settled on *Deadly Friend*.' The screenplay by *Brainstorm* scripter Bruce Joel Rubin (who later wrote *Jacob's Ladder*, *Ghost* and *My Life*) told of a fourteen year-old genius named Paul Conway (played by *The Little House on the Prairie* actor Matthew Laborteaux) who falls in

Below: A deadly friend — Kristy Swanson malfunctions.

love with the girl next door called Samantha (Kristy Swanson, later the star of the film *Buffy the Vampire Slayer*). When she is killed by her abusive father, Paul sets out to resurrect Samantha using parts from his home-made robot Bee Bee, with less-than-terrifying consequences.

'There were seven or eight producers and they all had their idea of what the film should be,' recalls Craven sadly. 'Then the marketing department came in at the very end and did a study and found out that I had this enormous horror following, so they immediately rewrote the script and had me do more horror in it. So the film became a hodge podge, then it was censored heavily by the MPAA [Moving Picture Association of America]. They made us submit the film thirteen times. So, for instance, the Anne Ramsey scene, with her getting killed by the basketball, was completely decimated.'

Deadly Friend features much of Craven's trademark iconography, particularly the dream sequences: 'They were mine, but they came very late. It was after the film was shot and the producers said, "Let's put some dream sequences in". Frankly, I didn't want to do those. You go into a studio and you find you have to make all these decisions to please people. Originally it was a straight sort of macabre love story between this boy and girl. I originally wanted it much quieter, but I was overruled. The things that were added later were a nightmare sequence between her and her father and the basketball scene. The basketball scene was my favourite (Anne Ramsey was originally killed another way), and the ending of her lurching up out of the morgue drawer was new. So there was a lot of, "Let's make it a Wes Craven film". I was actually afraid that would become a cliché Wes Craven touch. I've grown suspicious of putting dreams in my films.'

Writer Bruce Joel Rubin worked closely with Craven and observed the frustrating production process for *Deadly Friend*: 'I was a gun-for-hire,

Below: *Paul (Matthew Laborteaux) shows off his robot Bee Bee.*

and really tried to write a deep and heartfelt movie out of it. Then we showed the picture to a bunch of Wes's fans, who hated it. All they wanted was guts, so the studio told me to give them six more scenes, each bloodier than the last. We ended up having Anne Ramsey's head bashed in with a basketball. That really destroyed our love story, and everyone still blames me for the ending. That robot coming out of the girl's head belongs solely to [the studio], and you don't tell the head of Warner Brothers that his idea stinks!'

The interference Craven and Rubin suffered on *Deadly Friend* may have affected the film, but it didn't destroy their friendship. 'As far as production went, *Deadly Friend* was one of the happiest experiences I've ever had on a film,' admitted Rubin in a *Fangoria* interview. 'I love Wes and he let me on the set and adopted my kids as pro-

duction mascots. It also let me buy a house...'

For the scenes chronicling the transplant of the robot brain into Paul's girlfriend's body, Craven called on the advice of retired neurosurgeon William H. Faethe. 'He was very helpful on all the anatomical details,' explains Craven. 'Because the whole movie was based around the brain operation, we researched the subject very carefully. I studied anatomy a great deal and researched into the art of brain surgery and brain exploration, which is one of medicine's most fascinating frontiers. Dr Faethe was instrumental in guiding us through all that.'

The suburban setting of *Deadly Friend* echoed *A Nightmare on Elm Street*, and was a deliberate choice by Craven, who felt that enough other films were satisfying the audience's need for exotic locations: 'It's my theory that familiar

Above: *Craven returns to suburbia, his favourite haunt.*

Above: Anne Ramsey was on the receiving end of more than just Kristy Swanson's hands in Deadly Friend.

locations are not in themselves horrific, but they contain memories where horrific things take place when we're children. To me the most poignant and powerful area of our memory is childhood, and that almost exclusively takes place in regular, residential houses. That's where you encounter most of the really primal events of your experience, and that's why you're afraid of the attic, the basement and the dark.'

Craven wasn't attracted to the story of *Deadly Friend* because Samantha goes on a killing spree when she's revived as an undead monster. He was much more interested in exploring the adults around her, all of whom seem to be monsters in human skin: 'The scares don't come from her, but from the ordinary people, who are actually much more frightening — a father who beats a child is a terrifying figure. That's the one

person you're afraid of in the movie... The idea is along the lines that adults can be horrible, without being outside what society says is acceptable.' Unfortunately, *Deadly Friend* turned out to be a flop at the box office.

Playing a vibrant teenager turned into a zombie robot was a challenge for sixteen year-old actress Kristy Swanson, making her feature film début in Craven's film after years of television bit-part work. 'Wes wasn't convinced I could handle the role,' admitted Swanson, who, ironically, went on to feature in Jeffrey Bloom's disappointing version of *Flowers in the Attic*. 'Eventually he changed his mind. He was always encouraging me, prodding me in subtle ways to get me to give a scene everything I could. There were some days when we were behind schedule, or a particular scene was not working, where he would get a little upset, but I found Wes Craven to be a very patient man.'

Swanson found herself caught up in the studio's attempts to strong-arm Craven into making the film more visceral than he'd intended. 'Script changes were being made, a title change was being discussed and there was a lot of discussion about just how violent and bloody the movie would ultimately be,' she told *Fangoria*. 'The effect of the basketball hitting the face was added after the fact, but Wes kept at me to throw it as hard as I could to indicate great speed. I must have tossed that ball a hundred times.'

Although new to big screen acting, Swanson was proud of her work in *Deadly Friend*, and her reappearance in *Buffy the Vampire Slayer* showed her affinity for the horror genre: 'Many people consider horror films as the kind of dues paying pictures you must do to get exposure. I don't agree. A well-made horror film is just as legitimate as any other kind of movie.'

The critics were not kind to *Deadly Friend*, and Paul Attanasio, writing in the *Washington Post*,

summed up many reactions: 'Director Wes Craven works some humor out of Paul's timid sidekick, Tom (Michael Sharrett), who regularly advises that things have gone too far, and the movie has its occasional Cravenisms — just when you're tiring of the robot's cutesy antics, the old woman opens up with her shotgun, and there's a fairly spectacular effect in which a woman's head is pulverized by a basketball. But it also has its familiar Craven miscues, like "nightmare" sequences that fool no one, and a "surprise" ending that makes no sense. On the whole, *Deadly Friend* is a routine horror movie, poorly photographed (by old-time cinematographer Philip Lathrop) and poorly performed (with the exception of New York stage actress Anne Twomey, as Paul's mother).'

As a follow-up to his groundbreaking *A Nightmare on Elm Street*, *Deadly Friend* was a major disappointment. Thankfully, it proved to be nothing but a creative misfire, as Craven went on to make three very distinctive films that marked him out as a leading genre auteur. ∎

Below: *'A very patient man' — Craven directs his young cast.*

Raising the Dead

After the disappointment of *Deadly Friend*, Wes Craven entered a creative phase during which he produced three of his most accomplished works. Finally, aged forty-nine, he had enough power in the film industry to exert control over the projects he wanted to be involved in.

Still determined to broaden his horizons, Craven was looking for a project which would rise above the run-of-the-mill fright flicks he was being offered: 'For a long time I'd been looking for a crossover piece that would use the benefits and momentum of my reputation as a horror director to get me into more of an adult venue.'

Executive producer Rob Cohen (later to direct the Dennis Quaid movie *Dragonheart* and the Sylvester Stallone thriller *Daylight*) was trying to track Craven down through his old agent when he had a chance meeting with Craven's current agent, Andrea Eastman. Complaining that Craven's agent never returned his calls, Eastman promptly informed him that he had in fact been dead for some time. 'I'd only ever had two agents in my life at that point,' says Craven. 'The last one had died. Of course, I'd left him earlier. As a matter of fact, at his funeral someone leant over to me and said: "See what you've done".'

Cohen was representing the Taft/Barish company, who had a project they thought would be perfect for Craven. Producers David Ladd (son of actor Alan Ladd) and Doug Claybourne had bought the film rights to a recently published book called *The Serpent and the Rainbow*, about the experiences of an anthropologist in Haiti. '*The Serpent and the Rainbow* was based on a non-fiction book written by a Harvard ethno-botanist

by the name of Wade Davis,' explains Craven. 'He specifically studies cultures and the use of plants as either psychotropic devices or as things for curative purposes. His book was brought to me by the producers who already had the rights to do it and had a script underway.'

Reading the book, Craven discovered a fascinating true story which followed up many of the concepts he had been exploring in his films, including altered states of consciousness and the boundaries between nightmares and the waking world: 'Once I'd read the book, I signed on right away without seeing the script. I knew that anything made from it would be wonderful. Wade

Opposite: Marielle (Cathy Tyson) falls under the spell of Gaston (Badja Djola) in The Serpent and the Rainbow.
Left: Don't lose your head — Craven faced quite an ordeal filming in Haiti.

Above: Bill Pullman, previously known mainly for his comedy roles, as Dr Dennis Alan.

Davis was approached by a pharmaceutical firm and a financier and was given the assignment to go into Haiti and try to penetrate the voodoo cults and find out whether there was any truth to the rumours about zombies. They were thought to be mythological, but they were actually people that had been poisoned by a drug that made them appear to be dead for a period of time, at least ten hours. Wade Davis had this incredible adventure, meeting a magician in the interior of Haiti who makes these powders. He discovered there is indeed a tribal judgement where a person who affronts the tribe is made into a zombie, believed to be dead and in fact buried alive.'

Craven also drew inspiration from a real-life case that was related in Davis' book: 'There was a man by the name of Clairvius Narcisse who died in Port-au-Prince [the capital of Haiti] in an American clinic and was declared dead by an American doctor. He appeared alive again twelve years later, and that's what broke the whole thing open. Apparently, the creation of a zombie is a two-part business. The first is that they're given the powder without their knowledge, sicken and appear to die, usually within a period of two days. The heartbeat and respiration are so faint that it's not discernible, unless a doctor knew specifically

what to look for. He's then buried and the person that poisoned him comes back to wait for him to revive. Meanwhile, the person who's a zombie is fully conscious the whole time. Clairvius Narcisse could tell every detail of his funeral. They are then dug up, beaten and told that their souls have been taken. Then they are given a second drug, a very powerful hallucinogen, and this process was interrupted by the death of the person doing this to Clairvius and he escaped. He stayed away for twelve years and was eventually identified by his sister.'

Richard Maxwell had the job of writing a script from the often dry and scientific prose of Davis' true-life account of his adventure in 1982 in pre-revolutionary Haiti. Davis was searching for the drug which induced the zombie state, with the aim of bringing it back to the United States for use in medicines. The inevitable dream sequences were written by Craven after Maxwell had left the project: 'I had the entire climax of the film done as a nightmare under the influence of the drug in order to rationalise what the previous screenwriter had left me with. I felt that, the film being about voodoo and the research into voodoo and how much we found that it influences the interior of the mind, there could be a great deal of dreams and hallucination in the film. It's an organic, natural part of it. It was actually very powerful to expand the film in that way.'

There was also a political dimension, which allowed him to make a more adult movie than he'd done in recent years: 'In the seventies and eighties, voodoo had been corrupted by Duvalier [Haiti's then dictator] and used for political terrorism. So the film was about that adventure of Wade Davis [played by Bill Pullman] and it had this very strong political element in the confrontation with the Ton Ton Macoute [the Haitian secret police]. It also had the love story between Bill Pullman and Cathy Tyson. Wade Davis was guided on his search by a beautiful young Haitian woman, and they did fall in love, so major elements of the movie parallel Wade

Davis' life.'

This was to be a commercial film that needed elements of adventure, romance, politics and conflict, all of which could be drawn out of the source material. There was one thing missing — Craven's archetypal strong villain: 'We created an antagonist for the Davis character, Dr Dennis Alan, to go up against. The villain is the symbol for all the terrorism going on in the country, and Alan takes it upon himself to get rid of him. Essentially, it's still Davis' story of looking for the zombie drug. All the elements of voodoo, zombies and Haiti's exotic mystery were so good that it would have been a mistake to mess with them. Wade Davis was pretty happy with the film. He understood we were making a commercial sort of picture.'

In keeping with Craven's desire to broaden his range, he aimed to make a much more rounded film than he'd done before: 'It was my first movie out of the genre in the sense that it had a love story and politics and a big budget of $11 million. It had big crowds, 4,000 people in one scene. On the other hand, when the whole third act takes place within a hallucination of the main character when he's poisoned by this substance and we go

inside his mind, it's pure Wes Craven stuff.'

Producer David Ladd agreed that this was more involved than Craven's previous supernatural outings: 'There is a difference. Horror films owe nothing to truth, while stories of terror stem from some aspect of reality, as this one does.'

The Serpent and the Rainbow was also the first film to take Craven out of the United States: 'It was a very important film for me in the sense that it gave me the chance to expand my palette and shoot on actual locations in Haiti. It was quite an intensive piece to shoot, working with full-blooded voodoo people all the time. We were working within a very narrow window between two revolutions in Haiti, where things were very unstable.'

Craven took his first trip to Haiti late in 1986 in the company of David Ladd, to scout possible locations for the film and to make themselves known to the powerful local politicians and voodoo witch doctors. It was the beginning of a terrifying experience which made the nightmares on Elm Street look like pleasant dreams.

Awakened in the middle of the night by their voodoo hosts, Craven and Ladd were taken to a field where a party seemed to be in progress. As

Left: The Serpent and the Rainbow *gave Craven the chance to create a uniquely unsettling atmosphere.*

Below: Craven
auditioned
scores of Haitian
dancers and
performers for
his film.

Bottom:
Casting a spell
— myth and
magic on the
set.

he got used to his surroundings — the music, the drinking, the dancing — it dawned on him that this was no ordinary party, but a voodoo ceremony. A pig was suddenly produced and slaughtered about five feet away from the startled director. The gathered throng began screaming and the blood from the pig was collected in buckets and circulated to be drunk. As the bucket drew closer, Craven grew paler. The priest in charge did not make his guests drink the blood, which came as a huge relief to Craven: 'We were lucky, because, based on what we had already learned about voodoo, you can be in serious trouble if

you don't drink it.' It was a taste of things to come during *The Serpent and the Rainbow*'s turbulent production.

The pig incident didn't alter Craven's tentative plans to shoot at least part of the film on location in Haiti — the first American feature film to do so: 'Originally we were going to shoot it in Mexico somewhere, but when we went to Haiti to scout around we discovered it had so much potential. It's got great scenery and presence and we were able to get hundreds of extras really cheaply.'

Back in the United States before shooting, Craven had an uphill struggle casting some of the roles: 'I kept running up against this problem people had with the subject matter. As soon as you say "voodoo" or "zombie" people think it's some old B-film. For the male lead we had a budget of about $1.5 million. The studio wanted a name, but we had to go with an unknown as no one would take it. I mean, we showed it to every leading man, as far as Kyle MacLachlan, and they all turned us down. Kevin Bacon, everyone. At one point they even tried to get Al Pacino, which was insane. Pacino as an anthropologist? Come on!'

Finally Craven found Bill Pullman, who at the time was best known for his comedic role as Captain Lonestar in Mel Brooks' *Star Wars* spoof *Spaceballs*: 'We were lucky to get Bill Pullman, and he was pleased to have a role which showed what he could do — there's Indiana Jones style adventuring, some love scenes, good hero stuff.' Pullman has gone on to become an under-rated leading man, with his appearances as the President in *Independence Day* and a moody jazz saxophonist in David Lynch's bizarre and brutal *Lost Highway*.

Craven needed a strong, emotive actor for the leading part, as the character faced a roller-coaster dramatic arc. 'Usually, the script has an early scene where the villain behaves in an extreme and unpredictable way that goes far beyond the bounds of normal behaviour,' he explains. 'There is violence and aggression in his action that

leaves the audience terribly frightened. The second step is to take the hero, strip him of his usual panoply of defence and support, whether that is a wife, language, friend, vehicle or clothes. By degrees, you take the hero deeper and deeper into isolation and helplessness. Once you strip him of those customary aids, he discovers resources from an entirely different source. He learns to cope on a different level, on a solitary, spiritual level where all strength comes from his own being.

'As the hero goes increasingly into his own vulnerability, the villain gains increased strength. His impact grows in directly inverse proportion to the amount of time he is seen on screen. A hovering threat is most effective; the audience supplies details from its imagination that are much more powerful than anything expressed by the film-maker.' It was Bill Pullman's job to pull off the emotional and physical exertions Craven would put *The Serpent and the Rainbow*'s hero through.

The other roles were easier to fill, and many of Craven's first choices fell right into place: 'I go for villains to be as nasty as they can be and Zakes Mokae had no problem with it. I had some criticism about that — the white hero and the black villain, but it's about a black religion, a black country, black culture. There's the Paul Winfield character, who's very intelligent, political and powerful. And there's Cathy Tyson, who's independent and the love interest. We had some trouble in the southern states [of the USA] because of the love scenes between the white guy and the black girl.'

Craven arrived back in Haiti with his cast and crew in late February to begin principal photography on 9 March 1987. The first thing the director did was arrange a blessing for the movie from the local voodoo *bokor*, a witch doctor. Protection from evil spirits was granted and Craven set out to film for thirty days in Haiti's grim, unhealthy slums and cemeteries. A rough shoot was expected, but nothing like the problems they actually faced. Almost all of the cast and crew were ill on the second day of their stay in Haiti. The sickness,

manifested in the form of nausea, vomiting or dizziness, persisted throughout the location shoot, but Craven himself escaped. 'I felt protected,' he declared, 'and was determined not to be invaded by what was going on.'

Illness was not the only spectre stalking the production. Tales abound of crew members so affected by the voodoo atmosphere that they were unable to work. Incidents of hallucinations among the crew were legion, some more serious than others: 'People were having wild hallucinations. One person went completely mad after talking to a magician and had to be shipped back to the United States. He snapped out of it five days later. Very strange events were happening all the time, so it was quite an adventure to make.'

Above: The love story in The Serpent and the Rainbow *was based on Wade Davis's own experience.*

The man supposedly driven mad by Haiti was, in fact, screenwriter Richard Maxwell. In the country to work on some script re-writes, he had arranged a meeting with a voodoo *bokor* for research purposes, but Maxwell found the experience very unsettling and tried to get back to Los Angeles. He lost the ability to write and ended up locking himself in his hotel room, before heading straight to the airport and grabbing the next flight out. Back in the States, he suffered for four more days, before awaking on the fifth with no memory of any of the events that had transpired since his meeting with the magician.

Other strange occurrences dogged the production throughout March 1987. Bill Pullman was not immune to the fear and unease spreading through the cast and crew and claimed to have seen a green cow with television screens for eyes. Another crew member was convinced he had seen a long dead general on horseback. The general had approached the man and pleaded with him to give him the colour blue. Actor Paul Winfield believed his colleagues may have had visions, but there was a more mundane explanation than voodoo curses. 'I don't attribute any of that to supernatural occurrences,' he said of the general weirdness that surrounded the film. 'I

was very curious about the locals who would put themselves in a trance. One put himself in a trance and started speaking in tongues. You could see a physiological change take place in his face. I'm a pretty good actor, but to have cheekbones seem to sharpen — I don't think that's something I could do. I'm not saying it was fake, but as an actor watching this "performance", I could see its mechanics.'

Winfield faced one of the film's trickier set pieces when, in a dream sequence, a scorpion had to emerge from his character's mouth. Although the actor agreed to do the scene for real, Craven opted to use a fake head and special effects. 'I was willing and ready to do it,' Winfield told *Starlog*. 'I had talked to the scorpion handler and was mentally prepared. We even considered making an appliance mouthpiece that the scorpion could crawl out of. It would have made a great story for me to tell at dinner parties. Wes was against it — he felt there was too much chance of something going wrong, even though the scorpion had been de-poisoned and was relatively harmless.' Instead, a dummy head was made from a lifecast of Winfield: 'They gave me it to keep, but I finally decided it was too freaky to have around the house.'

Right:
Conditions in Haiti were far from comfortable.

Winfield watched Craven at work coping with the many problems that arose, and came away impressed by his director's skills and abilities: 'He's an amazing man. He has the driest sense of humour I've ever encountered. I would have to listen twice to make sure he was joking, because he always had the straightest face. It was nice to be around someone in this business I could really learn from — and I don't mean just about camera angles and that kind of boring bullshit. He's conscious that there's another world outside the set, that there's more to life than just how much money you make.'

Every morning the cast and crew working on *The Serpent and the Rainbow* awoke to another oppressive Haitian day and made their way through the streets, which ran with raw sewage in ditches, to the day's location. Craven had secured the co-operation of the Haitian government and the Department of Culture, so the film crew were under the protection of the local militia and a village police station served as the payroll base for the employment of thousands of locals as extras. Recruiting the extras was not a problem for casting director Sue Parker, but reigning in their excitement sometimes was: 'Rather than asking people to offer us all their enthusiasm and co-operation, quite often we had to restrain them from supplying too much. Haiti is a land rich with unusual talents. We had to prevent a number of extras from volunteering to show how they could self-combust and burst into flames with the aid of voodoo spirits. Other suggestions came from extras who wanted to show they could eat glass, crunch hot coals and fly with no technical assistance. "Pretence" is a hard word to introduce into the language of people who have had no previous filming experience.'

A desire to show off bizarre skills was not the only problem the crew faced with the locally recruited extras. 'Things had been pretty tense all along,' recalls Craven. 'There were a number of bombings and we were faced with riots because the estimated 2,000 extras we were using kept

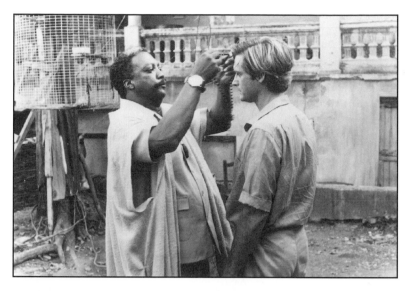

asking for more money. We were right in the middle of shooting when they went on strike. They surrounded the entire company and began throwing stones. They were ready to do us in. The producers and I had an immediate conference with them and negotiated a higher fee. At that point, we realised how dangerous the country had become for us.'

After that incident, Craven decided it was time to call a halt as things were becoming too risky for his cast and crew: 'We left the country the next day. It became apparent in many ways that the place was a time bomb, so we had to get out. I wish it were different. All of us came away

Top: Paul Winfield as Lucien Celine — prepared to swallow scorpions for his art.
Above: Wes Craven, first assistant director Bob Engelman and friend.

Right: Craven on location with producers David Ladd and Doug Claybourne. **Opposite above:** The Serpent and the Rainbow *proved the ideal home for a trademark nightmare sequence.* **Opposite below:** *Police brutality — Peytraud (Zakes Mokae) asks Dr Alan a few questions.*

feeling very much attached to Haiti...' As the crew finished the last scheduled scene at the airport, they took the opportunity to hop on a plane that was being used as a prop and leave the turbulent island behind, relocating to the safer conditions of the Dominican Republic for the remaining eight weeks of production, where filming finally wrapped on 12 May 1987.

Craven was full of praise for his cast and crew, who'd put up with so much to capture what the director was looking for in his film: 'You have to be willing to work in unpleasant places, quite often swamps [or] graveyards, with a crew that possesses the same tolerance. You had to be there to see how well they performed under those circumstances. They were professional above and beyond the call of duty. Bill Pullman, in particular, had to perform some mighty physical moves, especially during the scenes in which he suffers the hallucinations. It's a joy to work with actors like Bill — someone who is able to encompass the ultimate in exhaustion, terror, disorientation, hate and anger, outside the range of any normal state of human experience. He was wrung out at the end.'

Craven really had some fun with Pullman's hallucination scenes, returning to some of the tricks he'd first dreamt up (literally) for *A Nightmare on Elm Street*: 'We all tend to stay within the lighted rooms of our own reality, but there are many other rooms in the house which are dark and unknown, and don't fit into the scope of acceptance. So we tend to avoid magic, voodoo, insanity, free consciousness, all those areas where we are in the dark, literally and figuratively, when we become like children.'

As before, Craven was inspired for certain scenes in *The Serpent and the Rainbow* by his night visions. An early scene playing up the sense of foreboding which dominates the film features a group of threatening figures in brilliant scarlet carrying a coffin across a Haitian landscape. This vivid scene had sprung from a dream Craven had when he began working on script revisions and was immersing himself in voodoo lore to maintain the film's authenticity.

After a more relaxing time filming in the Dominican Republic, Craven faced another nightmare when he returned to the States and began editing the picture. He was left with a three hour first cut that was far too long for a commercial release. 'A lot of that was talk,' he explains. 'There was too much talk.' Cutting it down to the more standard hour and a half, Craven paid particular attention to sound on his epic: 'Sound is profoundly disturbing. You can hear a faucet echoing off-screen and imagine a whole complex of dungeons. It can accomplish more than a million dollars' worth of carpenters' work on sets. In the Haitian culture particularly, there is so much drama in its natural background. Everyday living is accompanied by the acoustic punctuations of drama and rhythm. Standing on a Haitian balcony and hearing the drums far off in the hills, with the distant dogs barking — it is stirring and frightening.'

Craven was gratified by the favourable response to the movie at several test screenings, and *The Serpent and the Rainbow* was released in the United States on 15 January 1988. 'It was very well received critically, did well at the box office, and won Best Film, Best Director and Best Screenplay at the Madrid Film Festival. It was also a big hit in Japan,' he recalls. In the US alone the film grossed just under $20 million.

There was a bizarre postscript to the tale of *The Serpent and the Rainbow*. When the film was released on video in Britain in 1989, CIC video distributors thought it would generate publicity if they sent live Chinese rat snakes to 700 video stores nationwide to promote the film. Sure enough, it generated publicity, but not the type CIC were looking for as hundreds of video store managers called the RSPCA to have the snakes collected. 'It was unbelievable and pathetic,' said RSPCA spokesperson Diana Jones. 'We had to go around all the video shops collecting the snakes.' The manager of London's Video Palace told the *Evening Standard*: 'We were a bit perturbed when we got a package labelled "live animal inside". We had no idea it was being sent.' CIC claimed they had acted responsibly in mounting the offbeat publicity stunt. 'I spoke to the RSPCA before we did this and they had no objections,' said Paul Brett, marketing manager for CIC at the

time. 'It was intended as a talking point to draw attention to the film, and it worked.'

The Serpent and the Rainbow was one of three voodoo movies that were released around the same time, alongside Alan Parker's *Angel Heart* in 1987 and John Schlesinger's *The Believers* in 1988. 'We were all aware of each other's presence,' remembers Craven. 'Nobody got together and said, "Let's do this kind of film". It was one of those strange Hollywood coincidences. I think that was partially because the Wade Davis book had been out for a year. It is a fascinating subject. We think of it as this little corner of Haiti, but it is really their whole religion. Many elements are quite beautiful. It's a classic example, as Wade Davis said, of a racially despised sub-culture in the Caribbean, which is totally misrepresented because we've made it into this dark, nasty thing, but it's really like Catholicism.'

Treating voodoo as a serious religion and lacing the horror with elements of romance and adventure was important to Craven. It was *The Twilight Zone* episodes which had changed people's opinion of Craven's abilities: 'Suddenly people looked up and said, "My God, he can direct love stories, he can direct other things". That was the strength that got me *The Serpent and the Rainbow*. I think being typecast in horror has hampered me a great deal. I offended the power structure. I didn't offend the avant-garde film-makers, or the young film-makers, but the people in the established positions were very afraid of who I was. I've tried for years to move away from that. At the same time, I've had a lot of people write to me and say, "You should not walk away from something that you're so good at, because you have a real gift". I've had a real interior conflict with my own participation in

horror and I've decided that rather than acting as if I'm horrified by it and need to move away from it, I really do enjoy making them. I think that within the genre there is the capacity to do something quite significant and valid.'

With *The Serpent and the Rainbow*'s success, Wes Craven realised that he had the ability to combine his aptitude for horror with more mainstream themes or subjects and turn out good movies in the process: 'I had to do something I had never anticipated — I had to come to terms with the fact that I do have a capacity to generate horror films, horror images. Somehow those images from our own culture affect me profoundly and I'm able to put them onto film. There is an element that I enjoy that I denied for many years. I'm trying now to be more mature about it and say that I have to admit that there is a part of me that is this wild maniac, that loves these crazy images, that loves to scare people and enjoys going into these very dark labyrinths of human consciousness. I must not try to deny that outlet. I feel I can do that very well, and I feel that I can do a lot of other things well, so the

trick is not to just kick it out of my life but to make room for the other things as well.'

With that in mind, Craven signed a two-picture deal with Alive Films, who had a distribution agreement with Universal. Alive had recently been behind a couple of 'arthouse' hits in the States, including Lindsay Anderson's *The Whales of August* and Alan Rudolph's *The Moderns*. They'd already done a deal with horror filmmaker John Carpenter, giving him complete control of his own low-budget feature films. 'I'll be able to make a complete "Wes Craven film". I think that is such an opportunity,' said Craven at the time. 'I've never ever had that. That alone is worth doing a film for.'

Making *The Serpent and the Rainbow* changed Wes Craven in a way that no other film-making experience would: 'Haiti really mellowed me out. I almost died down there, and I experienced a lot of strange things. So, when I came through it all, not only alive, but healthy, I decided to begin taking my life a bit easier. The experience was definitely therapeutic. I've learned about another place and I've learned much about myself.' ■

Scary Movies

Although he had scored a commercial and critical success with *The Serpent and the Rainbow*, Craven had also suffered some personal loss in pursuing his vision. Soon after completing the film, he and his wife of five years, Mimi Meyer-Craven, were divorced. Mimi had appeared in her husband's films in a variety of roles, from Arcane's secretary in *Swamp Thing* to a nurse in *A Nightmare on Elm Street* and *Chiller*. She went on to notable TV guest appearances in episodes of *Seinfeld* and the short-lived *Nowhere Man*, plus a featured role in David Twohy's time travel TV drama *The Grand Tour* (aka *Disaster in Time*) in 1992. During publicity interviews for *The Serpent and the Rainbow*, Craven claimed to be handling it 'pretty well'.

Craven's next feature grew out of his attempts to develop further ideas for television. Pitched to the Fox network as a TV show about the experiences of serial killers, *Dream Stalker* was deemed too controversial and quickly dropped. 'There was a killer who can get into people's bodies and take over their electro-magnetic field as [Horace] Pinker does,' recalls Craven of the idea that evolved into his next movie, *Shocker*. 'There was a young kid that was a very unlikely psychic, able to dream whatever murders this man was committing, and so identify and locate him. The killer would have been different every week.'

Although Chris Carter's serial killer show *Millennium* later aired to critical acclaim, television wasn't quite ready for such Craven images at the end of the eighties: 'Fox had problems with it. They thought it would have been too violent, too negative, too difficult for the audi-

ence to know and identify with the killer. They had it a year before they finally passed on it, and by that time I was in pre-production on *The Serpent and the Rainbow*.'

It was during the making of his voodoo epic that Craven's new producer partner Marianne Maddalena told him about a film called *The Hidden*, directed by Jack (*Freddy's Revenge*) Sholder, which featured an alien inhabiting various human bodies, in a similar way to Craven's *Shocker* villain.

Opposite: A real Shocker — *Mitch Pileggi as electro-villain Horace Pinker.*
***Below:** Wes Craven tries the chair for size.*

Right:

Jonathan Parker (Peter Berg), robbed of everyone he loves in Shocker.

'Our original inspiration was a film one,' admits Craven, candidly. 'It was Howard Hawks' *The Thing from Another World*, which had probably been the inspiration for *The Hidden* too. We felt that if we extended the ideas about how Horace Pinker could move around we could make it. I was reading a book about television which said that when people watch television they have brainwaves almost identical to those when dreaming. I realised that here was a parallel world to Freddy's dream world, because it is entered into every night by people's minds and it enters their minds. That's how the third act of *Shocker* came about.'

Shocker begins with football jock Jonathan Parker (Peter Berg) dreaming about the murder of his foster family. He awakes to discover that it has really happened, and is able to pin the blame on homicidal TV repairman Horace Pinker (Mitch Pileggi). Pinker is electrocuted, but instead of dying he's transformed into an evil entity able to use energy waves to move around and take over other people's bodies. Soon, he's

out for vengeance, resulting in a battle between Jonathan and Pinker through the landscape of television itself. Jonathan is helped by the ghost of his girlfriend Alison (Cami Cooper), who was murdered by Pinker, and is shocked to discover that there may be a closer connection between himself and Pinker than he thought.

Craven was up front about his hopes for Horace Pinker: '*Shocker* was a good option because it gave me the chance to create another Freddy and to have a big piece of it. *Nightmare* and Freddy gave me great credibility, but not a great payday. So when Alive Films came to me and said they'd like to have a *Nightmare* series too, and that they thought I could do it again, I jumped at the chance.'

Catching lightning in a bottle twice proved more difficult than Craven had imagined. He signed a two-film deal with Alive Films, which gave him control over the projects, a similar arrangement to the one they had made with John Carpenter for *They Live*. Both Craven and

Pileggi's *Shocker* contracts had options for two sequels built in, but this proved a little optimistic. There were other reasons for Craven to tackle *Shocker*, though: 'This film has a real strong love story to it. That was important to me. I've always had the notion, and I think it shows in my films, that "death is not the end" is a jumping off point for horror. If you believe that, you've also got to believe that goodness and strength and love are immortal too. Those latter elements are very much present in this film, especially when Alison's spirit comes back to help Jonathan ultimately triumph over Pinker.'

Casting his new villain proved problematic for Craven, who was faced with duplicating the success of Robert Englund as Freddy: 'We did not look for anybody who looked like Robert Englund. We were looking for somebody with the same quality, an undiscovered actor with that kind of talent.' After dismissing rock star Mick Fleetwood because of his strong connections with Fleetwood Mac, Craven settled on Pileggi, an actor who had been toiling as a villain-for-hire in TV and low-budget

movies, but who found greater fame as FBI Assistant Director Skinner on Chris Carter's phenomenally successful *The X Files*. 'We had one basic rule toward casting the character of Horace Pinker,' remembers Craven. 'That was that we would know him when we saw him. When Mitch Pileggi walked in, we knew we had our man.'

'I just went in and acted crazy,' Pileggi told *Fangoria*, describing his unusual audition for the part. Asked by the casting director to tone down the yelling, Pileggi returned to read for Craven and Maddalena: 'I came in and did it, and I must've done a pretty good job because I noticed that Marianne was getting quite frightened and moving to the other side of the room. I went home and got a call two weeks later to come back and see if I could handle the physical stuff. Marianne once again started to move across the room to get away from me. I figured by that point that I had at least convinced her.'

Pileggi also convinced Craven that he'd found his new Freddy and shooting began in April 1989 under the title *No More Mr Nice Guy*. 'It's a strange

Left: *Peter Berg and Ted Raimi (cult director Sam Raimi's brother).*

feeling, having created something and fought to get it made and then see another organisation own it,' said Craven of the *Nightmare* series when he was preparing to film *Shocker*. 'Rather than sulking in the corner or doing something really nasty, I go out and compete with them. It's my way of saying "I can do it again; can you?"'

Craven found roles in his new film for his daughter Jessica (as a counter girl) and son Jonathan (as a jogger), as well as casting himself as the neighbour who asks 'Was that real?' at the end. Furthermore, Jonathan worked behind the scenes as a post-production apprentice editor and visual effects co-ordinator. Craven also made room in *Shocker* for *A Nightmare on Elm Street*'s Heather Langenkamp (as 'Victim'), director Sam Raimi's actor brother Ted (as 'Pac-Man') and even Craven's *Nightmare 3* co-writer Bruce Wagner (as the executioner). There was also an uncredited appearance by *Star Trek: The Next Generation* actor Brent Spiner as a talk show guest.

Below: No more Mr Nice Guy.

Alive had to have a print to Universal Pictures by 25 September, since they aimed to open the film in late October 1989. The biggest headache was the ground-breaking, innovative special effects that were required to show Pinker's various abilities, using new film and video technology. Having worked on video during the shooting of *The Twilight Zone*, Craven was intrigued by the possibilities of combining it with film on *Shocker*, and he hired an opticals expert who'd also worked on *The Twilight Zone* to explore the areas of interaction between the mediums.

'We had a great deal of fun with the flexibility of video in opticals,' remembers Craven, who saw ways to facilitate scenes that would otherwise have been more difficult. 'There's one scene where the hero picks up the television remote control and beeps the shit out of Pinker, making him reverse, freeze, fast-forward and everything else. For me, it was a way of saying video is a big part of our culture, so why not admit it and get

Left: Craven with Timothy Leary, in costume as Shocker's TV evangelist.

the two things working together?'

Craven recruited cinematographer Jacques Haitkin, who'd worked with him since *A Nightmare on Elm Street*, and they set about developing a series of techniques to combine video effects with film. This was before computer generated imagery came to dominate the production of special effects. 'I sat down and designed shots around those effects,' says Craven, who was faced with solving the problem of integrating Jonathan and Pinker with violent newsreel stock footage during the climactic television chase. 'I wanted to create the idea that these two were fighting their way through the backdrop of violence in our culture. So, you see the atomic blast at Hiroshima, a bloody raid in Vietnam, soldiers using flame throwers — Jonathan and Pinker are actually in those scenes as they're happening.'

As well as that bravura special effects sequence, Pinker disrupted several types of TV show in footage Craven created himself. One featured a TV evangelist played by the late Timothy Leary — Craven's nod to drug culture. Four months were spent on post-production, and it was then Craven realised that *Shocker* might not live up to his ambitions: 'I would be a liar if I didn't say that we got in over our heads. If we had to do it over again, we'd be much more terrified. As you go along, you realise it's getting bigger and bigger, you keep solving problems and you somehow manage to make it happen.'

Nevertheless, *Shocker* failed to fulfil its potential, which naturally disappointed Craven, especially after *The Serpent and the Rainbow*. *Shocker* grossed $16.5 million at the American box office: 'It got some good reviews. I don't know quite what happened with that. There were a couple of things that were bad for the film. One was that we had an alliance with a company that produced heavy metal music, and so the score was influenced by heavy metal, which was to the detriment of the picture, although I didn't know

Above: *Mitch Pileggi and Jessica Craven pose for the cameras.*

to video, at a fraction of the cost.'

Always keen to work on the cutting edge of special effects, Craven had been happy to delegate the responsibility, a decision he regretted: 'We kept waiting for them to come in and he kept saying there were minor problems and he'd give us all the scenes all at once instead of a bit at a time. Then we went to dinner with him at his request and he just burst out crying and said it was not working. It was hopeless and we should have killed him.'

Craven tried to salvage something from a terrible situation, with no extra time or money available: 'There was a mad scramble over a period of a month, not only to reconceptualise all of the opticals, but also to have them re-done, which meant that, as it was a short period of time, they had to be spread all over town. All the negative had been lost in one way or another and the guy had virtually had a nervous breakdown. We were finding negative under the work benches in his lab, in the trunk of his car, in boxes next to other negatives — it was total chaos. It was an absolute nightmare, the worst I've ever had.'

Despite the setbacks, Craven was able to salvage a very watchable, if compromised, film from the mess: 'We felt happy just to have a film at the end of it. I still like that film a lot, and I like the idea of the son finding out that the father is the murderer and still being able to separate himself from that. I feel in many ways that it's not a catastrophe, it's just much less than it could have been.'

Years after these events, Craven was sanguine about what, at the time, had been a real-life nightmare: 'Sometime those things happen. Making a film is like a war — sometimes you're lucky to get out with your skin, you know. In fact, there was real active talk of doing a sequel to both *Shocker* and *The Serpent and the Rainbow*, at slightly lower budgets, but [with] the same basic creative freedom. I wasn't going to direct them, but I would have been executive producing.' Neither sequel ever happened.

it at the time. Having seen the picture completed, it did not work. We were too far into our commitment to those people to replace the score.'

That would have been bad enough, although a lot of horror fans did like the heavy metal soundtrack on *Shocker*, but far harder to recover from was the disaster which occurred during the production of the key special effects sequences. 'The second thing that happened was that we had an extraordinary calamity,' recalls Craven with a shiver. 'The person in charge of the optical special effects, which were legion, completely collapsed. When we were supposed to be taking delivery of all of the opticals, we discovered that none of them were ready. In fact, the whole process that he told us he could use to do these did not, in fact, work. It was an innovative new process by which we would be pulling mattes from film transferred

Writing in *Cinefantastique*, critic Bob Morrish saw the flawed nature of *Shocker* and lamented that Craven had failed to live up to expectations: 'After the first few minutes, it seems that Craven has graduated to a new level of film-making... but the film spins out of control in the attempt to create a "new Freddy". Craven flashes moments of creative brilliance in *Shocker*, but until he learns a sense of restraint, he will never realise his significant potential.'

Craven knew he faced a battle with the censors over *Shocker* and attempted to pre-censor himself to minimise the time the film would spend shuttling back and forth between the MPAA and Alive Films: 'It's a fun film. There are a few scenes that are a little gory, but it's more of a chase and special effects film than a slasher film. On screen there are only two scenes of someone actually being stabbed, and they're very short. It's done without a lot of explicit footage.'

These precautions didn't stop the MPAA returning the first submitted print as unsuitable for the R rating Craven was contractually obliged to deliver. 'In the last five years they [the MPAA] will not say it's a particular shot; they will just say it's too intense overall,' he explained to *Cinefantastique* at the time. 'More and more they're bringing into it the question, "What if a child should see it?". It's a very strange argument, because it leaves no place to approach an adult audience. It's a serious issue because I don't make my films for children to see, and there should be a way for keeping children out of these films so that you can make them for a healthy adult audience. I told them it's my job to be intense.'

Several cuts were made to *Shocker* in order to gain an R rating, but there was one scene in particular that Craven regretted losing, as it was a signature moment in his attempt to build Horace Pinker up as the next Freddy Krueger. Out went the shot of Pinker spitting out the fingers he had just bitten off a prison guard, leading him to comment: 'Finger lickin' good'. Craven knew the jokily horrific moment worked with an audience: 'In our test screening, the audience stood up and cheered that — it was a phenomenal moment.'

Craven felt that the censors seriously under-

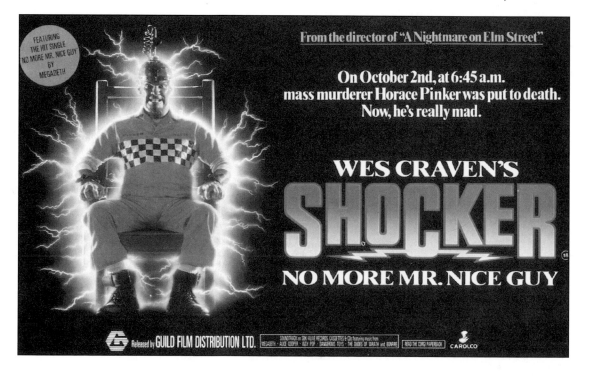

estimated the capacity of audiences to cope with and enjoy horror movies: 'It's a put-down of the audience to think they're so impressionable that they're going to be damaged by this stuff, a put-down by people who are tremendously smug control freaks. I think what they're really afraid of is that the audience will get out of control. They are so terrified of kids and the underclass of America that when they see audiences screaming and yelling and laughing, they're terrified the audience will be coming over their well-manicured lawns to get them next.'

Despite Craven's ambitions to create a new movie monster in Horace Pinker, *Shocker* was not a big enough success to give Mitch Pileggi a second chance to wreak havoc over the airwaves. This was much regretted by Craven, who believed there were many areas that could still be explored: 'Universal never felt it did the business they wanted to. *Shocker* was an expensive movie to make, and the studio probably felt they did not get the franchise character they were hoping for. I would still love to do a sequel, though. It's something that's primed to go off in a million

different directions.'

Perhaps as a result of his latest tussle with the censors and his failure to replicate the success of Freddy Krueger, Craven again began to look beyond the horror genre after completing *Shocker*, although he had a commitment to deliver another horror picture for Alive Films: '*The Serpent and the Rainbow*, *The Twilight Zone* and even *Shocker* have gotten a lot of attention. I'm looking to do something out of the genre, probably next. Then I'll come back and do my next Alive/Universal genre film. *Shocker* was really hard, so I wouldn't mind doing one of those films where two people sit in a cafe and talk to each other!'

Craven's ambition to create a long-running TV series had been an ongoing struggle over the years. After *Shocker*, he turned to television again as an outlet for his material, creating a comedy show as far removed from the horrors of Horace Pinker as it was possible to get. 'With *The People Next Door*, the situation was that I basically came up with the idea and co-wrote it with a friend,' says Craven of his short-lived 1989-90 series. 'We got it sold. There was the addition of a second

Right: The Nightmare Cafe, where lives are changed and wrongs put right.

team that rewrote the idea. At the time I was too busy to actively work on the show. Everyone knew that I was not on the set, wasn't doing the hiring and firing and was not the film-maker. However, it was presented as a "Wes Craven show", because I was the creator.'

The People Next Door, starring Jeffrey Jones (*Beetlejuice*) and Mary Gross (*Saturday Night Live*) quickly flopped on the CBS Monday lineup in 1989: 'That was very frustrating because I was working on *Shocker* at the time, and I had to give up control of that series. Right after we conceived it, the series was turned over to another group of people. With *Nightmare Cafe* [a later TV series], I gave up on any semblance of a personal life to work round the clock on the first five episodes.' The failure of *The People Next Door* didn't keep Craven away from the small screen while he considered his options for another cinema outing, however.

While looking for a non-horror project, Craven cast Mitch Pileggi as Keller, head of an LAPD department, in his TV movie *Night Visions*. Again, Craven seemed ahead of his time as *Night Visions* was a psychic cop show, a genre which proliferated in the wake of *The X Files* and *Millennium* a few years later.

This two-hour TV movie, which could have served as a pilot for an on-going series, centred on young college graduate Sally Peters (Loryn Locklin) who lands a job with the LAPD and is teamed up with tough detective Tom Mackey (James Remar). Relying on her psychic abilities, Sally is able to crack the case of a notorious serial killer which has baffled the cops. Her special skill allows Sally to put herself at the scene of future murders — as the victim. Her ability appears to be the result of a traumatic childhood, and she relies on the straight arrow Mackey to keep her on the right side of madness.

As well as directing, Craven was also credited as executive producer and co-wrote the teleplay with Thomas Baum. Following on from *Shocker*, Craven cast Timothy Leary in a cameo role.

'From a film-making view it was an interesting experience,' says Craven of *Night Visions*. 'The actors were fine and overall we got a good looking picture for a television budget.'

Night Visions was not picked up by broadcaster NBC as a series because the film was finished too late for the autumn 1990 schedule, although the option of the series being renewed as a mid-season replacement or for a series of sequel movies remained open. 'I was a little disappointed that the network didn't get behind it more,' says Craven. 'What happened was, they had a test screening and one of the main characters tested weak. At that point, the network just lost interest in the film.'

Nevertheless, he kept trying to get a Wes Craven inspired concept on to television, tackling *Nightmare Cafe* next: 'I've taken my lumps when it comes to TV. That's alright, though,

Above: *Freddy's revenge — Craven was reunited with Robert Englund (Blackie) for* Nightmare Cafe, *alongside Lindsay Frost (Fay) and Jack Coleman (Frank).*

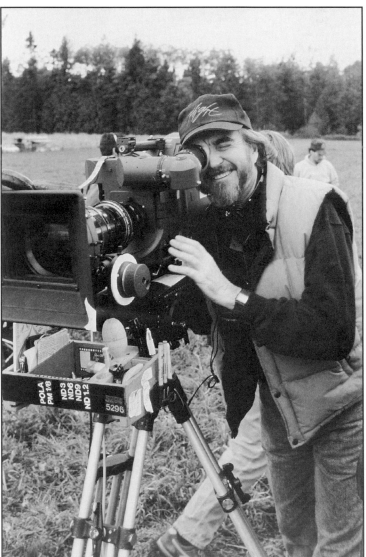

because I've pretty much known what I was up against. Television is much more restrictive when it comes to horror and dark fantasy, so you do have to be careful. I was not worried about *Nightmare Cafe*. It was not going to be a blood and guts show, it wasn't *Freddy's Nightmares*.'

Nightmare Cafe has been the most artistically successful of Craven's television exploits so far. The series pilot was shot between *Shocker* and Craven's next horror feature film for Alive, *The People Under the Stairs*. Described by Craven as '*Cheers* meets *The Twilight Zone*', *Nightmare Cafe* had great potential that was rarely exhibited in the handful of episodes which made it to the screen.

The pilot, made by MCA/UA for NBC TV, was co-written by Craven with *Night Visions* colleague Thomas Baum and directed by feature film director Philip Noyce, best known then for *Dead Calm*. 'It is a concept about two people who inherit a café that's somewhere between life and death,' said Craven while working on the project. 'They serve as moderators and participate in the stories. People in the real world come to experience their worst nightmare, their turning point, their comeuppance or their breakthrough. They see their lives on television and disappear into the stories. The people in the café make bets on how it's going to come out and go into the story to influence it. Robert Englund plays three characters, including the resident cynic.'

Cast in the pilot as the first two characters to stumble across (and ultimately stay in) the Nightmare Cafe were Lindsay Frost (brother of *Twin Peaks* co-creator Mark Frost) and Jack Coleman. More importantly for Craven, the series provided another chance to work with Robert Englund: 'He approached me about the role of Blackie in the show. At first I didn't think he could handle playing what is essentially the older character, but then I realised that Robert's in his forties, and more than able to play an older type, so I went with him. He's a totally different character than Freddy. Blackie is a shyster-lawyer type.'

The pilot was successful enough to be picked

up by NBC as a mid-season replacement, with an order for a further five episodes during the post-production period on *The People Under the Stairs*. Although busy with the feature film, Craven found it difficult to say no to the opportunity to run his own TV show, but at the same time his attention was divided. He was also contracted to direct at least one of the remaining episodes: 'We wanted to do more of those, beyond just the six episodes. It was a difficult series to conceptualise how it went on and we were sort of feeling our way and we were having fun. I think the audience were having fun, but the network were feeling uneasy about it. They couldn't quite pigeon-hole it.' The series initially aired between January and April 1992, and Craven took the opportunity to work in a professional capacity with his son Jonathan. Since appearing as the boy with the balloon in *The Last House on the Left*, Jonathan Craven had worked closely with his father on *Shocker*, helping to sort out the problems with the visual effects. *Nightmare Cafe* gave

Jonathan his first opportunity in the producer's chair, under his father's guidance. The experience served him well when it came to producing his first feature film, *Mind Ripper*.

Wes Craven also indulged himself when it came to directing his episode of *Nightmare Cafe*, called 'Aliens Ate My Lunch'. It was a comedic look at the alien abduction phenomenon, packed with bizarre items such as flying cows and a group of circus midgets who might have been aliens. Craven's ideas wouldn't have looked too out of place in one of the more off-beat episodes of *The X Files* a few years later.

'The stories were good and the premise was interesting,' maintained Craven of *Nightmare Cafe* after it had been cancelled. 'What ultimately sunk us was the late timeslot and the unwillingness of the network to give us a longer look at a different time. Despite that, it was wonderful to work with Robert Englund again.' Craven's renewed relationship with Englund was to sow the seeds of their fruitful collaboration on *Wes*

Craven's New Nightmare.

Craven had other television ambitions in his search for the right formula to develop a long running series: 'We did a second pilot for the network called *Laurel Canyon* [directed by Tim Hunter]. That's a canyon here in Los Angeles which is very quirky and full of show business people, dope dealers and back-to-nature types. We wanted to do a horror soap opera based there. We had a murder which was central to the first plot and it was completed right when the head of the network was called to testify in front of a congressional committee [looking at television standards], and they dropped it like a hot potato.'

Following *Laurel Canyon*, Craven and Marianne Maddalena decided that they had given television their best shot and should focus on films once more: 'After that we concluded that TV was not really that fruitful a place. All of our agents were saying, if you can get something that goes into syndication you can retire for the rest of your life. First, that shouldn't be the first reason for doing

something and second, I think it's such a distant carrot. The networks don't really know what they want. They change their minds all the time, they change where they put you in the schedule.'

Like Craven's breakthrough film *A Nightmare on Elm Street*, his first feature film of the nineties came from an old newspaper cutting which had been lying in the director's files for quite some time. Craven's script for *The People Under the Stairs* was drawn from an article in the *Santa Monica Evening Outlook* in 1978 about an apparently normal couple who had kept their children locked up in their home all their lives. Craven was fascinated by the macabre story and wrote an eighty page treatment, followed by a script called *The Puzzle*. Three-quarters of the way through, Craven gave up when he was unable to think of an ending: 'When I'd get the chance between films, I would take it out and try to get the second and third acts to work. I knew I'd have one hell of a film once I got that problem solved. What appealed to me was the thought of a hid-

Right: The People Under the Stairs *set — Craven directs young actor Brandon Adams.*

Left: *The people under the stairs.*

den truth that was radically different from the surface appearance, and the fact that this was taking place in a neighbourhood where, supposedly, people were enjoying the good middle-class life. Also the idea that beneath the surface of apparent normality can be found these strange aberrations of behaviour; these two people who appear to be completely well-behaved can, in secret, perform these atrocities on their own children.'

Dreams came to Wes Craven's rescue once more and salvaged *The People Under the Stairs*. While attending the Brussels Film Festival in 1990, Craven claimed to have dreamt and remembered the entire film, from frame one to the end: 'I dreamed I was writing this picture, then I woke up. I began writing and in four hours had the entire story down. It was a major breakthrough.' As well as the newspaper story and the dream ending, Craven was aware that much of the film's material had been in his subconscious for a long time: 'This movie is really getting at something that's been in and out of my dreams

for years. There were visions of houses, finished and unfinished, that branched off into long winding galleries. *A Nightmare on Elm Street* got into that dream to a certain extent, but this film was taking it all the way.'

The People Under the Stairs follows a black teenager named 'Fool' (Brandon Adams, making his feature film début) who, desperate to help his poverty stricken family, agrees to accompany some friends (among them *Pulp Fiction*'s Ving Rhames) on a burglary attempt. The house they choose, however, turns out to be an inescapable maze of booby traps and torture devices, presided over by a dangerously deranged couple known only as Man and Woman (played by *Twin Peaks* stars Everett McGill and Wendy Robie).

Craven characterised the film as 'a modern fable and myth. A film I'm very proud of and happy to do. Horror films generate our modern mythology. Freddy Krueger is like the Minotaur. These modern mythological figures [Man and Woman] stand for psychological states, such as unexpressed fear, that don't get expression very much in modern culture. I think horror films are very viable if they're thought through that way — not just a bunch of knives flashing.'

Craven saw *The People Under the Stairs* as a result of the skills he'd learnt as a film-maker over the years. 'I don't know if what I'm going through now is so much a new beginning as it is a transition of sorts,' he told *Fangoria* magazine at the time. 'I feel more settled and more mature than I did two pictures back. I'm continuing to follow that inner voice, whatever it is.'

Despite dreaming up solutions to the script problems of *The People Under the Stairs*, Craven was determined to exclude any dream imagery from the film, fearing that after *The Serpent and the Rainbow* and *Shocker* it was becoming too pre-

Below: Craven with Everett McGill, on a cigarette break.

dictable: 'I see this as more along the lines of my earlier work like *The Last House on the Left* and *The Hills Have Eyes*. It's a very real and primitive situation that is not dreamlike and does not rely on electrical circuits. I see it as something very symbolic. The kids going up against Man and Woman are representative of small groups standing up to larger groups. The house, with all its claustrophobic spaces and hiding places stands for civilisation run amuck. The generations that have lived in it have got more and more crazy until the present one is totally locked into madness. It compares the two sides of normality and abnormality and shows how they interlock. In this piece, the family of the young apprentice to the burglars is actually much more intact and normal than this bizarre semblance of a family that lives in the mansion and is quite mad.'

With the central duo of *The People Under the Stairs*, Craven was returning to one of his most successful themes — the broken family: 'I try to find the basis for fear and horror in the world around me. Ideas that come out of families which are fractured or disturbed in some way are the most profoundly terrifying things to me. There's something about innocent children being held captive and abused by people they are supposed to look up to and trust that touches a very large and unpleasant nerve. The idea of parents as monsters represents an almost quintessential evil in people.'

The film also drew on Craven's own childhood: 'In many ways, a rigid upbringing gives a real kick start to your imagination. It can weigh heavily on your wild years, because it tells you, no, you can't do anything. So when you break free, you really break free. But another very real advantage to such a background is that it preoccupies you with the major issues of being alive. It makes you ask ultimate questions all the time. I've always felt that I was on solid ground when I was making movies about families. *A Nightmare on Elm Street*; *The Last House on the Left*; *The Hills Have Eyes*: they were all tied to the interworking of families and they all scared the hell out of people.'

Left: A return to visceral horror — Woman (Wendy Robie) prepares to skewer Alice (A.J. Langer).

So it proved with *The People Under the Stairs*. Everett McGill and Wendy Robie were cast as Craven's latest twisted monsters, but the fact that they had played a husband and wife on David Lynch's weird TV series *Twin Peaks* was not instrumental to their casting, according to Craven: 'That wasn't deliberate, actually. They were just both perfect for the roles. They were the best that I saw. Wendy just came in for the audition — I didn't know she was on *Twin Peaks* until Marianne told her how much she enjoyed her on the show. Everett was just the best of the guys who came in. After I cast them, I thought, "God, this is really weird". Woman had to be very manipulative and clever. She's someone who has taken neatness to maddening heights [also a trait of Robie's *Twin Peaks* character]. Man was a much more beastly creation, a wily and brutal person. I'd like to say that their creation was all in the script, but Everett and Wendy came up with some very strange twists that enhanced what I'd written.'

By June 1991, Craven was completing princi-

pal photography and faced a five week post-production schedule before the film was handed over to Universal for a Halloween 1991 release in the United States. Making *The People Under the Stairs* had not been an easy task, although it was his most personal effort in many years. Describing filming as 'horrendous', Craven had to deal with shooting on a difficult and constricting set, as well as working with dogs, children and many tricky special effects: 'We were shooting in a lot of confined places: ducts, chimneys and closets. The way we filmed those cramped areas was integral to the psychological approach we took.'

A larger budget than he'd had on *Shocker* helped Craven to have the sets he needed to reflect the psychological states of the house's twisted inhabitants: 'I like exotic material, but I like budgets that allow me to do it thoroughly. The kind of material I do calls for a lot of camera set-ups.'

The People Under the Stairs proved to be a big hit, taking over $5 million on its opening weekend in the United States. The film finally grossed just over $24 million — the first time one of Craven's movies had crossed the $20 million barrier at the domestic box office since *A Nightmare on Elm Street*. However, the drama's sociological and political subtexts were not clear to all. Craven found that his attempt to mix domestic political commentary with the kind of realistic horror he'd pioneered in *The Last House on the Left* was not widely appreciated, particularly in America. 'Nobody in the United States understood that,' he recalls. 'It was certainly meant as a political allegory. Critics Siskel and Ebert claimed the two antagonists were meant to be Nancy and Ronald Reagan. That was not true, it was not meant to be that specific. They're just conservatives, or actually, people who would elect Nancy and Ronald.'

Despite the general failure to grasp the movie's

political allegory, Craven was happy to note that *The People Under the Stairs* did seem to have made inroads into the American consciousness: 'The only thing I heard about in this country that was gratifying was a political cartoon which ran when Bush was seeking election, which had Bush creeping up these rickety stairs and it had our *The People Under the Stairs* logo and was captioned 'Terror On the Way to the Polls'. Underneath were all the poor and disenfranchised.'

After *The People Under the Stairs*, Craven considered his next project. Among the options was a script called *Shades of Gray*, a ghost story based on a novel about a West Point professor's research into the haunting of one of the military academy's oldest dormitories. He also worked on an adaptation of the comic book *Dr Strange* with Akiva Goldsman, but the project stalled while still

Below: There's always a lot of hanging around on a movie set.

in development.

Despite a continued ambition to work 'out of the genre', Wes Craven was enjoying the most successful period of his creative life when he finished *The People Under the Stairs*. Although drawn from someone else's source material, *The Serpent and the Rainbow* had proved the ideal vehicle for his obsession with dream imagery, showing that he could produce a hit mainstream adventure. Critically, he was at his highest point since *A Nightmare on Elm Street* in 1984. Although fatally flawed and undermined by terrible production problems, *Shocker* featured enough trademark Craven touches to be a memorable example of the director's craft. With *The People Under the Stairs* he returned to his film-making roots, albeit with more resources and a larger film-making palette at his disposal. At last, Craven felt secure enough to make peace with his position as the number one auteur of Hollywood horror.

'I'm typecast as a horror film-maker,' he finally acknowledged after *The People Under the Stairs*. 'I know it, but that's not necessarily bad. I've got a lot of power within the genre that has not been afforded me outside of it. Look what I've got when I'm doing genre films — I've got my own production company, script and cast approval, and I don't have to show dailies to anybody. I'm able to make films that are personal and unique, without any interference. I could not go outside horror and do that.'

The power Wes Craven now had within the horror genre would allow him to work with a major star for the first time in his career and to make a final, fateful return trip to Elm Street and the nightmares of Freddy Krueger. ■

Above: *Lights, camera, action — Craven shows Everett McGill exactly what he wants.*

New Nightmares, New Success

It was the morning of 12 September 1994 when Wes Craven received the good news about his film *Wes Craven's New Nightmare*. A birthday celebration was already taking place in trailer nine on the Paramount lot for one of Craven's production team. That morning the director and his team, then deep into pre-production on the Eddie Murphy movie *Vampire in Brooklyn*, received the Hollywood trade papers with the first reviews of Craven's eagerly awaited return to Elm Street.

Wes Craven's New Nightmare had been no ordinary project and it started in a most extraordinary and unexpected way. 'It began with Bob Shaye asking me to come into New Line because he had heard that I had some problems with the way the business side of *A Nightmare on Elm Street* had gone over the last ten years and that had been instrumental in me not wanting to participate, not just creatively but business-wise, with New Line,' says Craven of the meeting late in 1992 that sparked off the *New Nightmare*. 'There followed about a good hour's very frank discussion between him and me... and I'll just leave it at that.'

These detailed discussions resulted in the business side of the Freddy Krueger empire being resolved once and for all, to Craven's evident satisfaction: '[Shaye] listened carefully and in the subsequent month made good on all the things that I felt had been left unattended, so that was the first half of why I came back [to work for

Opposite: Star quality — Eddie Murphy convinced Craven to direct Vampire in Brooklyn. *Left: Heather Langenkamp and Miko Hughes watch* A Nightmare on Elm Street *in* Wes Craven's New Nightmare.

New Line]. There were significant payments and the beginning of a very uniform and predictable accounting of profits and so forth. Then he asked me if I'd be interested in bringing Freddy back again, one more time. This is included in the movie — I say, "I thought you'd killed Freddy off", and he says, "Yes, but we fear we may have killed him off too soon".'

It was the one thing Craven had more or less ruled out — another tussle with Freddy Krueger. This time, though, he was determined it would be different. Craven was now in a position to retain creative control of the project and to revive Freddy again on his own terms and in a totally unique way: 'I always felt that under wonderful

Below: A decade after A Nightmare on Elm Street, *John Saxon and Heather Langenkamp are reunited to face a real-life evil.*

circumstances I'd love to get my hands on the franchise one more time. When I realised it would be the tenth anniversary and the seventh film, it was attractive to come back from a position of strength and do it. So, we agreed — that's Bob Shaye, Sara Risher, Mike DeLuca, the creative heads of New Line and myself and my producer Marianne Maddalena — that unless we could bring back Freddy in a way that wasn't farcical, like saying it was all just a nightmare, just a dream and Freddy isn't really dead, we wouldn't do it. If we couldn't do it in some way that was justified, then we wouldn't do it at all.'

Craven had an idea lurking at the back of his mind after seeing Robert Altman's Hollywood satire *The Player*, in which various movie stars appear playing themselves. Central to his concept was securing the return of Heather Langenkamp to the *Elm Street* fold for a third time: 'I decided that if I were to do it, I would want Heather to star in it. I felt for me she epitomised the spirit of *A Nightmare on Elm Street*. I called her up and we hadn't seen each other for some years, so we had lunch and discussed how our lives had gone, we talked about New Line Cinema and everything else.'

Since *A Nightmare on Elm Street*, Langenkamp had been stalked by an obsessive fan over several years. She'd gone on to star in a cult TV series called *Just the Ten of Us*, but the harassment had continued. 'There were letters and phone calls,' Langenkamp remembered. 'You never know what a sick mind is going to focus on.'

As Craven heard about Langenkamp's own experience, he saw a way to bring Freddy back in a more realistic and even more frightening mode than before. 'There were a few incidents, especially one that had come out of Heather having made the first film and having gone on and done a television series,' says Craven of his star's real-life fears. 'The attendant fame had caused her some real difficulties and frightening moments. So, I left that meeting thinking I would love to work with Heather, who looked terrific and was very bright and enthusiastic about doing the picture. I realised that things that happened in real life were just as dramatic as things that happened in fiction, especially the whole dramatic environment surrounding *A Nightmare on Elm Street.*'

As before, the final ingredient that allowed Craven's ideas to fall into place came from a dream, a trusted source of creative inspiration: 'I had a dream, as happens quite often in my work. The dream was that Freddy and a whole bunch of us from New Line were at a cocktail party. Robert Englund was there in costume, acting like the burlesque Freddy that I felt he had become, and I felt in the dream that in the background was a shadowy figure that was moving parallel to Robert — his own darker shadow, completely apart from that party and it felt very frightening. I awoke with that and was trying to puzzle out what this dream might mean, when it occurred to me that when I first wrote *A Nightmare on Elm Street* I was trying to account for something in human nature, in the human race, that had been here since day one and went all the way back to Cain and Abel, one half of humanity rising up to club the other, running right up to events in the world today.'

Craven's dreams of a shadowy Freddy figure and a growing desire to comment on both the nature of film and fear itself formed the basis of Craven's *New Nightmare*: 'If there were a series that I had begun around this character [Freddy], and that series was to stop production, that wouldn't mean that this eternal evil being or entity would be stopped — it would simply be out there without a name. At the same time, there was this whole view of horror films, questions about whether horror films harmed children. My conclusion was that, as I never felt these things were harmful, the good that they do and why they are so popular is that they somehow give shape and form and name to this unknowable, very frightening and very destructive thing. They somehow contain it, not to the extent that they stop it, but to the extent that they make it

a bit more bearable. So, Freddy, by being in the series of movies, captures a bit of the evil and makes it knowable to us.'

Craven set out with an audacious ambition — to reduce the series of six New Line Freddy movies to mere fodder for his own final Freddy film set in the real world of horror movie making: 'The simple way to put it is, what if New Line stopped making the *Nightmare* series and unintentionally released the spirit of Freddy to go where he will, and he decides to cross over into our reality. His only limitation is that he

Above: *Robert Englund as himself in* Wes Craven's New Nightmare.

Above: Surprise entrance — Robert Englund as Freddy Krueger on a TV chat show.

must pass through the actress who played the character who first defeated him. I proposed that to New Line and they went for it surprisingly quickly, so I began writing.'

Setting his film in the real production offices of New Line and the sound stages on which the *Nightmare* films had been made, Craven had an ideal opportunity to take a swipe not only at New Line and some of the personalities involved in the Freddy saga, but at other industry targets. Key in his sights was the Motion Picture Association of America, the censors who had tampered with so much of Craven's work: 'It was an opportunity for many things. There is a lot of humour in the film and skewering of various people. There is a strong treatment of the "Do horror films harm or help children [debate]". There is a central figure called Dr Heffner, which

was the name of the guy who headed the MPAA, and her feeling is that horror films are definitely injurious to children. Heather's child [Miko Hughes] in the film goes through what appears to be a nervous breakdown, which the Dr Heffner character blames on him having seen Heather's films and having a mother who has acted in these films. Of course, it's really a result of being assaulted in his dreams by Freddy.'

Craven also took care to make his new film follow on quite closely from his original Elm Street excursion. In the first movie there is much talk of earthquakes being connected to the Freddy character and it was a theme Craven picked up with a vengeance: 'The film did have an eerie life of its own. We had a theme of earthquakes in the film being antecedents to the appearance of Freddy and this was long before the quake in LA. We filmed all of our major earthquake scenes and cut them together and we're looking at them, thinking "We've gone a bit extreme here", with things falling down in the house. We'd never had an earthquake like that in Los Angeles. Needless to say, shortly afterwards the historic earthquake [17 January 1994, 6.8 on the Richter scale] struck Los Angeles, and we were amazed by how accurate it was. We also had the problem of where to shoot the aftermath of the earthquake, and suddenly we were sending the second unit out to film just about anywhere and we got all this remarkable footage of Heather driving by actual collapsed freeways and so forth. It was really spooky.'

Creatively, Craven knew he was taking a gamble. Could he successfully resurrect Freddy after failing to create a Freddy-type villain in Horace Pinker? Could he convince an audience to follow him and his actors on this remarkable journey beyond 'the fourth wall'? Craven was setting out to shatter his audience's suspended disbelief by bringing Freddy into the 'real world' of the production of the *Nightmare* movies. As ever, Craven felt he knew his audience: 'I thought that the smartest and most interesting thing for me to do would be to try and address an audience that might have been fifteen or eighteen at the time of the first film, and now it's ten years later, so they might well have children. I decided to do a film about people who have a young child, rather than about teenagers worrying about whether they're coming home too late. I was interested in doing a film for more mature audiences, so the challenge was to do a film that both audiences would like.'

Production commenced in November 1993 in Los Angeles, shooting in New Line Cinema's real-life offices on Robertson Boulevard. Craven set himself and his fellow executives a challenging task — to play themselves convincingly on screen.

Craven had acted before, following up his appearance in an episode of *The Twilight Zone* and a quick cameo at the end of *Shocker* with

another cameo in John Carpenter's horror compendium *Body Bags*. 'It was kinda fun,' says Craven of his turn in the Carpenter-directed segment 'The Gas Station'. 'I played a complete drunken lecher, which proved surprisingly easy. I'd never turn down a job — it's a lot easier than directing, that's for sure!' After *New Nightmare*, Craven would play Dr Arnold, a professor, in Vincent Robert's *The Fear*, and a counsellor in Stephen William's TV movie *Shadow Zone: The Undead Express*. He later popped up briefly in *Scream* as Fred, the irascible janitor, wearing an

Below: Evil never dies — Freddy claws his way into the real world.

Above: New Nightmare, *new costume — the revamped make-up and glove.*

oddly familiar hat and red and green striped jumper. However, Craven doesn't have any plans to appear in front of the camera more permanently: 'Maybe sometime in the future when it's appropriate. I don't want to become a Quentin Tarantino and wear out my welcome.'

Craven, at least, was used to acting, but the question was whether New Line Cinema boss Robert Shaye could pull it off. 'After his scenes were done he was immediately talking about re-shoots, because he thought he was terrible,' laughs Craven. 'In fact, he was quite good. Everybody came back to play themselves because

it's pretty much about all our lives. It worked within the context of the film, but I don't really think of myself as much of an actor.' Returning from the original film were actors John Saxon, Nick Corri and Tuesday Knight, and playing themselves alongside Craven and Shaye were Marianne Maddalena, Sara Risher and Mike DeLuca. Also billed as playing 'himself' was one Freddy Krueger.

Bringing Freddy back after announcing so publicly and finally that the character was dead was a big risk for Craven and New Line, but they felt the new storyline justified it. 'Nobody could imagine how we could do one more Freddy,' admitted Craven at the time. 'It's a different Freddy, we've redesigned him, so you don't have the feeling that this is the same old Freddy. We have Robert Englund doing a press appearance in his old costume, and afterwards you feel the presence of the new Freddy behind the old. It addresses a lot of things, both positive and negative, about our business, about critics.'

No one could play this new Freddy except Robert Englund, but when he first heard about his character's return from the grave, he was sceptical about how he'd explain to fans of the series that he was back again. 'People will think we lied to them,' he worried. 'I can understand how they might have been disappointed by the idea of another one, but Freddy is darker, bigger and stronger. He's broken out of the constraints of the previous movies.' Englund had to approach the role of Freddy with a fresh eye, and not simply rehash the vaudeville act he'd developed during the *Nightmare* sequels: 'Wes' script didn't allow for the expected Freddy stuff, so I found myself having to do an about-face in terms of playing him in a more pronounced, evil way.'

Also returning from the first film was David Miller, glad to have another chance to revise his original Freddy make-up for this new, darker character. 'Everybody wanted something different,' he told *Fangoria*. 'It was to be a new look, but one that still looked like Freddy. What I came up with was something a bit meaner looking. The make-up has more of a splitting skin rather than burned look, basically a streamlined design.' Miller regarded his new Freddy make-up to be the definitive version and a vast improvement on those he'd applied for the fifth and sixth entries in the series: 'For those films I had to basically stick with the commercial-style Freddy, which had moved a long way from the original concept, so it was very rewarding to design a new Freddy who was more intimidating. It was also great working with Wes again, because he really knows how to work with the character and make Freddy far scarier than a guy in rubber make-up.'

Returning to Elm Street allowed Craven to echo some of the more famous moments of his original, but with more up-to-date effects technology, so the revolving room scene made a reappearance, along with a modified phone-tongue and a spooky boiler room. The Freddy glove was also revised and became more of Freddy's hand rather than the home-made version seen in the original. Craven was keen to use less optical effects than the previous *Nightmare* movies and return to more traditional, in-camera special effects, but that didn't stop him giving in to the temptation to create his own version of the traditional Freddy climax: 'At the end Heather falls a mile down in "Freddy Hell", which was a very advanced digital matte painting combination shot.'

For production designer Cynthia Charette, 'Freddy Hell' was a creative challenge. 'We started by studying the history of hell through such works as Dante's *Inferno* and the writings of the Roman poet Virgil, among others,' she explains. 'We found a parallel in each ancient civilisation that was represented by entering hell through an opening and landing in water.' So, Heather Langenkamp slides down a ramp through a twenty foot tall carving of an open-mouthed Freddy and lands in a Greco-Roman pool. There were a few familiar items scattered about "Freddy Hell",

which had seven entrances, this being the seventh film in the series. 'In what we called the river Styx room,' points out Charette, 'familiar icons that we have seen in earlier *Nightmare* films were cast about, as if in a sewer, reminding us of the evil Freddy had visited upon the children of previous movies.'

Special effects were also used in scenes that were intended to be more realistic than fantastic: 'There was a sequence where Miko Hughes is wanting to get home and must cross this freeway,' recalls Craven. 'He closes his eyes and simply walks across eight lanes of traffic. Obviously

Above: *Bloody Hell — Heather Langenkamp tries to follow the* New Nightmare *script.*

Above: An impressive feature film début — Miko Hughes in Freddy Hell.

imposing the structure of the first film on her, until she finally yields to playing that character in the last act.' Playing herself as well as Nancy gave Heather Langenkamp pause for thought as she committed to Craven's *New Nightmare*. It's unlikely that she would have returned to Elm Street if Wes Craven hadn't been behind the camera. 'It was hard enough before, living with the fact that my name would always be associated with the character I played in the *Nightmare* films,' she told *Imagi-Movies*. 'Now, I'm having to handle the fact that my real name will always be up there on the screen as well. In a way, I've sacrificed my name for these films. It's scary for me, and I'm still trying to deal with that.'

Craven set out in his *New Nightmare* to make the film much more 'real' than the previous sequels. Aware that fans of the Freddy movies had become discontented with the direction they'd taken, and frustrated that he'd lost control of the series after his script contribution for *Dream Warriors*, Craven put characters and story before special effects: 'I've found talking to the fans that they think the *Nightmare* series was just more of the same, with Freddy getting sillier and sillier. I have nothing against special effects *per se* — usually I can't afford them! My real wish in any film is that the characters are important and the plot important, not contrived as a result of a committee or a director and a bunch of special effects people saying, "OK, what razzle-dazzle effects can we do". It should come out of their hearts and souls. This certainly did with me — it's very much about my own life and the lives of people I know. That engages an audience at a level that does not cost a lot of money.'

Craven had a larger than normal budget for the forty-eight day shoot, and even found that New Line were so keen to bring Freddy back properly they were willing to release additional funds when needed: 'We punched up the ending a little, after the previews. New Line were enthusiastic enough to put a little more money into it. We actually came in on budget and on schedule,

we couldn't do that for real. That was quite an extraordinary special effects sequence, but it's not something you look at and say, "Oh, those are special effects". It looks real, and my filmmaking philosophy has always been that actual practical effects, things done physically, are always stronger.

'The idea is that Heather must play Nancy one last time in order to capture Freddy,' continues Craven, 'and she's resisting this. Freddy keeps which is quite unusual.' During the pre-publicity for genre magazines like *Fangoria* and *Cinefantastique*, Craven put his showman's hat on, playing up rumours of a haunted shoot, scary nightmares and tales of things going bump on soundstages. Nothing could have been further from the truth. 'The shoot in general had a great spirit,' he confirms. 'The crew was very, very excited about it. We had an editor, Patrick Lussier, who had worked with me on *Nightmare Cafe* in Canada, but had never cut a feature before. We strongarmed New Line into letting us use him, and he was so good and so fast that we had almost always had fully cut scenes, with sound effects and music, about two days after we'd shot a scene. We were cutting on Lightworks [a digital editing system now common in Hollywood]. I would come in a day or two after shooting a sequence and call the crew together before that day's shooting and play for them a two or five minute scene which was exactly what we'd been working on a few days before. There

was a tremendous sense of knowing how the film was progressing, which I've never had on another picture.'

The end of the shooting schedule was a memorable time for several of the key people who'd been involved in the original *Nightmare* ten years before. 'The night we wrapped was extremely emotional,' remembered Langenkamp. 'There was not a dry eye on the set. This was a kind of ten year reunion with a lot of the same people. And to see people grow and change — some people had kids, some had got married — was really nice.' Craven agreed that, despite himself, he was caught up in the moment: 'I never cry at the end of films, but she [Langenkamp] had me in tears. On her last shot, she just thanked everybody so beautifully and spoke so warmly about how vulnerable she had been and how she had done something very important for herself.'

The last thing to be settled on was the title, with Craven at various times subtitling *A Nightmare on Elm Street* 7 with *The Real Story* or

Below: *Déjà vu — some things never change for Heather Langenkamp.*

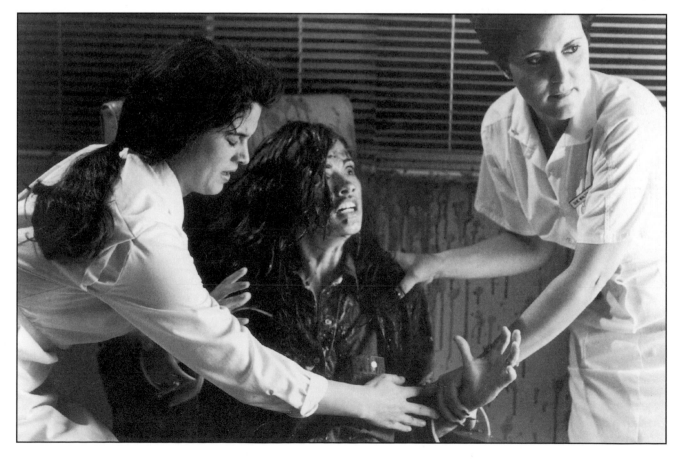

From the creator of
"A Nightmare on Elm Street."

WES CRAVEN'S
NEW NIGHTMARE
This Time The Terror Doesn't Stop At The Screen.

OCTOBER 1994

The Ascension. 'New Line were rather shy of using the number,' claims Craven, 'because they think if you have a high number on a sequel everybody goes, "Oh, it's the seventh, why go to see it?".' Putting Craven's name in the title was thought to give the new movie a connection to the series source material, making it clear that this was a Freddy feature from his original creator, yet offering something 'new' in the *Nightmare* mix.

Released on 7 October 1994 in the United States, *Wes Craven's New Nightmare* was the director's biggest critical hit to that date. The reviews

in the daily trade papers that Craven and his team working on *Vampire in Brooklyn* received were unanimous. 'An ingeniously conceived and devilishly clever opus,' was how *Daily Variety* described his latest venture to Elm Street. Rather than a horror movie, *Variety* saw *New Nightmare* as an 'amusingly self-referential thriller' which should 'earn some admiring reviews'. Reviewer Joe Laydon added: 'When he isn't playing fast and loose with what's real and what isn't, Craven drops a few intriguing hints that he's had mixed feelings about the influence of his and other people's horror pix.'

The Hollywood Reporter dubbed *Wes Craven's New Nightmare* 'a sly and imaginative look back both into the *Nightmare* phenomenon and the nature of horror films' making for 'cannily engaging entertainment with some cheeky insights into the Freddy phenomenon.' In an unusually good review for a horror film, they called it 'both intelligent and generically grounded.'

After putting so much effort into making *Wes Craven's New Nightmare* and receiving rave reviews, the film earned rather lukewarm box office receipts. It just scraped past the $18 million mark in the United States, making it the lowest grossing of the *Nightmare* films. 'I admit there was something of a risk in not featuring Robert [as Freddy] as much as some may have wanted,' says Craven. 'I wasn't real sure about the ad campaign, but I was happy that the film received some of the best reviews I've ever gotten.'

He'd said it before, but this time Wes Craven felt he really was finished with Freddy, although it might not be the end of the road for the character: 'Unfortunately, I don't think this will be the end of Freddy. I think it's my final word, but I hear New Line is talking about bringing Jason [from the *Friday the 13th* series] in with Freddy, and I've been around New Line enough to know that they're actively pursuing it.' In fact, the 'Jason vs Freddy' concept had been mooted at New Line after the third *Nightmare* movie. New Line distributed *Jason Goes to Hell: The Final Friday* and held the rights to both characters. The comic coda of *The Final Friday* showed Jason's discarded hockey mask being retrieved by a familiar razor-fingered gloved hand. Mike DeLuca even asked Craven if he wanted to helm such a picture: 'I've talked to Wes about it. He has other things on his plate. Of course, [he was] the first person I solicited for any interest or ideas.' However, several draft scripts later, Freddy's return still seems mired in development hell.

Even before the critical success of his *New Nightmare* was assured, Craven had taken on a new project: '*Vampire in Brooklyn* was supposed to be a horror-comedy with Eddie Murphy.' Murphy, whose career was in something of a slump at the time, wanted to make a horror movie rather than his more traditional comedy. To that end, he approached Craven, the man who'd made *The Serpent and the Rainbow*, one of Murphy's favourite films. There were several big attractions for Craven. It was to be a studio film,

something he hadn't really done since the disappointing experience of *Deadly Friend*. Craven was keen to do a comedy, and he rarely got the chance to work with big Hollywood stars, so saw the Eddie Murphy vehicle as a way of broadening his range. It was a mistake waiting to happen — the wrong film made at the wrong time, for all the right reasons.

'It came from something that Eddie and his brother Charlie had written and developed and they brought me in,' remembers Craven. 'It turned out that Eddie and his brothers were all big fans of *The Serpent and the Rainbow*. They interviewed me and I guess they liked what they heard. Eddie wanted it to be an Eddie Murphy-Wes Craven film, a collaboration between the two of us. Eddie would recite whole chunks of dialogue from *The Serpent and the Rainbow* and *The Hills Have Eyes* — it was hilarious. It's a very comedic script, which was one of the things that really attracted me to it. I wanted to do some-

Left: Wes Craven directing Eddie Murphy in Vampire in Brooklyn.

*Right: Craven
with Eddie
Murphy in full
make-up as
Maximillian,
the last true
vampire.*
*Below: Craven
with (l-r) John
Witherspoon,
Kadeem
Hardison, Zakes
Mokae and
Allen Payne
filming* Vampire
in Brooklyn.

thing a little bit away from simply scaring people. For Eddie, it was just the opposite: he wanted to do something that was scary. We combined our talents in two different fields and came up with this collaboration.' It was a misguided alliance. Each party pursued a different agenda, resulting in a confused and disappointing horror-comedy outing which, considering Murphy's star power, ultimately failed at the box office.

All things considered, Craven was happy to take on the direction of *Vampire in Brooklyn*. 'I would have been foolish to deny that it was a step up in terms of the profile of actor I work with, although it's not something I would have pursued of and for itself,' he says. 'Stars can give you a certain leverage in the making of a film, and people take you a little bit more seriously, which in turn brings better funding and more control over the project.'

A mounting series of problems served to derail the film, from script rewrites, a rushed production schedule and the opinions of the star and director to troubles with the make-up and budget. *Vampire in Brooklyn* turned into an exer-

Left: Wes Craven, Angela Bassett and Eddie Murphy on the set.

cise in lateral thinking rather than a creative process. The first step taken by Craven and producer Maddalena was to rework Charlie Murphy's screenplay. As the script was being rewritten, Eddie Murphy's third *Beverly Hills Cop* movie opened to scathing reviews and poor box office. 'It had become sort of open season on Eddie,' notes Craven. '*Beverly Hills Cop 3* really hurt him, but in a sense the failure of that film may have actually helped Eddie, because it made him more secure in his own mind that it was time to do something different.'

The search for 'something different' on *Vampire in Brooklyn* was to be the film's downfall. 'We did some re-writing of the script with two writers we brought in,' remembers Craven. 'Chris Parker and Michael Lucker were brought in to unify it a bit more, to make it make a bit more sense.' It was only when neophyte writers Parker and Lucker set to work that they realised that the two Murphy brothers, Craven and the studio executives at Paramount were all keen to influence the final screenplay. 'This was our first produced script,' Parker explained to *Fangoria*, 'and we didn't want it to be the only Eddie Murphy movie that had no humour. Once we'd started, we'd get these notes. Paramount wanted funny, funny, funny. Eddie wanted a change for himself. Everybody wanted something.'

Eddie Murphy had come up with the idea of doing a black vampire film in the tradition of the 1972 cult classic *Blacula* and its sequel *Scream, Blacula, Scream!* The script, based only on the title *Vampire in Brooklyn*, was begun by Murphy's

Above: The Vampire in Brooklyn shoot was complicated by input from studio, star and director, all of whom were looking for different things.

brother Charlie and his cousin Vernon Lynch. The first draft was straightforward horror, lacking any of Murphy's usual comedy material. A deal was done with Paramount, which had just dropped its *Friday the 13th* series, and was keen to develop a new horror film for the Halloween slot. Having Eddie Murphy attached to the script was a sure thing as far as the studio suits were concerned. They saw only one problem — the script wasn't funny. By February 1994, Parker and Lucker were on board with orders to 'make it funny'. 'Paramount made it very clear they wanted Eddie to be funny,' confirmed Parker.

They were about to start work when they were asked to go to New York to meet the star. Eddie Murphy made his case plain to the writers. He wanted to play a villainous character and star in a movie with more scares than laughs, almost directly contradicting what Paramount wanted. Adding

a vampire love interest and a male cop as a romantic rival, Parker and Lucker set out to put their own stamp on the film. Their script draft did the rounds of Craven, the Murphy camp and the studio heads, to general acclaim. There was no doubt that it was a vast improvement on Charlie Murphy's first effort, but all the interested parties just could not be satisfied. 'Paramount wanted funny, Eddie wanted edge. He felt he had to show the audience something they hadn't seen from him before,' Lucker told *Fangoria*. Parker found the process frustrating, despite enjoying the opportunity to work with a director whose work he admired: 'Wes is very knowledgeable about what frightens people and was invaluable in the process, but we'd finish a draft and Paramount would come back with a note that said they wanted it funnier. Once Eddie made it clear he liked what we were doing, that made it easier for Paramount to accept certain things.' For Lucker the toughest thing was 'balancing all the requests. We were being hit by a lot of experienced, smart opinions and we had to make them all go together.'

Craven was happy with the script as he prepared to shoot it. 'It has a very nice love story in it and a lot of action,' he said of the elements added by Parker and Lucker. 'It's the story of a vampire from the Bermuda Triangle. Eddie plays Max, the last of a tribe of vampires. He is seeking a young woman who he knows had a vampire for a father. In the lore of these vampires, this is a person who can be converted over to a full, intelligent vampire, as opposed to somebody who gets bitten and turns into a zombie vampire. He knows she's in this strange place called "Brooklyn". He comes crashing in and discovers to his dismay that Rita (Angela Bassett) is a rookie cop and her partner, Warren Justice (Allen Payne), is in love with her. It's sort of a love story triangle between these three people. Rita doesn't know she has anything vampire in her, but she believes in the supernatural, although her partner is the most straight, by the book guy you can imagine.' Rounding out the cast were several familiar faces from Craven's previous work, including Nick Corri (*A Nightmare on Elm Street*), Zakes Mokae (*The Serpent and the Rainbow*), Mitch Pileggi (*Shocker*) and Wendy Robie (*The People Under the Stairs*).

Craven declared a mutual admiration between director and star: 'Eddie felt he was doing something in a genre he was not used to, and he told me several times, "This is your genre. You know what works here". Eddie is playing the vampire very straight. It's not like a goofy vampire at all. He wants it to be tense and scary.'

With a fifty-five day shooting schedule, Craven only spent three days on location in Brooklyn, with the rest of the New York scenes recreated on Paramount's back lot or the streets of Los Angeles. The remainder of the time was actually spent working on tiring and dispiriting night shoots, often in cold and damp conditions. The budget limited what Craven could do.

'In comparison to other films I've done, it was a pretty good bank-roll,' he admits, but there were costs associated with a star-driven studio picture. 'Obviously, when you're shooting an Eddie Murphy picture you're not going to use a non-union crew.'

Working on a studio film again meant Craven had to hone his diplomatic skills, especially when production delays mounted due to problems with Murphy's vampire make-up. Howard Berger, of the KNB effects house who had worked with Craven on *The People Under the Stairs* and *New Nightmare*, saw the director in action. 'Everybody was a little tense,' he said, when it

Below: Craven at work on set, as Angela Bassett prepares to awaken.

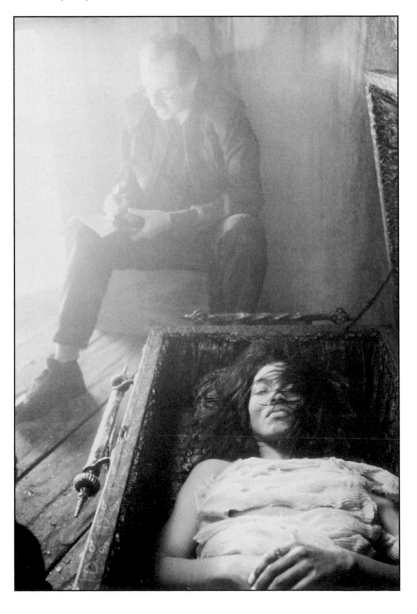

became evident that the make-ups would have to be used without being tested before filming, due to the tight schedule. 'It sort of tortured Wes, y'know. Wes had to play the studio game a little bit.' As well as playing the vampire in various different make-ups, Murphy also played an assortment of other characters which required extensive cosmetic applications.

The opening harbour collision sequence was one of the more elaborate challenges for Craven. Using ships obtained from the Coast Guard, who confiscate vessels used in crime, Craven orchestrated 'some precision driving and crashing. It was done by having a pilot on the ship and a tugboat lashed to it on the side away from the camera guiding it. The tug and ship captains were in constant contact. It was amazing how we were able to get that ship to hit its marks.'

Tragedy struck the production on 3 November 1994 with the death of thirty-two year-old

stuntwoman Sonja Davis, regular stunt double for actress Angela Bassett. Taken to hospital following a fall that went wrong, she died eleven days later of massive head injuries.

The accident appalled Craven and Maddalena. 'All I can say is it was a very sad time for all of us,' Maddalena declared. 'It was horrendous. It's probably one of the worst things I've personally ever been through.'

Production on *Vampire in Brooklyn* carried on after the accident, wrapping in January 1995. It opened to mixed reviews, many attacking Murphy for not being funny enough and Craven for not being frightening enough. Neither star nor director could win. The film grossed $20 million in America — fine for a Craven film, but a severe disappointment to Paramount Pictures, who were expecting an Eddie Murphy blockbuster.

Roger Ebert, of the *Chicago Sun-Times*, said *Vampire in Brooklyn* suffered from 'an amateur-

Below: Craven works on a scene with Eddie Murphy in one of several character make-ups as Preacher Pauly.

night screenplay stapled together from a story by himself and his brothers... contains scenes that I think are supposed to be funny'. *Entertainment Weekly* said the film contained 'lame gags. Its one lingering image is that of Eddie Murphy trying, and failing, to rise from the dead.' For *USA Today* the film was an 'anaemic horror show', while the *San Francisco Chronicle* agreed, calling the film 'muddled in its mix of horror and comedy genres.'

'I happen to think it's a pretty good film,' says Craven. 'I'm not ashamed of it. I think the timing of it was not good, in that Eddie Murphy was so under attack and expected to be funny or else. Eddie, on that film, just wanted to be the opposite. He wanted to play a dark character, not for laughs, to be scary and evil. And, of course,

Paramount wanted it to be funny, so you end up with this thing that's neither fish nor fowl.'

In response to *Vampire in Brooklyn*'s poor reception, Craven was even more determined to pursue his goal of a move to the mainstream: 'Frankly, I'm sick of doing films that get released at weird times of the year. I would like a summer release or a Christmas release. You get an audience at those times of the year that's going to look for intelligence and a good story. Who knows? I may end up getting rediscovered.' A rediscovered Wes Craven releasing an intelligent film with a good story at Christmas? Who would have thought that little over a year later he would be making American audiences *Scream* to the tune of $100 million at the box office. ∎

Above: Craven directs Angela Bassett as Rita and Eddie Murphy as Guido in the restaurant scene from Vampire in Brooklyn.

Someone has taken their love of *sequels* one step too far.

SCREAM 2

DAVID ARQUETTE   NEVE CAMPBELL   COURTENEY COX   SARAH MICHELLE GELLAR   JAMIE KENNEDY   JERRY O'CONNELL   JADA PINKETT   LIEV SCHREIBER

THE NEW THRILLER FROM WES CRAVEN

DECEMBER 12 IN THEATERS EVERYWHERE

Scream & Scream Again

Before Craven came across Kevin Williamson's script *Scary Movie*, which later became *Scream*, he had a variety of potential projects in development. One of these saw 'Wes Craven' used as a horror brand name, attached to the title of *Mind Ripper*, a film produced by his son, Jonathan.

Broadcast on HBO in October 1995 and released on video outside the United States, *Mind Ripper* began life as a potential third *The Hills Have Eyes* film. Jonathan had cut his producing teeth on his father's TV show *Nightmare Cafe* and had the *Mind Ripper* screenplay in development for several years, originally under the title *The Hills Have Eyes 3*. That was changed to *The Outpost* when shooting began in Bulgaria in autumn 1994, and became *Mind Ripper* for release outside America.

'It's not called *The Hills Have Eyes 3*, and the story has very little to do with *The Hills Have Eyes* films,' explained Craven as *Mind Ripper* was in production and he was preparing to work with Eddie Murphy on *Vampire in Brooklyn*. 'My son's producing it and it's being shot in Bulgaria and produced by Kushner-Locke, an LA outfit, half of which is Peter Locke, who was my partner on *The Hills Have Eyes*. I just talked to my son yesterday who said that they are one day behind schedule, halfway through shooting and he's exhausted! It's an interesting story about a government installation in the middle of the desert, where people are doing biological experiments on what could easily be a member of the *Hills* wild family, but nobody felt there was a real strong franchise there.'

Locke, who owns the rights to the *The Hills Have Eyes* titles, and Craven agreed that the likelihood of developing a successful franchise on the back of the first two films so many years after their initial release was remote. With the second film's commercial failure the concept seemed dead, although Craven had often toyed with his own idea for a third movie set on an alien planet and featuring a different strain of mutant: 'After what happened to *The Hills Have Eyes Part II*, I felt like I owed it to the fans of the series to end it on an up note.' That desire led to a screenplay, co-written by Craven and his *Dream Warriors* collaborator Bruce Wagner, which relocated the *Hills* series to a hostile planet in outer space: 'That script had Earth researchers running afoul of a new kind of mutant.' Passing the idea on to Jonathan, Craven and Locke were happy to let him take the basic concept in a new direction.

Opposite: Scream *again* — *Wes Craven was happy to return to the* Scream *franchise.* **Below:** *Director Joe Gayton, star Dan Blom and producer Jonathan Craven on the set of* Mind Ripper.

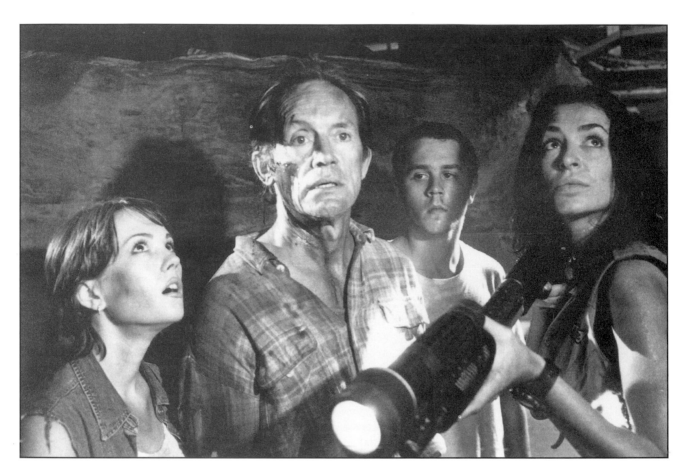

Above: *Lance Henriksen heads the cast of 'monster-on-the-loose' thriller* Mind Ripper.

Director Joe Gayton cast Lance Henriksen (*Aliens*, *Millennium*) as the creator of a superhuman soldier who has to feed on human brains to survive. Rounding out the cast were Claire Stansfield, John Diehl and Natalie Wood's daughter Natasha Wagner. The biological killing machine of the title was played by Swedish actor Dan Blom.

Filming in Bulgaria was an inexpensive option compared to building sets and shooting in Hollywood, but it led to a series of production problems. 'We did end up in some unimaginably horrific places, like the atomic centre where Jonathan had to take a Geiger counter through every day before we went in, to check the radiation levels were safe,' Gayton told *The Dark Side*. 'Frankly, after the first two days I was ready to leave. I wanted to quit. I didn't think it was ever going to work. Then something kicked in on the third day. I think the multi-national crew started becoming enthusi-

astic and getting pride in what they were doing.'

For Gayton, the premise of *Mind Ripper* was simple, and he tried to keep the gore to a minimum. 'It's a classic haunted house movie,' he claimed. 'A group of people are trapped in a confined space with something they created stalking them.'

Craven encouraged his son's producing endeavours, and the finished product clearly reminded him of some of his own low budget efforts: 'It turned out pretty well for a first film on a limited budget shot in a hellish place. I mean, you try and make Bulgaria look like the United States!'

In the hiatus between *Vampire in Brooklyn* and the phenomenal, unexpected success of *Scream*, Craven was developing a series of potential projects. *Original Sin*, a sexual thriller with a screenplay by Joe Eszterhas, was one option, but Craven was probably wise to leave this one on the shelf. Around the same time, Craven teamed up with Malcolm McDowell for an unrealised project called *The Monster Butler*, based on a book about an actual case of a con man who impersonated a butler, then became a thief and a murderer.

Keen on animals and wildlife, Craven had never had a chance to reflect this interest on the screen. He hoped *The Cage*, a script drawn from a novel by Audrey Schulman about a woman who joins a perilous all-male expedition to photograph rare polar bears, would allow him to do so, but nothing came of the project.

Although eager to leave horror behind, Craven was contacted by independent producers Miramax with a script from Edithe Swensen (TV's *Tales From the Dark Side* and *Monsters*) for a proposed remake of the classic poltergeist movie *The Haunting*. It came close to production, and Craven was very interested in making the film: 'My take on that film would have been to do something with the same sense of class, but utilising modern tools. Obviously, it would have been a more contemporary view of what is scary, using the psychodynamics between the mother and the daughter which cause the house to resonate with its own haunting. We couldn't find a way to do it

that matched the original approach of not showing anything. That's what it's famous for, but everyone expects to see the monster these days. We came up against the problem of how to keep it scary, but modern.' Miramax let their option on the project lapse, allowing Steven Spielberg's Dreamworks to snap it up. 'They're pursuing it actively with a completely different team,' says Craven. 'Miramax just decided not to renew their option. They were never completely comfortable with any of the drafts, and didn't want to go for a new writer.'

Although *The Haunting* did not go ahead, it had opened doors for Craven at Bob and Harvey Weinstein's Miramax, one of the most powerful mini-studios in Hollywood. Miramax had another script ready to go into production, with no director attached, but one star, Drew Barrymore, already signed on. The screenplay, by novice writer Kevin Williamson, was a self-referential examination of horror films called *Scary Movie*.

Williamson had studied theatre before pursuing a career as an actor in New York. Television opportunities brought him to Los Angeles, where he'd also turned to writing. His inspiration came from the stalk 'n' slash horror movies he grew up watching: 'I can remember seeing the film

Left: *Natasha Wagner in mortal danger.*

Halloween over and over again when I was ten years old. It scared the living hell out of me, not to mention Wes Craven's *A Nightmare on Elm Street*. I was so scared my leg got a cramp and I couldn't leave the theatre when the movie ended.'

In his *Scary Movie* script, Williamson set out to pay tribute to slasher movies and take a retrospective look at the genre. Favourites which he cited as inspirational during the writing of *Scary Movie* included *When a Stranger Calls*, *Prom Night* and *Terror Train*, as well as the films of Wes Craven and John Carpenter. 'I didn't want it to be a horror movie which appealed just to teenage boys,' explained Williamson to *Entertainment Weekly*. 'I wanted it to appeal to everybody, across

Below: Casey Becker (Drew Barrymore) relives Kevin Williamson's house-sitting scare.

the board, the way *Halloween* did. I would play the soundtrack to *Halloween* while I was writing this movie.'

In line with the self-conscious tone of *Wes Craven's New Nightmare*, Williamson intended *Scary Movie* to be populated by teens who had watched the same fright flicks as the writer and were aware of the rules of the game. 'It's really just all these characters talking about horror movies,' he admitted. 'That's what appealed to Hollywood, that's what they saw as different and new.'

Williamson wrote the script in three days. He locked himself in a Palm Springs hotel room and hammered out a story he'd been thinking about for a while: 'I got the idea from watching a Barbara Walters special on the Gainesville murders. I was broke, house-sitting for a friend to pay him back for money he'd lent me for groceries, and I was scaring the hell out of myself. I thought I heard a noise. I walked the house with a butcher knife and a phone and called a friend while I searched the place. We got into this huge discussion, testing each other on horror movies. And that's how *Scream* was born.'

Williamson began to realise that he had not finished his story, and there was much more to be done with his characters. He wrote a synopsis for two proposed follow-up films, attached it to the first screenplay and passed the whole lot over to his agent: 'The sequel was planned before we sold the first one. Along with the script for *Scream*, I submitted a five page treatment for *Scream 2* and *Scream 3*. I was not being ballsy or over-confident. I was just suggesting that, if they bought this script, they would have a possible franchise on their hands.'

Scary Movie was offered up by Williamson's agent in a spec script sale which sparked a bidding war among the Hollywood players, including Universal, Paramount, Morgan Creek and producer/director Oliver Stone. 'At the end of the day it was Bob Weinstein [of Miramax] and Oliver Stone duking it out. Stone offered more money, but I had to ask myself who'd make the better film,' said Williamson.

With a script packed with references to classic horror movies and a hip young star attached, Miramax needed to find the right director. At the same time, Wes Craven had just dropped out of the struggle to remake *The Haunting*. It was the ideal match, a union made in horror movie heaven, but Craven took some convincing: 'I was approached pretty early on. I suspected they thought they could get me one way or another. We were sort of in business developing *The Haunting*, but when Miramax decided to put that into turnaround, they immediately offered me this. I had already turned it down once, but finally I just thought it was really worth it. It was sort of like being shown the script to *Pulp Fiction*. You know in some ways you're going to get into trouble with the MPAA, but you also know that you've got a piece of material that is very unusual in its force and power and wit, and you'd be stupid to pass it up.'

Craven was not wildly enthusiastic about the film before he started shooting, although the screenplay had been re-written since he'd first seen it: 'I had heard about it before and was interested, but I had gone through this struggle of trying to separate myself from the horror genre and here was something with this strong, scary opening sequence. I thought, this is the kind of sequence that you can do and never be forgiven for. The critics will hate it and audiences will be repulsed.' Even after almost thirty years, Craven was haunted by memories of the fierce reaction he'd suffered after making *The Last House on the Left*: 'As it turned out, these were all unfounded fears, of course. When I heard Drew Barrymore was attached, it changed. I had meetings with Kevin Williamson and we found the script was generating its own heat and we were attracting the kind of cast I'd never worked with before. It had a great buzz on it.'

Craven faced a decision. More determined than ever to leave horror behind, he now had the opportunity to revive the slasher movie. He knew

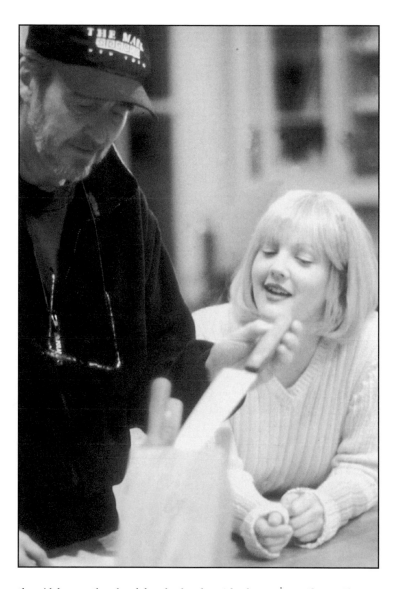

there'd be another hard-fought battle with the MPAA if the script were filmed as written, and he seriously wondered if he still had the stomach to continue to fight the censors who had bedevilled his career. Although the NC-17 rating had been introduced, most of Craven's films were still contracted to be rated R, meaning days, weeks or possibly months of to-ing and fro-ing between the producers and the MPAA to get an acceptable cut.

As he considered the script afresh, Craven decided that he'd be better off making the film rather than leaving it to someone else. 'I make movies about fear,' says Craven, coming to terms

Above: Choose your weapons — Craven directs Drew Barrymore in Scream.

Above: The Scream — Edvard Munch couldn't have anticipated the feature film potential of his original painting. **Right:** Not so friendly — Courteney Cox as Gale Weathers.

with his place as a film-maker. 'Scream confirmed my belief that horror films are great character pieces. They get in deep under the skin of human psychology. Kids today have fears and they need a way to process their terror in a positive and funny manner. Scream accomplished this with scenarios of intense anxiety as well as playfulness.' The possibility of the concept becoming a franchise, depending on the success of the first, was another temptation, and Craven is pleased with his work: 'The style and the humour and the scares are the best of what I've done over the years. It's about kids who are fascinated by horror films, and somebody is killing them off and using the clichés from those kinds of movies. There are scenes in it straight out of that genre, and in that sense it looks like a slasher film, if you want to use that term. But around that is this sort of sophisticated murder mystery dealing with kids in real life. It's much more naturalistic, about lives that are being invaded by this world that they have only looked to for amusement. It's also darkly funny.'

Craven came to savour Scream as a chance to offer a swan song to the genre, but there was one thing he went to great lengths to avoid: 'No dream sequences, nothing like that. I feel after almost thirty years in the genre that I can't just continue to do straight horror films. You don't see all these conventions and clichés without imitating yourself. You have to at least let the audience know that you are aware of it. It's recognised as a cultural phenomenon. It was like a challenge. I was saying to myself, "You know the films you've done, Wes, always sort of broke boundaries and barriers and got you into trouble? This will definitely do that. Are you up to it?" And I just said, "Yeah, let's do it". As Bob Weinstein said to me, "You really kicked ass".'

Relating Williamson's powerful screenplay to his own gritty earlier work gave Craven a way of approaching Scream: 'I felt it had the best of my older films, such as The Last House on the Left, which unflinchingly stays on long moments you can't believe you are watching, and not only that, you can't believe we haven't cut away. At

the same time, it has wit and sophistication that is fascinating.'

Casting proved key to *Scream's* success, and having one-time Hollywood wild-child Drew Barrymore already on board gave Craven a clue as to the direction to take in filling the other teen roles. He wasn't simply looking for 'Freddy fodder' to fall under the knife of *Scream*'s Edvard Munch-masked killer, but high-profile young actors who could bring an extra dimension to the film: 'I've usually tried to find talented actors who haven't really had a big breakthrough. Johnny Depp, I guess, is the classic example, and also [*Shocker*'s] Peter Berg. In this case, I had people who had quite a body of work behind them. They're very skilled actors who brought a lot to the set.'

The casting process saw Craven back up Barrymore, who dominates the opening section of the film, with fashionable faces from success-ful TV series. The leading role of Sidney Prescott went to *Party of Five* star Neve Campbell. Her first significant film role had been as one of the four teen witches in *The Craft*. Courteney Cox, from the hit sitcom *Friends*, landed the role of cynical TV hack Gale Weathers. Skeet Ulrich (who'd also been in *The Craft* with Campbell) played the boyfriend under suspicion, along with David Arquette (brother of Patricia, who starred in *Dream Warriors*), Jamie Kennedy (as Randy, the horror movie geek prime suspect who's full of the rules necessary to survive the film) and Matthew Lillard (as Stuart). 'Matthew Lillard got into it with incredible ferocity,' says Craven of the actor who steals many of his scenes, espe-cially towards the end. 'The actors brought a lot. I had the kind of atmosphere on set where they could improvise or ad lib, and a lot of that we kept in — Matthew, especially, was very free and brought a lot to his role. Skeet Ulrich really nailed his character. I told Neve at the begin-ning, "This is going to be an incredibly physical role and very emotional. You'd better prepare for that". She gave a thousand per cent every day. There was a tremendous amount of running,

fight scenes, falling, climbing over roof tops and a high emotional pitch all the time for some fifty-odd days. They all threw themselves into it with incredible enthusiasm.'

Whatever praise he might have for the screen-play and cast, the ultimate success of *Scream* lay in Craven's hands: 'I think I brought a lot to the film. There were a lot of improvisations and the physical staging of a lot of the scenes, [like] the stuff in the house and in the garage, were very different to the way they'd been scripted. Some other scenes we simply improvised on the spot.'

Pre-production saw Craven and his producers searching the United States and Canada for the perfect disturbingly peaceful town. They finally settled on locations close to home in Sonoma County, Northern California, including the towns of Santa Rosa, Healdsburg and Tomales. The open-ing sequence, where Drew Barrymore is torment-ed by the spooky caller with the in-depth knowl-edge of horror films, was shot in a private resi-dence deep in the mountains of Sonoma with a vineyard in the ten acre grounds. Healdsburg police station stood in for Woodsboro police sta-tion in the movie. An abandoned house in

Above: *It's a scream — Skeet Ulrich, Jamie Kennedy and Matthew Lillard under pressure.*

Tomales provided the ideal location for the final series of night scenes which make up *Scream*'s climax. The 200 acre ranch overlooked the Petaluma Hills and the Cotati Valley and the house was packed with antique furniture purchased locally, with elaborate gothic paintings created by the *Scream* art department hanging on the freshly painted, rust-red walls. As usual on a Craven film, the production team were only too happy to play up rumours that there had really been some mysterious, gruesome deaths in the house.

Craven was very happy with the completed film, but he was also aware that he faced a battle with the MPAA. 'I was ecstatic with the results. It came out just terrifically. We got an incredible response from early press, media and test audiences, so I was very happy with it,' he told *Fangoria*. 'We had to cut some stuff, but not that much. One thing the MPAA said was, "You cannot have any movement [of innards]". We had a shot where guts fall out, but we had to use just the part where they're already out. We had to shorten the shots of people hanging. They objected to moments throughout the film. The worst part was the ending, which is very intense.

The MPAA flatly announced, "You're miles from it. You'll probably never get an R rating". Well, we did, but it took endless screaming and crying and writing letters and paring it back somewhat. None of the test viewers said it was too gory, but the MPAA was just hysterical about it.'

Craven had feared the tussle — not because he thought he'd lose, but because of the time and energy he was required to expend struggling to get his vision past the censors. Again, it caused him to consider making small, quiet movies instead: 'After this episode with the MPAA, I feel like my days are numbered in this genre, because they're just on me. When I do my best work, that's exactly what they want me to cut out of the picture. In a sense, I'm a director who can do something very well, but I am not allowed to put it on screen. Ultimately they get you, like they did on this one, on intensity. That just makes me nuts. The final thing we had to do was submit the soundtrack, and they said the soundtrack was too intense! Too loud, too frightening, too scary. They're getting everybody. I feel I can't make a movie like this any more...

'I think it's been ruined for me. I can see the

Right: Freddy flashback — Neve Campbell and Rose McGowan share a Heather Langenkamp phone experience.

handwriting on the wall. I can't do what I do best. It will not be allowed to get to my audience. It's very frustrating and it feels tragic and wrong and obscene that they do that. But right now, those people are in control and they can tell you if a film goes on or not. It's always been a pain, but it depends on a film's profile. With *Vampire in Brooklyn*, the one where we had a name star, we had no cuts whatsoever, and I believe *The Serpent and the Rainbow* had no cuts. On the other hand, *A Nightmare on Elm Street* had several cuts that really hurt to make, and some, like *Deadly Friend* and *Shocker*, had severe cuts that really disrupted many sections of the films and made a hash of them.'

When *Scream* was screened for the Weinstein brothers, they were so pleased with the result that they were determined to keep Craven on board as part of the Miramax family. He was immediately offered a two picture deal, and gladly accepted, setting only one condition — that Miramax allow him to make a mainstream, non-horror film and give it a decent distribution. The

Weinsteins agreed. They also added a condition of their own, that Craven's next film should be the sequel to *Scream* outlined in Kevin Williamson five page addendum to the first screenplay. Whether the follow-up would go into production largely depended on the success or failure of the first movie in the run up to Christmas 1996 — the coveted holiday spot Craven had previously sought for his films.

'I'm holding my breath,' he said before the film opened. 'It's a very, very competitive time. The stars certainly won't hurt it, but whether their heat will work in this particular season or whether we'll be buried under *Beavis and Butt-head* [*Do America*, released at the same time], who knows?'

The success of *Scream* was slow to build. The film had cost about $14 million, one of Craven's highest budgets, and Miramax were confident of taking at least double that at the box office. It opened well enough, taking $6.3 million over the weekend from 20 December 1996, and instead of falling off, the box office take increased in weeks two and three, taking $9 mil-

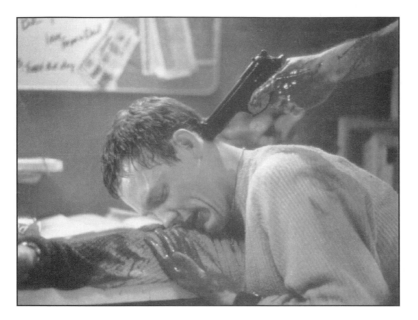

Above: Playing dead — Stuart (Matthew Lillard) takes his love of scary movies too far.

lion and then over $10 million respectively. Great reviews and exceptional word of mouth meant that the film stayed around. As well as drawing a widely-based audience, *Scream* also benefited from much repeat viewing. 'People are coming back three, four, five times,' Miramax co-chairman Bob Weinstein told *The Hollywood Reporter*. 'Some of them know every line in the movie. Normally, it's four weekends and you're gone, but this one stuck around for twenty-six weeks in wide release. It was almost frightening.' Not expecting this kind of success, theatres had not been booked for long runs, so *Scream* briefly disappeared from cinemas before being re-released in April 1997 to even bigger box office success. By early June the film had passed the all-important $100 million mark, making it a horror blockbuster of unprecedented proportions. The film won the MTV Award for Best Film, confirming its cool status, and Neve Campbell was nominated for Best Female Performance.

Success brought its own problems for *Scream*. Sony Studios suddenly decided the film's title was too close to their 1996 SF flop *Screamers*. They appealed to the MPAA, hoping to force Miramax to pay a fee for use of the title, which could amount to thousands of pounds for every

day the film remained in theatres. 'The movies couldn't be more different, so it never made sense,' says Craven. 'This was just part of a power struggle between Disney [Miramax's parent company] and Sony.' Although a court judgement initially went against Miramax, the dispute was later resolved quietly.

That wasn't the end of *Scream*'s troubles, however. Amazed by the film's box office performance, rival studios claimed Miramax were overstating the grosses by up to $20 million. A Miramax spokesperson denied the accusation: 'We're very proud of the success of this movie and we stand by our numbers.' The story came back to haunt the company with a vengeance when they released *Scream 2* a year later.

There were other problems too. The film was banned in Japan after the press linked it to a series of child murders. It was a familiar story to Craven, who was still smarting from the claims of copycat teen suicides made at the time of *Dream Warriors*, and the issue was raised again during the release of *Scream 2*. On the advice of local distributors, Miramax decided not to release *Scream* in Japan following a statement by police linking 'splatter' films with the discovery of the decapitated body of an eleven year-old boy and two further attacks on ten year-old girls. 'No one in Japan has even seen *Scream* yet,' claimed Steve Klane, Miramax's head of international marketing, in spring 1997, 'so there's no way it can be an influence.' Nonetheless Miramax cancelled the June 1997 release to avoid being caught up in the controversy, promising the film would be seen at a later date.

The Japanese embargo was not a worry for Craven. His film had taken enough at the United States box office alone to make it a smash hit, and the biggest earning film in his career: 'We expected $20 to $30 million. That would've been fine. We [Craven and Maddalena] had no experience of a film taking anything over $20 million. It changed the perception of me around town. A lot of people who hire directors don't go to see horror movies, but they did go to see *Scream*. As well as the tension and scares, it showed I could do comedy. I'm now at least regarded as someone who can do thrillers and opinions have changed of my work.' Craven was happy to direct the sequel, hoping for a similar hit and the promised opportunity to direct a mainstream movie for Miramax.

'The Weinsteins want to make movies like *Scream* that redefine the genre and bring the prestige back,' observes Craven. Bob Weinstein saw the company's work with Craven and Williamson as more than simply an investment in talent. 'I always liked how Steven Spielberg, George Lucas and Francis Ford Coppola all hung out together and had their own little family. Now we have our little family. I think *Scream* definitely showed there was an audience that was overlooked for a long time. You just have to get the right cast of young, cutting-edge stars, a soundtrack with exactly the music they want to hear, and make a good movie. It's such an easy formula, right?' said Weinstein, ironically.

When the sequel to *Scream*, called *Scream Again* and *Scream Louder* during production, before becoming just plain *Scream 2*, began shooting in Atlanta on 16 June 1997, the first movie was still playing in cinemas. Miramax wanted to push ahead as fast as possible with the sequel, aiming to release the film in the same Christmas holiday spot one year after the original. It meant a tight schedule for Williamson, Craven and his cast and crew.

Naturally, everyone was nervous about repeating the success of the first film. 'We had the briefest of sketches from Kevin for the other two films,' recalls Craven, 'and we didn't really think beyond the first when shooting it. We all liked the premise and we had a lot of the good continuing cast returning, not just the villain, which is normal in these franchises. We did have worries about repeating the success of the first.'

The survivors of the first film reunited, joined by a new ensemble of rising stars. Screenwriter Kevin Williamson claimed, 'We had people come

in and audition for the film who don't usually audition.' Wes Craven notes, 'Everybody wanted to be in the sequel. We were able to cast bit parts with big stars.' It was quite a change in circumstance for the director who'd had trouble getting actors to sign up for *The Serpent and the Rainbow* a decade before.

Scream 2 became a who's who of potential future stars, including Jada Pinkett, *Sliders'* Jerry O'Connell and TV's *Buffy the Vampire Slayer* Sarah Michelle Gellar (also in Williamson's post-*Scream* hit *I Know What You Did Last Summer*). Even Tori Spelling got in on the act following satirical digs at her expense in the first movie — she really does play the part of Sidney in *Stab*, a movie-within-a-movie based on the events of the first film. 'Most of us [in *Scream 2*] were around fourteen when *Nightmare* came out,' said Jada Pinkett, ruefully. 'That makes Wes, like, a total hero.'

Bottom: Big in Japan — the Scream *press tour comes to the Yubari International Fantastique Festival, with the traditional mashing of the melons.*

Above: Stab in the dark — Jada Pinkett, Scream 2*'s first victim, queueing to see the film-within-a-film, starring Tori Spelling as Sidney.*

The *Scream 2* cast all had to sign legal waivers holding them liable if they were responsible for leaks of sensitive information relating to the screenplay. Realising that a large part of *Scream*'s success came from trying to figure out who was behind the mask, the sequel was filmed under a heavy blanket of security. The only leak came when forty pages of what purported to be the screenplay appeared on the Internet in spring 1997. Craven responded by posting a note on his own website, Wes Craven's World: 'I can tell you that the script, although genuine, is a very early rough draft. Many notable changes were made through the filming. Most notable would be the ending.' To stop the new climax from leaking out, the last ten pages were reportedly printed on dark red paper which could not be photocopied, faxed or scanned, and they weren't even issued to the relevant cast members until the final two days of shooting.

'There has always been a degree of secrecy on my films,' claims Craven. 'It wasn't this bad on the first *Scream*. People thought it was just another horror film, and admittedly we felt we'd be doing well if it made $30 million. Now, all of a sudden, we have a movie that everybody, not just genre people, are interested in. That tends to change things.'

Following the pattern of the first film, *Scream 2* sees a minor star bumped off right at the beginning — this time it's Jada Pinkett, who's at the cinema to see the film *Stab*, drawn from a book, *The Woodsboro Murders*, by TV hack Gale Weathers (Courteney Cox). Two years after *Scream*, Sidney Prescott (Neve Campbell) is a drama student at a midwestern college where horror movie buff Randy (Jamie Kennedy) is studying film, giving Williamson and Craven a great opportunity to discuss the merits or otherwise of most sequels. Cotton Weary (Liev Schreiber, briefly glimpsed in the first movie) has finally been released after his wrongful imprisonment for the murder of Sidney's mother, and may be out for revenge. Deputy Dewey Riley (David Arquette), whose nerves have never fully recovered from events in *Scream*, turns up to protect Sidney... or does he have a darker motivation? 'I could be the killer. Anybody could be the killer. It's that kind of movie,' declared Arquette. Craven and Williamson play games with the audience, gleefully admitting that 'sequels suck' and setting up almost every cast member as a possible suspect, right up to the last few scenes of the movie.

Craven felt the pressure to deliver while making *Scream 2*: 'It has been tougher than the last one. There has been very little time for mistakes and reshoots. We lost a whole day due to damage to the negative in Georgia, and there have been a lot of what I call technical reversals. We've had to go fast, it has been difficult physically and I didn't get much sleep.' The scheduled release date of 12 December loomed large as editing and post-production continued into the autumn.

Craven was keen to downplay *Scream 2*'s status as a sequel, despite tackling those issues head on in the film class discussions featured in the movie: 'This film actually feels more like an element of a trilogy rather than a sequel. We're basically continuing the development of Sidney and the people around her as they face another threat. I'm proud to be a part of this, whereas I wouldn't have been proud to be a part of *A Nightmare on Elm Street 2*.'

On top of the $23 million production budget, *Scream 2* also boasted a marketing spend of between $15 and $20 million, a sure sign of Miramax's faith. Opening on almost 3,000 screens across the United States to rave reviews, the film quickly made a big impression on ticket sales. *Variety* reported an opening weekend box office take of $39.2 million for *Scream 2*, wildly out-stripping even the most optimistic predictions, making the film the biggest non-summer opening ever. The film had taken almost double the highest December opening figure, set the previous year by *Beavis and Butt-head Do America*.

The joy was to be short lived, however. Within days, Miramax admitted to over-estimating the box office by some $6 million. The revised figure had *Scream 2* grossing $32.9 million over the first three day weekend, so *Ace Ventura: Pet Detective* held on to the top spot as the biggest non-summer opening. Miramax blamed the mistake on an over-counting of screens on which the film was

playing — it opened on 2,663 screens instead of the 3,112 initially stated. The confusion didn't harm the film, though, as it reached the $100 million mark by the end of January 1998, far quicker than its predecessor.

Returning from a holiday in Switzerland and Africa to enjoy his success, Craven was shocked to see that the *Scream* films had been connected to a copycat killing in the USA. Gina Castillo of Lynwood, California, was allegedly murdered by her fourteen year-old son and two nephews on 15 January 1998. When arrested, the boys claimed to have been inspired to carry out the killing by *Scream* and *Scream 2*. 'They admitted to homicide investigators that they killed the mother after getting the idea from the movies,' said a sergeant. 'We think the movies are behind it.'

The police claimed that the killers had planned to buy 'grim reaper' style costumes, masks and voice boxes similar to those featured in the *Scream* movies. It is alleged that the boys went ahead with the stabbing even though they could not afford the disguises. A Miramax spokesman said simply that the company was

Left: A wanted man — is Cotton Weary (Liev Schreiber, far right) the killer?

'saddened by the tragic death,' and Wes Craven refused to be drawn into the debate.

Whether Craven will also direct the third *Scream* movie depends on Williamson. 'Kevin Williamson has first refusal on the opportunity to direct number three written into his agreement with Miramax,' says Craven. 'I would be happy to do it and Kevin may decide it would be good to have the original director do all three. It's certainly a fascinating thing to think of, as a film-maker, to do a trilogy. There are very few film-makers that have actually done it. To do it well would be quite an accomplishment.'

Williamson is determined that part three will see the end of his involvement in the franchise: 'I won't be a part of *Scream 4*, *5*, or *6*. I'm done. Three stories and that's the end of it.' Miramax chairman Bob Weinstein might be reluctant to let his new found success come to an end so easily: 'If we ever did get to a *Scream 4* it wouldn't happen for at least three years, and there'd be all new characters and a whole new conception. Right now, though, we all see the franchise ending at

three.' Even Craven, who had his fingers burned previously with the *A Nightmare on Elm Street* sequels is willing to entertain a return to *Scream* territory: 'If there's a continual clamour for more, I'll be there, but it will have to wait a few years.'

Having finally earned the respect of the film industry by making his mark at the box office, Craven found himself able to tackle films outside of the horror genre. Close to his heart are his plans to write and direct a semi-autobiographical film about growing up in a religious household. Craven's own upbringing had been considered as potential subject matter for a film, but the closest he'd come was *Deadly Blessing*: 'I think there are interesting issues in growing up fundamentalist in America that are not tackled on film or in the media... With the resurgence of the right-wing religious groups, it represents a lot of the country, but you never see films about it... I'd like to look at those beliefs and the influences they have on people's lives. It'd be a low budget, small film, not strictly autobiographical. They always say write about what you know when you

Below: *Teens in peril — Jerry O'Connell (back) and Elise Neal (far right) join the* Scream *team.*

start out, although *The Last House on the Left* was pretty far from my real life. It's something that I definitely want to do and for about a minute I had a deal with a studio before they went out of business, so the film folded.'

Despite that setback, Craven is still working toward getting something of his own life experience onto the cinema screen: 'I just closed a deal to write a script about growing up in Cleveland, which will be a straight coming-of-age film. Except it'll be the story of Wes Craven growing up, so it'll have a lot of nightmares.'

Another project Craven was involved in was a remake of Herk Harvey's 1962 cult movie *Carnival of Souls*. Craven was intrigued by the idea of remaking this creepy little film, which had been made on a shoestring budget. Later, Adam Grossman, who'd scripted the remake, was also hired to direct, with Craven offering support in an advisory capacity.

In fact, Craven has lent his name and experience to a series of productions he has had little creative involvement in. As well as his work on *Carnival of Souls*, Craven's name above the title of *Wishmaster* helped the film make the top ten in America shortly after *Scream*.

Wes Craven's New Nightmare was the first sign that the director was now something of a horror brand name: 'That was quite unusual — there have been few other directors who have their names in the title [John Carpenter is prime among them]. There is an awareness now in the audience that directors are ultimately the ones who can make or break a picture. You are the one who makes it for an entire year. You are not an actor who comes in for six weeks, or an editor who isn't part of it until it's shot. There is no one else, except the producer, involved for so long.' However, Craven's experiences with *Wishmaster* made him more careful about attaching his name to other people's projects, as he was not entirely happy with the aggressive marketing of the film: 'I want to be cautious. The problem is keeping control of the way your name is used

after you sponsor something. I saw ads on buses around New York [for *Wishmaster*] where my name was bigger than the film title. I want to be careful about using my position like that again, finding the right product to endorse.'

This name recognition allows Craven to effectively 'sponsor' the work of newcomers, and his involvement as an executive producer can open doors that might otherwise have remained closed: 'The next step is to executive produce and find young directors that I think are really good, as well as young writers. Sort of nurture a new generation.' Craven even considered a possible return to academia: 'In 1988 I taught a masters class in directing that I found a lot of fun. As I advance into my silver years, I might at some point start teaching again. It's very time intensive and I think the best way to teach is at the level where you take on one or two people that are working with you in the business and have already proven themselves in some way. I'm much more of a believer in learning by doing rather than through reading books or doing something within the school context. I mean, I never went to school to learn to make movies.'

Also on the horizon is a timely return to television. Craven enjoyed some success with *Nightmare Cafe*, but has never created a lasting TV

Above: The original Carnival of Souls — *remade for release in 1998 as a 'Wes Craven presents...' project.*

concept. Early in 1998, Craven struck a deal with Fox to produce a pilot called *Hollyweird*, with series potential, and began laying the groundwork for a series of TV movies which he would produce under the umbrella title *Wes Craven's Realms of Fear*. The overall concept for this series of films, to be directed by young up-and-coming talent, had been developed for a Wes Craven branded computer game entitled *Principles of Fear*. 'The company went out of business and we retained the rights,' he explains. 'Some of that has gone into the TV concepts.'

As well as securing his place as a film-maker, the success of *Scream* brought Craven a new outlet for his talents — novel writing. Through a friend, Craven met literary agent Ellen Geiger of Curtis Brown Ltd, who suggested that she could put together a book deal if Craven had any ideas for horror or science fiction novels.

'[Writing] was what I started out intending to do,' says Craven. 'It is an alternative to movies. If it ever came to a situation where I couldn't get a movie under way, writing books is an alternative, frankly. It is also a way of retaining more control over the work, there's just you, no producers and no worry over how to achieve things, no special effects to worry about. It's just you and the reader.'

Craven developed an idea he'd had for twenty years based around cloning, and wrapped it up in a thriller plot. His agent managed to secure an amazing $1 million deal with publishers Simon & Schuster in February 1997. 'It's a vindication,' declares Craven of his book, called *The Fountain Society*, 'when people acknowledge that you can do more than just horror. The novel is along the lines of *Three Days of the Condor*, with a dose of cutting-edge medical science. I'd like to do it as a film.'

The director's next feature project will be *Fifty Violins*, a dramatic treatment of the Oscar-nominated documentary *Small Wonders*. At the time of writing, Craven is enthusiastic about the progress of the film, scheduled to start shooting in summer 1998: 'Part of my Miramax deal, *Fifty Violins* has been wonderfully adapted by writer Pamela Gray and is moving forward quite rapidly, with Madonna attached as the lead.'

It appears that Wes Craven has no plans to retire: 'No. I'll keep working, unless I have a heart attack or something that makes me physically incapable of working. I enjoy work too much to ever stop.' He has maintained a widely varied

Right: Craven on location, filming Scream.

career, despite concentrating on horror movies. 'It's unusual to have spent an entire career, almost, making scary pictures,' he notes. 'I often think why haven't I done better or done things differently. I think, though, I've been able to do things in the horror genre that I couldn't have done anywhere else. There is a lot of freedom, a lot less supervision or interference, although I've had some of that too. Certainly, the last few of my films have been entirely under my control, which is a good position to be in.'

Craven's religious background still gives him cause for thought as he reflects on his career: 'I don't know what the progress of my own soul has been through horror, but I do know that it has been important for me to do it. I grew up with Satan and God and a clear distinction between good and evil. The first opportunity I had to make a movie was to make something scary, so I did, but I think something had been exorcised. It's been good for me to do it.'

Wes Craven has repeatedly re-invented the horror genre, not content simply to churn out slasher and scare movies, and has always been happy to discuss the deeper meaning behind his films. Notoriety came early, and perhaps Craven has failed to capitalise on it, struggling instead to escape the genre.

Although his critical stature has grown steadily, Craven's audience remained small but faithful. It was rare for any of his films to gross more than $20 million at the United States box office until the *Scream* films fulfilled the potential shown by some of his earlier work. 'My strongest stuff has been at the beginning and end of my career, although I guess you'd have to put *The Serpent and the Rainbow* into that category,' he says. 'It's a good feeling that so much of my better work has come later on. I think there's been a long-term growth for both the genre and my work over the years. Consequently, people have been willing to be involved in my later films, whereas on my middle films, I was not that well known. Disasters like *Swamp Thing* and *Deadly*

Friend would pop up [occasionally].'

Despite the knocks he has taken, Craven seems destined to continue going his own way, even if it means suffering for his art: 'I always think that I'll never work again. And I've gone broke several times in my career and lost everything. But the biggest motivation, I guess, is that I would never want to go back to really working for a living. I'm having too much fun.' ∎

Above: Wes Craven at work, 'having too much fun' to stop now.

Filmography

As Director:

The Last House on the Left
aka *Sex Crime of the Century/Night of Vengeance/Krug & Co/The Men's Room*
USA, 1972. 88 mins.
Screenplay by Wes Craven.
Prod Co: Sean S. Cunningham Films.
Cast: Sandra Cassell (Mari Collingwood), Lucy Grantham (Phyllis Stone), David A. Hess (Krug Stillo), Fred J. Lincoln (Fred 'Weasel' Padowski), Jeramie Rain (Sadie), Marc Sheffler (Junior Stillo), Gaylord St James (Dr John Collingwood), Cynthia Carr (Mrs Estelle Collingwood), Ada Washington (Ada), Marshall Anker (Sheriff), Martin Kove (Deputy), Ray Edwards (Mail Man), Jonathan Craven (Boy with Balloon, uncredited).

The Hills Have Eyes
USA, 1977. 89 mins.
Screenplay by Wes Craven.
Prod Co: Blood Relations Co.
Cast: Susan Lanier (Brenda Carter), Robert Houston (Bobby Carter), Martin Speer (Doug Wood), Dee Wallace (Lynne Wood), Russ Grieve (Big Bob Carter), John Steadman (Fred), James Whitworth (Jupiter), Virginia Vincent (Ethel Carter), Lance Gordon (Mars), Michael Berryman (Pluto), Janus Blythe (Ruby), Cordy Clark (Mama), Brenda Marinoff (Katy), Arthur King (Mercury).

Stranger in Our House (TV Movie)
aka *Summer of Fear*
USA, 1978. 96 mins.
Screenplay by Glenn M. Benest & Max A. Keller, based on the novel *Summer of Fear* by Lois Duncan.
Prod Co: Inter Planetary/Finnegan Associates/NBC TV, tx 31/10/78.
Cast: Linda Blair (Rachel Bryant), Lee Purcell (Julia Trent), Jeremy Slate (Tom Bryant), Jeff McCracken (Mike Gallagher), Jeff East (Peter Bryant), Carol Lawrence (Leslie Bryant), MacDonald Carey (Professor Jarvis), Fran Drescher (Carolyn Baker), James Jarnagin (Bobby), Sierra Pecheur (Nurse Duncan), Billy Veck (Sheriff), Patricia Wilson (Mrs Gallagher), Gwil Richards (Dr Morgan), Frederick Rule (Mailman), Helena Makela (Beverly Hills Lady), Nicole Keller (Elizabeth), John Steadman (Vet), Kerry Arquette (Anne), Kim Wells (Female Rider), Beatrice Manley (Marge Trent).

Deadly Blessing
USA, 1981. 102 mins.
Screenplay by Matthew Barr, Glenn M. Benest & Wes Craven, based on a story by Matthew Barr & Glenn M. Benest.
Prod Co: Inter Planetary/PolyGram Filmed Entertainment.
Cast: Maren Jensen (Martha Schmidt), Susan Buckner (Vicky), Sharon Stone (Lana), Jeff East (John Schmidt), Lisa Hartman (Faith), Lois Nettleton (Louisa), Ernest Borgnine (Isaiah Schmidt), Colleen Riley (Melissa), Douglas Barr (Jim Schmidt), Michael Berryman (William Gluntz), Kevin Cooney (Sheriff), Bobby Dark (Theatre Manager), Kevin Farr (Fat Boy), Neil Fletcher (Grave Digger), Jonathon Gulla (Tom Schmidt), Chester Kulas Jr (Leopold), Lawrence Montaigne (Matthew Gluntz), Lucky Mosley (Sammy), Dan Shackleford

(Medic), Annabelle Weenick (Ruth Schmidt), Jenna Worthen (Mrs Gluntz).

Swamp Thing
USA, 1982. 91 mins.
Screenplay by Wes Craven, based on the DC Comics character.
Prod Co: United Artists.
Cast: Louis Jourdan (Dr Anton Arcane), Adrienne Barbeau (Alice Cable), Ray Wise (Dr Alec Holland), David Hess (Ferret), Nicholas Worth (Bruno), Don Knight (Ritter), Al Ruban (Charlie), Dick Durock (Swamp Thing), Ben Bates (Arcane Monster), Nannette Brown (Dr Linda Holland), Reggie Batts (Jude), Millicent Meyer (Arcane's Secretary), Karen Price (Arcane's Messenger), Bill Erickson (Young Agent), Dov Gottesfeld (Commando), Tommy Madden (Little Bruno).

The Hills Have Eyes Part II
USA, 1984. 88 mins.
Screenplay by Wes Craven.
Prod Co: New Realm/VTC.
Cast: Tamara Stafford (Cass), Kevin Blair (Roy), John L. Bloom (Reaper), Colleen Riley (Jane), Michael Berryman (Pluto), Penny Johnson (Sue), Janus Blythe (Rachel/Ruby), John Laughlin (Hulk), Willard E. Pugh (Foster), Peter Frechette (Harry), Robert Houston (Bobby Carter), David Nichols (The Psychiatrist), Edith Fellows (Mrs Wilson), Lance Gordon (Mars), Susan Lanier (Brenda Carter), Brenda Marinoff (Katy), Martin Speer (Doug Wood), Virginia Vincent (Ethel Carter), James Whitworth (Jupiter), Arden Roger Meyer (Man with Towel).

Invitation to Hell (TV Movie)
USA, 1984. 96 mins.
Screenplay by Richard Rothstein & Wes Craven (uncredited).
Prod Co: ABC TV, tx 24/5/84.
Cast: Robert Urich (Matthew Winslow), Joanna Cassidy (Patricia Winslow), Susan Lucci (Jessica Jones), Joe Regalbuto (Ted Peterson), Kevin McCarthy (Mr Thompson), Patricia McCormack (Mary Peterson), Soleil Moon Frye (Chrissie Winslow), Barret Oliver (Robbie Winslow), Nicholas Worth (Sheriff), Virginia Vincent (Grace), Greg Monaghan (Pete), Lois Hamilton (Miss Winter), Michael Berryman (Staff Member), Gino De Mauro, Jason Presson.

A Nightmare on Elm Street
USA, 1984. 91 mins.
Screenplay by Wes Craven.
Prod Co: Media Home Entertainment/New Line Cinema/Smart Egg Pictures.
Cast: John Saxon (Lt Thompson), Ronee Blakley (Marge Thompson), Heather Langenkamp (Nancy Thompson), Amanda Wyss (Tina Gray), Nick Corri (Rod Lane), Johnny Depp (Glen Lantz), Charles Fleischer (Dr King), Joseph Whipp (Sgt Parker), Robert Englund (Fred Krueger), Lin Shaye (Teacher), Joe Unger (Sgt Garcia), Mimi Meyer-Craven (Nurse), Jeff Levine (Coroner).

Chiller (TV Movie)
USA, 1985. 96 mins.
Screenplay by J.D. Feigelson.
Production Company: Frozen Man Productions/Polar Films/CBS Entertainment Productions, CBS TV, tx 22/5/85.
Cast: Michael Beck (Miles Creighton), Beatrice

Straight (Marion Creighton), Laura Johnson (Leigh Kenyon), Dick O'Neill (Clarence Beeson), Alan Fudge (Dr Stricklin), Craig Richard Nelson (Dr Collier), Paul Sorvino (Reverend Penny), Jill Schoelen (Stacey), Anne Seymour (Mrs Bunch), Russ Marin (Dr Sample), Mimi Meyer-Craven (Nurse Cooper).

The Twilight Zone
USA, 1985. TV Series, 7 x 22 min segments.
Created by Rod Serling.
1 A Little Peace and Quiet (CBS, tx 27/9/85)
(w. James Crocker, with Melinda Dillon).
2 Shatterday (CBS, tx 27/9/85)
(w. Alan Brennert, based on a short story by Harlan Ellison, with Bruce Willis).
3 Wordplay (CBS, tx 4/10/85)
(w. Rockne S. O'Bannon, with Robert Klein, Annie Potts).
4 Chameleon (CBS, tx 4/10/85)
(w. James Crocker, with Terry O'Quinn, John Ashton).
5 Dealer's Choice (CBS, tx 15/11/85)
(w. Don Todd, with Dan Hedaya, M. Emmet Walsh, Morgan Freeman).
6 Her Pilgrim Soul (CBS, tx 13/12/85)
(w. Alan Brennert, with Kristofer Tabori, Gary Cole, Anne Twomey).
7 The Road Less Travelled (CBS, tx 18/12/86)
(w. George R.R. Martin, with Cliff De Young, Margaret Klenck).

Deadly Friend
USA, 1986. 91 mins.
Screenplay by Bruce Joel Rubin, based on the novel *Friend* by Diana Henstall.
Prod Co: Warner Brothers.
Cast: Matthew Laborteaux (Paul), Kristy Swanson (Samantha), Michael Sharrett (Tom), Anne Twomey (Jeannie), Anne Ramsey (Elvira), Richard Marcus (Harry), Russ Marin (Dr Johanson), Charles Fleischer (Voice of Bee Bee), William H. Faeth MD (Dr in Sam's Room).

Casebusters (TV Movie)
USA, 1986. 60 mins.
Screenplay by George Arthur Bloom & Donald Paul Roos.
Production Company: Walt Disney Co, ABC TV, tx 25/5/86.
Cast: Pat Hingle (Sam Donahue), Noah Hathaway (Jamie), Virginya Keehne (Allie), Gary Riley (Anthony 'Ski' Zabrowski), Sharon Barr (Mrs Bonner), Tim Russ (Dixon), Ebbe Roe Smith (Joe Bonner).

The Serpent and the Rainbow
USA, 1988. 98 mins.
Screenplay by Richard Maxwell, A.R. Simoun & Wes Craven (uncredited), based on the book by Wade Davis.
Prod Co: Universal Pictures.
Cast: Bill Pullman (Dr Dennis Alan), Cathy Tyson (Marielle Duchamp), Zakes Mokae (Dargent Peytraud), Paul Winfield (Lucien Celine), Brent Jennings (Mozart), Conrad Roberts (Christophe), Michael Gough (Schoonbacher), Paul Guilfoyle (Andrew Cassedy).

Shocker
USA, 1989. 110 mins.
Screenplay by Wes Craven.

Prod Co: Carolco Pictures/Alive Films.
Cast (in order of appearance): Mitch Pileggi (Horace Pinker), John Tesh (TV Newscaster), Heather Langenkamp (Victim), Peter Berg (Jonathan Parker), Jessica Craven (Counterperson), Cami Cooper (Alison), Richard Brooks (Rhino), Sam Scarber (Cooper), Ted Raimi (Pac Man), Michael Murphy (Lt Don Parker), Bruce Wagner (Executioner), Jonathan Craven (Jogger), Timothy Leary (TV Evangelist), Wes Craven (Man Neighbour), Holly Kaplan (Woman Neighbour), Brent Spiner (Talk Show Guest, uncredited).

Night Visions (TV Movie)
USA, 1990. 90 mins.
Screenplay by Thomas Baum & Wes Craven.
Prod Co: NBC TV, tx 30/11/90.
Cast: Mitch Pileggi (Keller), James Remar (Tom Mackey), Jon Tenney (Martin), Penny Johnson (Luanne), Loryn Locklin (Sally Peters), Francis X. McCarthy (Dowd), Bruce MacVittie, Mark Lindsay Chapman, Timothy Leary.

The People Under the Stairs
USA, 1991. 102 mins.
Screenplay by Wes Craven.
Production Company: Universal Pictures.
Cast: Brandon Quintin Adams (Fool), Everett McGill (Man), Wendy Robie (Woman), A.J. Langer (Alice), Ving Rhames (Leroy), Sean Whalen (Roach), Bill Cobbs (Grandpa Booker), Joshua Cox (Young Cop), John Hostetter (Veteran Cop), George R. Parker (Attic Cop).

Nightmare Cafe
USA, 1992. TV Series.
Created by Wes Craven.
Directed by John Harrison, except 'Aliens Ate My Lunch' (tx 3/4/92) directed by Wes Craven.
Prod Co. MCA/UA, NBC TV.
Cast: Jack Coleman (Frank Nolan), Robert Englund (Blackie), Lindsay Frost (Fay Peronivic).

Wes Craven's New Nightmare
USA, 1994. 112 mins.
Screenplay by Wes Craven.
Prod Co: New Line Cinema.
Cast (in order of appearance): Heather Langenkamp (Herself), Miko Hughes (Dylan), Matt Winston (Chuck), Rob LaBelle (Terry), David Newsom (Chase Porter), Wes Craven (Himself), Marianne Maddalena (Herself), Gretchen Oehler (Script Supervisor), Tracy Middendorf (Julie), Cully Fredricksen (Limo Driver), Bodhi Elfman (TV Studio PA), Sam Rubin (Himself), Robert Englund (Freddy Krueger/Himself), Sara Risher (Herself), Robert Shaye (Himself), Cindy Guidry (Kim at New Line), Nick Corri (Himself), Tuesday Knight (Herself), John Saxon (Himself), Tamara Mark (Patrice Englund), Fran Bennett (Dr Heffner), Lin Shaye (Nurse with Pills), Jessica Craven (Junior Nurse with Needle).

Vampire in Brooklyn
USA, 1995. 100 mins.
Screenplay by Michael Lucker, Charlie Murphy & Chris Parker.
Prod Co: Paramount Pictures.
Cast: Eddie Murphy (Maximillian/Preacher Pauly/Guido), Angela Bassett (Rita), Allen Payne (Justice), Kadeem Hardison (Julius Jones), John Witherspoon (Silas), Joanna Cassidy (Dewey), Nick Corri (Anthony), Simbi Khali (Nikki), John LaMotta

(Lizzy), Zakes Mokae (Dr Zeko), Mitch Pileggi (Tony), Wendy Robie (Zealot at Police Station).

Scream
USA, 1996. 110 mins.
Screenplay by Kevin Williamson.
Production Company: Woods Entertainment/Dimension Films/Miramax Films.
Cast (in order of appearance): Drew Barrymore (Casey Becker), Roger L. Jackson (Phone Voice), Kevin Patrick (Steve), Neve Campbell (Sidney Prescott), Skeet Ulrich (Billy Loomis), Courteney Cox (Gale Weathers), W. Earl Brown (Kenny), Rose McGowan (Tatum), David Arquette (Deputy Dewey Riley), Matthew Lillard (Stuart), Jamie Kennedy (Randy Meeks), Liev Schreiber (Cotton Weary), with Linda Blair (Obnoxious Reporter, uncredited), Wes Craven (Fred the Janitor, uncredited), Priscilla Pointer (Maureen Prescott, uncredited), Henry Winkler (Principal Himbry, uncredited).

Scream 2
USA, 1997. 120 mins.
Screenplay by Kevin Williamson.
Prod Co: Craven-Maddalena Films/Konrad Pictures/Dimension Films/Miramax Films.
Cast (in order of appearance): David Arquette (Dewey Riley), Neve Campbell (Sidney Prescott), Courteney Cox (Gale Weathers), Sarah Michelle Gellar (Cici Cooper), Jamie Kennedy (Randy Meeks), Laurie Metcalf (Debbie Salt), Elise Neal (Hallie), Jerry O'Connell (Derek), Timothy Olyphant (Mickey), Jada Pinkett (Maureen Evans), Liev Schreiber (Cotton Weary), Lewis Arquette (Chief Louis Hartley), Duane Martin (Joel), Rebecca Gayheart (Lois), Portia De Rossi (Murphy), Omar Epps (Phil Stevens), Heather Graham ('Stab' Casey), Roger L. Jackson (Phone Voice), Kevin Williamson (Talk Show Host), Joshua Jackson (Film Class Student), Tori Spelling (Herself/'Stab' Sidney), Luke Wilson ('Stab' Billy), David Warner (Drama Teacher Gus Gold), with Wes Craven (Man at Hospital, uncredited).

As Producer:

Together (1971, associate)
Shocker (1989, executive)
The People Next Door (1989, TV Series, creator/executive)
Night Visions (1990, TV Movie, executive)
The People Under the Stairs (1991, executive)
Laurel Canyon (1993, creator/executive, dir. Tim Hunter)
Wes Craven's New Nightmare (1994, executive)
Wes Craven Presents Mind Ripper (1995, executive, dir. Joe Gayton, aka *The Outpost*)
Wes Craven's Wishmaster (1997, executive, dir. Rob Kurtzman)
Wes Craven Presents Carnival of Souls (1998, executive, dir. Adam Grossman)

As Editor:

You've Got to Walk It Like You Talk It or You'll Lose That Beat (1971, dir. Peter Locke)
The Last House on the Left (1972)
It Happened in Hollywood (1973, dir. Peter Locke)
Car Hops (1977, dir. Peter Locke, aka *California Drive-In Girls*)
The Hills Have Eyes (1977)

As Actor:

The Twilight Zone, 'Children's Zoo' (1985, dir. Robert Downey Sr), uncredited appearance
Shocker (1989), played Man Neighbour
Body Bags, 'The Gas Station' (TV Movie, 1993, dir. John Carpenter), played Pasty Faced Man
Wes Craven's New Nightmare (1994), played Himself
The Fear (1995, dir. Vincent Robert), played Dr Arnold
Shadow Zone: The Undead Express (TV Movie, 1996, dir. Stephen Williams), played Counsellor
Scream (1996), played Fred, the Janitor

Selected TV/Documentary Appearances:

Fangoria's Weekend of Horrors (1986, dir. Rex Piano, video)
Fear in the Dark (1991, dir. Dominic Murphy, Channel 4)
Hallowe'en (1994, dir. Rob Dustin, CBS)
Anatomy of Horror (1995, UPN)

Unreleased Project:

Tales That Will Tear Your Heart Out (1976)
Craven acted in and directed one segment of this unfinished anthology film, produced by Roy Frumkes.

Based on Characters Created by Wes Craven:

A Nightmare on Elm Street Part 2: Freddy's Revenge (1985, dir. Jack Sholder)
A Nightmare on Elm Street 3: Dream Warriors (1987, dir. Chuck Russell)
A Nightmare on Elm Street 4: The Dream Master (1988, dir. Renny Harlin)
Freddy's Nightmares (1988-90, TV Series, tx 8/10/88 to 12/3/90)
A Nightmare on Elm Street: The Dream Child (1989, dir. Stephen Hopkins)
Freddy's Dead: The Final Nightmare (1990, dir. Rachel Talalay)

The above cast lists are usually taken directly from the on-screen credits, so may be listed in either order of billing or of appearance.

Bibliography

Cooper, Jeffrey *The Nightmare on Elm Street Companion* (St Martin's Press, 1987)
Meyers, Richard *For One Week Only: The World of Exploitation Films* (New Century Publications, Inc., 1983)
Szulkin, David A. *Wes Craven's Last House on the Left* (FAB Press, 1997)

Magazines consulted include:

Cinefantastique *Imagi-Movies*
The Dark Side *Premiere*
Empire *Shock Xpress*
Entertainment Weekly *Starburst*
Fangoria *Starlog*
GoreZone